The Birds of the Latin Poets

The Birds of the Latin Poets

By
ERNEST WHITNEY MARTIN
Associate Professor of Greek

KALPAZ

ISBN: 978-93-5128-729-2(HB)

First Published in 1914
Indian Reprint in 2017

Published by

Kalpaz Publications
C-30, Satyawati Nagar,
Delhi – 110052
E-mail: kalpaz@hotmail.com
Website: kalpazpublications.com
Ph.: +91-9212142040

Cataloging in Publication Data—DK
Courtesy: D.K. Agencies (P) Ltd. <docinfo@dkagencies.com>

Martin, Ernest Whitney, author.
The birds of the Latin poets / by Ernest Whitney Martin.
pages cm
"First published in 1914"—Title page verso.
ISBN 9789351287292

1. Latin poetry—History and criticism. 2. Birds in literature. I. Title.

PA6029.N4M37 2017 DDC 871.009 23

TO

HENRY RUSHTON FAIRCLOUGH

PROFESSOR OF LATIN IN LELAND STANFORD JUNIOR UNIVERSITY

TRUE FRIEND AND TEACHER

Yet have I loved thy voice
Frail echo of some ancient sacred joy.

—SANTAYANA.

O Wanderer from a Grecian shore,
Still, after many years, in distant lands,
Still nourishing in thy bewilder'd brain
That wild, unquench'd, deep-sunken, old-world pain
Say, will it never heal?

—MATTHEW ARNOLD.

Quis volucrum species numeret, quis nomina discat?
Mille avium cantus, vocum discrimina mille.

—*Anth. Lat.* 733.

PREFACE

In the following pages I have attempted to present, in their own words, a tolerably full picture of the Roman attitude toward bird life as reflected in their greatest poets. To this end I have recorded, side by side, the important and the commonplace.

My collections of material are, I believe, fairly comprehensive down into the second century of the Empire. The thread is picked up again in the *Latin Anthology*. The appended index of the loc. cit. shows exactly what ground has been covered. These collections were begun in my undergraduate days and saved as marginalia at a time when some slight technical skill in taxidermy and ornithology made college and university possible for me. Omissions, errors, and the gap in the later poets may, of course, be checked from the *Archiv,* when finally completed.

Considerations of space and the check-list arrangement have made it necessary to omit, in the main, citations from the prose writers and references to birds in general. This general restriction of scope has led to other omissions as well, notably the sources and parallels from Greek literature. The poets of both peoples, after all, were but drawing from a common fund of traditional lore, the whence and wherefore of which had become obscured in many places by the lapse of untold years. This is particularly true in matters of astronomic lore, in augury, and in the various myths of metamorphosis. However, as to the Greek background, the curious reader may satisfy himself to weariness by turning to Thompson's indispensable *Glossary of Greek Birds*. As a ready aid to such readers I have given with each Latin bird-name a parallel synonym in Greek.

I have omitted for the most part any full discussion of astronomical and mythological problems. Such new light as may eventually be thrown upon these two clouded phases of the ancient view of bird lore will come, I think, from gleanings here and there in comparative literature, folklore and anthropology. In order that we may more fully appreciate the continuity of literary tradition and folk observation in this field, we must have a series of studies covering mediaeval and modern European literatures. A detailed study of the birds in the English poets is, perhaps, our most immediate need. Such a survey will command a very large field of readers. As my own contribution to this larger purpose, I may say that in three more years I hope to be able to tell the full story of the birds in our own American poets.

For the most part the Greeks and Romans held the same viewpoint as regards the birds about them. The latter still kept, as their chief exponents of bird song, the nightingale, swallow, halcyon and swan, with all their inherited myths and lore. But, in addition to this, the uninitiated, I believe, will be surprised at the really wide range of observation and sentiment which is encompassed by the Roman poets in this little corner of nature's realm. The consistent Roman attitude toward the song of birds is, to the modern reader, perhaps the most striking thing to be noted. It is simply this: that they nearly always felt a tone of sadness in the songs of their favorite song birds, where we are inclined to feel joy and ecstasy.

This prevalent Roman feeling is due, in my judgment, to the widespread ancient belief in the metamorphosis association. Their favorite birds were not thought of merely as birds *per se,* but rather as human beings who had been changed into the birds in question. The nightingale and swallow were still Philomel and Progne. This is probably the clue to the rather curious choice of the swan and halcyon as typical song birds. This Roman point of view is the key to the interpretation of the rather frequent literal descriptions of actual metamorphoses scattered through the Latin poets. Horace, assuming before our eyes the form of a swan, is an example of this peculiar usage. This attitude of mind is the basis of several epithets and derivations. Thus, as I still believe, *luscinia* is best taken as derived from **luges-cinia*. The wide use of *querulus* and related words takes on a new significance when once this basic attitude is taken into consideration.

As we shall see, practically the same species were noted and recorded in the spring and fall migrations; but, in this matter, similar geographical and climatic conditions were contributing elements.

In the matter of identification of species I have of course attempted nothing new. My single year in Italy, occupied largely with the technique of our craft, left scant time for woods, meadows and riverside. Besides, this is the task of years for a finished expert in the birds of Europe. Thrown back, therefore, upon the books, I have tried to catch the prevailing traditional identifications; and in their quest I have spent many pleasant days with Gesner and his kind. However, there still remain a few siftings in the final nomenclature, to be made from the little hints of place, season, color and habit, scattered through the remains of literature and art. These will break up some of the generic names into the probable species which the poets unconsciously had in hand.

Professor W. Warde Fowler has shown us the method with his observations on the crows, ravens and doves. And more recently, Boraston's article in the *Journal of Hellenic Studies,* Vol. 31, on the *Birds of Homer,* has made clear the possibilities of this manner of approach. It must be done, preferably by a native, on the ground; and it may well be the task of some future Italian Thoreau or Burroughs.

Most American village boys know at least the common local birds. But this living contact has been ignored in the rather colorless treatment of the Roman birds in our annotated editions. Possibly, therefore, the reader will be interested in the literary parallels from our American poets. For this particular phase of our study it would have been sufficient for the purpose in view to have taken only the greater poets of the last century, with such minor writers as are included in the later Anthologies of, let us say, Stedman and Sladen.

But as the work grew I became more and more interested in our older poets; so that, as a matter of fact, I have gone through the dusty pages of some hundreds of our all but forgotten earlier writers, and have included also the host of minor poets saved for us in the early anthologies of Kettell, Griswold, Duyckinck and many others. For the literary ornithologist in the earlier periods of our literature, from William Morrell and Jacob Steendam down to Philip Freneau and a generation beyond, there are many peculiar little antiquarian problems. Our birds were then as yet largely unnamed. Alexander Wilson in 1814 listed only two hundred and eighty-three species of North American birds; with Dr. Coues in 1882 the number has grown to nearly nine hundred. Throughout these earlier periods English influence is very strong, and one must be ever watchful for skylarks, mavises, rooks, throstles and nightingales. For the last mentioned, Anne Bradstreet, our first poetess, had a special penchant.

Naturally, in bringing together American and Roman birds, I have attempted no close scientific paralleling of species; I have tried rather to group the birds which have aroused similar reactions in the feelings of their poetic observers. Hence Roman nightingales have suggested American mocking-birds and even whippoorwills, while larks have been answered by bobolinks, and starlings by meadowlarks.

This hunt through our own poets was undertaken first, in order to find out just how much of the ornithological tradition of the classics had percolated, as it were, through time and distance to our own shores. It turns out that there is far more of direct imitation, translation and traditional reminiscence than we should have expected, and a surprising coherence in related observation. In checking over this material I have felt in quite a new way the truism that all literature is one, and that no particular literature can be fully understood alone. And I have felt with new force that Greek and Latin literature can never be divorced from English and American literature. In thus prowling through the literary underbrush of our own past, one comes to have a warm affection for our early bards, and to feel an admiration for the old classical training which everywhere shows its abiding influence. And finally, after counting the birds, one comes to believe with Burroughs, "that the birds are all the birds of the poets and of no one else."

Save that nightingales, larks, and the classic traditions of the halcyon and swan can never be quite forgotten, our poets are in the main content with our own native species. There is, of course, little or nothing from heraldic associations. The younger poets even have favorites to pit against classic *Philomel;* thus Stedman vouches for the cat-bird, Lanier for the mocking-bird, and Van Dyke, after hearing the nightingale on the banks of the Arno, "longed to hear a simpler strain—the wood notes of the veery."

In upper Austria, in 1845, Bayard Taylor, surrounded by the bird prima donnas of Europe, could still dream of our own meadowlark, oriole and mocking-bird. But General Albert Pike, it seems to me, was a bit overly American, in his youth, when he grouped mock-birds (*sic*) and humming-birds with Latona in a "rich and lustrous Delian paradise." Yet having noted this trifle, the classical teacher will pause with pleasure over his *Hymns to the Gods*—Neptune, Apollo, Venus, Diana and the rest—"written," as Griswold tells us, "at an early age, principally while he was surrounded by his pupils in the school-room." They are documents of a lost point of view. It is only fair to this very distinguished southern poet and scholar to add that the above offending passage was fully emended in a later edition of his works.

A complete study of the birds in our American poets is something yet to be done, but, in passing, we may note that they record over one hundred different species. Bryant has twenty-eight species; Emerson, Holmes and Lowell over thirty each; while Longfellow lists over fifty, and Whittier something beyond seventy. Their bird lore is nearly always exact and satisfying, and of very wide range and observation. Whittier still had an interest in the old hibernation fallacy of the swallow. Longfellow knew, for example, the recondite myth of the *swallow-stone* (Plin.

XI, 79; XXXVII, 27), and utilized it with great beauty in his *Evangeline*. Dr. Lebour (vid. *The Zoologist*, 1866, p. 523; Hartung, *Birds of Shakespeare*, p. 283) found this myth still a living tradition in Brittany; hence its reappearance in Acadia, where no doubt Longfellow came upon it.

In conclusion, I must thank a long list of teachers and friends for influences and suggestions leading toward a combination of interests, which have been in subsequent years an unfailing source of pleasure. From the earlier academic years I would mention Professor J. R. Kennan. To him the capture or observation of a rare migrant warbler or sparrow was just as important as the capture of an elusive ablative or optative. To Professor Charles E. Bates I owe more than I can ever repay. He was truly one of our great college teachers of Latin. He proudly belonged to the older school—to those who knew their Latin grammar by heart and by paragraph number, and who needed no text in presenting Horace. I owe a similar debt of gratitude to Professor Edward W. Claypole, whose Latin marginalia inscribed upon our notebooks in biology and the like, would now, I suppose, seem to be relics of an order of things that is no more. Pliny and 'il maestro di color che sanno,' were to him still doubly real. Natural science with him was invested with an atmosphere never quite forgotten by his scholars. It was my very good fortune to be under him for four years, in the preparation of a very considerable collection of American birds. From later years, to Professors F. F. Abbott, E. M. Pease, A. T. Murray and H. R. Fairclough, I would pay a student's grateful homage for years of kindly guidance and inspiration. Finally, I am greatly indebted to Professor J. E. Church, Jr., my colleague for two years at the University of Nevada, for unfailing kindness and patience in helping to prepare this rather long paper for publication.

E. W. M.

Stanford University, California,
April 1914.

[illegible]

Stanford University, California

The Birds of the Latin Poets

ACALANTHIS (ACANTHIS). Ἀκαλανθίς (ἀκανθίς). Goldfinch, thistle-finch. *Carduelis elegans.* Vid. Fowler, *A Year with the Birds,* p. 243. Note IV, RUSCINIA.

American literary parallels: Wild canary, summer yellow-bird, thistle-bird.

Celia Thaxter: *Yellow-bird.*

Roswell Park: *To a Goldfinch.*

> Send up your full notes like worshipful prayers;
> Yellow-bird, sing while the summer's before you.
> —CELIA THAXTER.

> Let the tiny yellow birds
> Still repeat their shining words,
> While across our senses steal
> Hints of things no words reveal.—CARMAN-HOVEY.

A summer evening scene with attendant background of bird-song:

> Tum tenuis dare rursus aquas, et pascere rursus
> Solis ad occasum, cum frigidus aera vesper
> Temperat, et saltus reficit iam roscida luna,
> Litoraque alcyonem resonant, acalanthida dumi.
> —VERG., *Geor.* III, 335.

Cf. Serv. in loc.: Alii lusciniam esse volunt, alii vero carduelem, quae spinis et carduis pascitur. Vid. Note IV, RUSCINIA.

> The thistle-birds have changed their dun,
> For yellow coats, to match the sun.—HENRY VAN DYKE.

> The yellow-hammer by the way-side picks
> Mutely the thistle's seed.—WILCOX.

The *acanthis,* with the nightingale, is represented (by implication) as endowed with great powers of song:

> Nyctilon ut cantu rudis exsuperaverit Alcon?
> Astyle, credibile est, si vincat acanthida cornix,
> Vocalem superet si dirus aedona bubo.
> —CALP. VI, 6.

A-poise upon the mullein's tipmost top,
And bending down its rod of gold,
The thistle-finch all liquidly lets drop
Melodies manifold.—MIFFLIN.

Vid. Robinson, *The Poets' Birds*, London, 1883, passim, for most of the European birds in this study as they appear in the poets of England. The author boldly assumes that the British poets (save Tennyson) know next to nothing at first hand of their own native birds and that in this regard they are vastly inferior to the poets of America. Naturally his treatment of the subject is wholly unsympathetic and unfair, though at times suggestive. The work is, however, so full of errors that it must be used with great caution. Cf. int. al. Swanton (Review), *A Literary Curiosity. Atlant.* 54, 398.

ACCIPITER. Κίρκος. Hawk. A general name for diurnal birds of prey. The accurate identification of the various species is impossible.

American parallel: Hawk.

The name is applied as a title of reproach to a rapacious man:

Inpure, inhoneste, iniure, inlex, labes popli,
Pecuniai accipiter avide atque invide.
—PLAUT., *Pers.* 408.

Disagreeable situations are proverbially called 'hawks'-nests':

Em, accipitrina haec nunc erit.
—PLAUT., *Bacch.* 274.

Hawks are not worth snaring:

Quia non rete accipitri tennitur neque milvo,
Qui male faciunt nobis: illis qui nihil faciunt tennitur
Quia enim in illis fructus est, in illis opera luditur.
—TER., *Phorm.* 330.

Cf. Cautus enim metuit foveam lupus accipiterque
Suspectos laqueos. —HOR., *Ep.* I, 16, 50.

If mind were immortal and subject to metempsychosis, the hawk would flee from its traditional prey, the dove:

Tremeretque per auras
Aeris accipiter fugiens veniente columba.
—LUCR. III, 751.

Cf. Coombs has a stand west of Nut meadow, and he says that he has just shot fourteen hawks there which were after pigeons.—THOREAU, op. cit.,[1] p. 116.

Birds at night are ofttimes aroused by dreams of the onslaught of hawks and birds of prey:

At variae fugiunt volucres pinnisque repente
Sollicitant divom nocturno tempore lucos,
Accipitres somno in leni si proelia pugnas
Edere sunt persectantes visaeque volantes.
—LUCR. IV, 1007.

Cf. The bird from out its dream
Breaks with a sudden cry.—HOWELLS.

Then half wing-openings of the sleeping bird,
Some dream of danger to her young hath stirred.—LANIER.

And sleeping birds, touched with a silly glee,
Waken at midnight from their blissful dreams,
And carol brokenly.—LAMPMAN.

The calls and cries of hawks and birds of the sea vary with their habits and environment:

Postremo genus alituum variaeque volucres,
Accipitres atque ossifragae mergique marinis
Fluctibus in salso victum vitamque petentes,
Longe alias alio iaciunt in tempore voces,
Et quom de victu certant praedaque repugnant.
—LUCR. V, 1078.

For the note of the hawk, vid. *Anth. Lat.* 762, 24.

Accipitres pipant milvus hiansque lupit.

Cf. also *Anth. Lat.* 733, 6; Wackernagel, op. cit., p. 50.

Cf. Hark, the sharp, insistent cry,
Where the hawk patrols the sky.—ROBERTS.

There shrieks the hovering hawk at noon.—BRYANT.

The hawk is portrayed as the foe of smaller birds:

Natura humanis omnia sunt paria: qui pote, plus urget, piscis ut saepe minutos magnu' comest, ut avis enicat accipiter.
(*Marcopolis.*) —VARR., *Men. Reliq.* 2.

[1]For list of works in this study, see Bibliography.

Cf. Forsitan hanc volucrem (i.e., accipiter) rapto quae vivit et omnes
Terret aves, semper pennas habuisse putetis.
—Ov., *Met.* XI, 291.

The hawk, in a simile describing the capture and slaying of the son of Aunus by Camilla, is portrayed as seizing a dove in mid-air:

Quam facile accipiter saxo sacer ales ab alto
Consequitur pennis sublimem in nube columbam,
Conprensamque tenet, pedibusque eviscerat uncis.
Tum cruor et volsae labuntur ab aethere plumae.
—VERG., *Aen.* XI, 721.

Cf. Hor., *Od.* I, 37, 17; Ov., *Met.* V, 604.

This dominant instinct to pursue doves as prey, is the survival of the militant spirit of Daedalion, who was metamorphosed into a hawk:

Illius virtus reges gentesque subegit,
Quae nunc Thisbaeas agitat mutata columbas.
—Ov., *Met.* XI, 299.

Cf. On steel-blue wings, with eyes intent on crime,
A hawk through tangled brush pursues the quail.—RICE.

Wild pigeons, early on the wing,
Woke overhead low thundering—
Blue, rearward columns mounting high,
Scared by the gray hawk's greedy cry.—HOSMER.

For the metamorphosis of Phoebus into a hawk, cf. Ov., *Met.* VI, 122.

Cf. Thee, bright-eyed hawk!
Soul-emblem, sunwards soaring, as to God.—BAILEY.

This militant spirit was a cause of hatred toward the bird:

Odimus accipitrem, quia vivit semper in armis.
—Ov., *Ars Amat.* II, 147.

Menelaus was mad in leaving Helen accessible to Paris:

Accipitri timidas credis, furiose, columbas.
—Ov., *Ars Amat.* II, 363.

Various bird enmities were lulled by Arion's music:

Et sine lite loquax cum Palladis alite cornix
Sedit, et accipitri iuncta columba fuit.
—Ov., *Fast.* II, 89.

Cf. With cawing crows that follow,
The hunted hawk wings wearily and screams.—CAWEIN.

The dove once smitten by a hawk never outlives its fear:

Terretur minimo pennae stridore columba
Unguibus, accipiter, saucia facta tuis.
—Ov., *Trist.* I, 1, 75.

The dove in airy speed may balk
Her swooping enemy the hawk.—HOSMER.

From swooping hawk may tear away
The partridge, and its haunt regain.—HOSMER.

Birds fleeing from hawks enter even the homes of men. In like manner Ovid turns to Messalinus:

Accipitremque timens pennis trepidantibus ales
Audet ad humanos fessa venire sinus
Nec se vicino dubitat committere tecto.
—Ov., *Ex Ponto*, II, 2, 37.

Cf.: Alauda accipitrem adeo timet, ut in hominum sinus confugiat, et loco manens vel in terra sedens capi se permittat.—ALBERTUS.

I cannot help admiring the great gray hawk. How bold, how bright, how swift he is! Let him but show his shadow and the shrieking hens scatter, flying to cover; and the blood-red cock, that braggart of the barnyard, hides his proud crest in fear.—CAWEIN, *Nature Notes*, p. 17.

Daedalus awaits the coming of Icarus even as the mother bird collects her brood when dispersed by the onslaught of a hawk:

Callidus medium senex
Daedalus librans iter
Nube sub media stetit,
Alitem exspectans suam
(Qualis accipitris minas
Fugit et sparsos metu
Conligit fetus avis).
—SEN., *Oed.* 899.

Idaeus is as helpless in saving his brother from Diomedes, as a mother bird is against a hawk:

Ut volucris, derepta sui cum corpora nati
Accipitrem laniare videt nec tendere contra
Auxilium nec ferre suo valet anxia nato,
Quodque potest, levibus plangit sua pectora pennis.
—SIL. ITAL., *Il. Lat.* 417.

For references to the hawk in auguries vid. Sil. Ital. IV, 103; Stat., *Theb.* III, 509; and supra Verg., *Aen.* XI, 721, sacer ales.

The metamorphosis of Daedalion into a hawk by Apollo, with some description of the bird in question:

Cum se Daedalion saxo misisset ab alto,
Fecit avem et subitis pendentem sustulit alis,
Oraque adunca dedit, curvos dedit unguibus hamos,
Virtutem antiquam, maiores corpore vires.
Et nunc accipiter, nullis satis aequus, in omnes
Saevit aves, aliisque dolens fit causa dolendi.
—Ov., *Met.* XI, 340.

A hawk, now a mere decoy, grimly mourns that the captured game is not his own:

Praedo fuit volucrum: famulus nunc aucupis idem
Decipit et captas non sibi maeret aves.
(*Accipiter.*) —MART. XIV, 216.

A sparrow while upbraiding a hare which had been seized by an eagle, is pounced upon by a hawk and is in turn rebuked by the dying hare:

Oppressum ab aquila et fletus edentem graves
Leporem obiurgabat passer: 'Ubi pernicitas
Nota,' inquit, 'illa est? Quid ita cessarunt pedes?'
Dum loquitur, ipsum accipiter necopinum rapit
Questuque vano clamitantem interficit.
Lepus semianimus: 'Mortis en solacium!
Qui modo securus nostra inridebas mala,
Simili querela fata deploras tua.'—PHAED. I, 9, 3.

For the Fable of the Hawk as arbiter between two quarrelling Cocks, one of which he seized, cf. Phaed., *Fab. Aes.*, App. II, 6.

A hawk, while befooling a nightingale, is caught by a fowler:

Accipiter ad lusciniae nidum dum sedet
Auritum speculans, illic pullos invenit.
Mater periclo mota prolis advolat
Supplexque, pullis ut parcat suis, rogat.
Accipiter: 'Quod vis,' inquit, 'faciam, si bona
Cantaris voce carmina modulatum mihi.'
At illa, quamvis excideret animus, tamen
Metu coacta est et cantavit denique
Dolore plena. Praedam qui captaverat
Accipiter illi: 'Non tu cantasti bene,

Et unum e pullis, apprehendit unquibus
Coepitque devorare. Ex diverso venit
Auceps et calamo clam levato perfidum
Visco contingit atque in terram deiecit.
Quicumque fraudes alii tendit subdolas
Timere debet, ne ipse capiatur dolo.
—PHAED., *Fab. Aes.*, App. II, 18.

For the Fable of the Hawk, Stork and Goose, in which the last is seized by the first, after a compact for protection with the stork, vid. Phaed., *Fab. Aes.*, App. II, 23.

ACREDULA. An unknown bird (?).

Acredula has been taken at various times as either a bird[1] (thrush, lark, owl, swallow, nightingale) or as a frog.[2] Cicero (*De Div.* I, 8, 14), translates the ὀλολυγών of Aratus, *Phaen.* 948, with *acredula.* Many therefore, following Aristot., *H. A.* 4, 9, 11, prefer to take *acredula* as a kind of frog. But ὀλολυγών, in the Greek tradition, is just as indeterminate as *acredula.*[3] In both Cicero and the *De Philomela*, the *acredula* is introduced in the midst of a category of birds. The descriptions of the song of the *acredula* (as a bird), with its touches of sadness, and the use of the word *cantus* agree with the ancient attitude toward bird-song in general. Furthermore, in his next chapter Cicero speaks specifically of the *ranunculi,* and a similar reference[4] appears later in the *De Philomela.* As we shall see, the song of birds at dawn and in the spring is fairly common in the classical poets. For these reasons it seems to me highly probable that *acredula* was understood in these passages as a bird.

[1]Cf. Gesner, op. cit., p. 76.

[2]So apparently Thompson, who does not cite ὀλολυγών in his *Glossary. Thes. Ling. Lat.* s. v. Genus ranarum ut videt. Isidorus records the double tradition, but apparently differentiates *acredula* (bird) from *agredula* (frog). *Orig.* 12, 7, 37: Eadem luscinia et acredula dicitur; *Orig.* 12, 6, 59: Agredulae ranae parvulae in sicco vel agro morantes, unde et nuncupatae.

[3]Cf. Schol. Theoc. VII, 139.

[4]Cf. with the passages below:

Vos quoque signa videtis, aquai dulcis alumnae,
Cum clamore paratis inanis fundere voces
Absurdoque sono fontis et stagna cietis.
—CIC., *De Div.* I, 9.

Garrula limosis rana coaxat aquis.
(*De Philomela.*) —*Anth. Lat.* 762, 64.

In this connection certain references to frogs in the American poets are of interest:

The croaking frogs, whom nipping winter kil'd
Like birds now chirp, and hop about the field.
(*The Four Seasons. Spring.*)
—ANNE BRADSTREET.

The frogs, nocturnal knights of song,
Are *nightly* wide awake;
I have no doubt they sing to sleep
The tadpoles small and great.—ABBOTT.

When Aristophanes in Greek
The tone essayed to hit,
"Pompholygopaphlasmasin"
Was near as he could get.
But this implies the bubbling sound
That voice in water makes:
Thy unimpeded, natural song
Was brekekex, koax.—BIGELOW (?).
(*Eolopoesis.*)

The frog's hoarse bassoon, and the loon's tremulous shriek.
—STREET.

Those guttural harps the green-frogs tune.—CAWEIN.

How dreary to be somebody!
How public, like a frog
To tell your name the livelong day
To an admiring bog!—EMILY DICKINSON.

I am sure the notorious frogs of Hor., *Sat.* I, 5, were part of the choir of spring. Vid. *Cl. Rev.*, 1901, p. 117 and p. 166. Vid. s. v TURDUS.

The vernal and matutinal songs of the *acredula*:

Et matutinis acredula vocibus instat,
Vocibus instat et adsiduas iacit ore querellas,
Cum primum gelidos rores aurora remittit.
—CIC., *De Div.* I, 8.

Vere calente novos componit acredula cantus
Matutinali tempore rurirulans.
(*De Philomela.*) —*Anth. Lat.* 762, 15.

The interpretation of Isid., *Orig.* 12, 7, 37: Luscinia avis inde nomen sumpsit, quod cantu suo significare solet diei surgentem exortum, quasi *lucinia*. Eadem et acredula, de qua Cicero in Prognosticis: et matutinos exercet acredula cantus.

For the form *acredula*, cf. Wackernagel, op. cit., p. 75: "So könnte auch das *edula*, worauf ausser *acredula* und *ficedula*, noch *monedula*, *querquedula* und (Isid., *Orig*. XII, 7) *coredulus* ausgehen, mit ἀείδειν und ἀηδών zu verbinden sein." The term *acredula* is still in use as the name of a genus of birds akin to the genus *Parus*. Cf. Newton, op. cit., p. 968.

For the onomatopoetic verbs of bird song in Latin, vid. passim *Anth. Lat.* 762; Wackernagel, op. cit. passim; Peck, *Onomatopoetic Words in Latin* (*Class. Studies in Honor of Henry Drisler*, p. 226).

AEDON. Ἀηδών. Nightingale.
Vid. s. v. LUSCINIA.

AFRA AVIS, (Libyca, Numidica). Μελεαγρίς, τέτραξ. Guinea-fowl. *Numida Meleagris*.

Described by Col., VIII, 8, 2; Africana est quam plerique Numidicam dicunt, meleagridi similis, nisi quod rutilam galeam et cristam capite gerit, quae utraque sunt in meleagride coerulea.

This is of interest, as it shows the difference between the Greek (Μελεαγρίς) and the Roman fowls. This agrees with the geographical distribution of the probable progenitors. Cf. Newton, op. cit., p. 399; Thompson, op. cit., s. v. v. supra; Hehn, op. cit., p. 358.

Guinea-fowls as table birds:

> Non Afra[1] avis descendat in ventrem meum.
> —Hor., *Epod.* 2, 53.

Cf. also Stat., *Silv.* I, 6, 78; II, 4, 28; vid. s. v. PHASIANUS.

> Si Libycae nobis volucres et Phasides essent,
> Acciperes, at nunc accipe chortis aves.
> —Mart. XIII, 45.

> Ansere Romano quamvis satur Hannibal esset,
> Ipse suas numquam barbarus edit aves.
> —Mart. XIII, 73.

[1]The guinea-fowl was brought to Italy after Hannibal's time. Cf. Hehn., op. cit., p. 309.

Nec frustum capreae subducere nec latus Afrae
Novit avis noster, tirunculus ac rudis omni
Tempore et exiguae furtis imbutus ofellae.
—JUV. XI, 142.

A Roman farm-yard scene:

Vagatur omnis turba sordidae chortis
Argutus anser, gemmeique pavones.
Nomenque debet quae rubentibus pennis,
Et picta perdix, Numidicaeque guttatae,
Et impiorum phasiana Colchorum.
—MART. III, 58, 12.

About my farm tame fowls should rove,
Geese and turkeys, ducks and dove;
Nor should I want the guinea-hen,
Which imitates the chatt'ring wren.—BELKNAP (Duyckinck).

He heard the chorus of the farm-yards, the jubilee of the birds.
—TROWBRIDGE.

The metamorphosis of the sisters of Meleager:

Post cinerem, cineres haustos ad pectora pressant,
Affusaeque iacent tumulo; signataque saxo
Nomina complexae; lacrimas in nomina fundunt.
Quas, Parthaoniae tandem Letoia clade
Exsatiata domus, praeter Gorgenque, nurumque
Nobilis Alcmenae, natis in corpore pennis
Adlevat, et longas per bracchia porrigit alas;
Corneaque ora facit, versasque per aera mittit.
—OV., *Met.* VIII, 538.

Cf. Ael. IV, 42; Plin. X, 38, 1; also Hyg., *Fab.* 174: At sorores eius praeter Gorgen et Deianiram flendo deorum voluntate in aves transfiguratae quae Meleagrides vocantur: at coniunx eius Alcyone moriens in luctu decessit.

ALCEDO (ALCYON). Ἀλκυών. Halcyon, kingfisher.
Alcedo ispida.
American parallel: Belted kingfisher.
Hosmer: *The Kingfisher.*
Luders (Stedman): *The Haunts of Halcyon.*
Maurice Thompson: *The Kingfisher.*

The halcyon is one of the four great song-birds of the Greeks and Romans. From early times it has been traditionally identified with the kingfisher, but the myths and associations, far more even than in the case of the swan, swallow and nightingale, resist rationalization. They seem hopelessly lost in the mystic symbolism of forgotten astronomic lore. In the Latin poets the whole treatment of the bird seems influenced by the metamorphosis idea, which as usual ascribes a tone of sadness, as if the bird were but continuing a former human sorrow. The American references to our own belted kingfisher are purely naturalistic and, as such, represent the one chief difference between the modern and ancient attitudes toward bird-life in general.

Alcedonia, the brooding period of the halcyons, is proverbially used to indicate a period of peace and quiet:

Tranquillum est, Alcedonia sunt circum forum.
—PLAUT., *Cas.* 26.

Iam hercle tu periisti, nisi illam mihi tam tranquillam facis
Quam mare olimst quam ibi alcedo pullos educit suos.
—PLAUT., *Poen.* 355.

And singing thoughts, like Halcyon birds,
Drift lightly o'er the waveless calm,
Near and more near the summer shore,
The isles of balm.—MACE.

Then, rocking near some cavern's emerald gleam,
Thou seem'st the soul of halcyonian days—
The restful Spirit of the sea supreme.—MIFFLIN.

Whose undulations rose and fell
Like ocean's soft and vernal swell,
When poets feign'd upon its breast
The wave-nursed Halcyon's floating nest.—WEBBER (Kettell).

And this the litany we pray:
That God who made may keep us free;
That storms may vex no more the sea,
Where, brooding 'neath a cloudless day,
Still sits Alcyone.—GORDON.

Art thou the bird of eld
That built its nest upon the cradling deep,
Owning a charm when wind and wave rebelled,
To hush them into sleep?—HOSMER.

Not there, not there Peace builds her halcyon nest:
Wild revel scares her from wealth's towering dome,
And misery frights her from the poor man's home.
Nor dwells she in the cloister, where the sage
Ponders the mystery of some time-stained page.
—EMBURY (Griswold).

Halcyon prophecies come to pass,
In haunts of bream and bass.—MAURICE THOMPSON

His is the halcyon table
That never seats but one,
And whatsoever is consumed
The same amounts remain.—EMILY DICKINSON.
(*Hope.*)

A simile seemingly illustrative of the habits and flight of the halcyon:

Alcyonis[1] ritu litus pervolgans feror.
—PACUV. (Ribb. *Trag. Rom. Frag.*, p. 149.)

Thine undulating flight
Mimics the billow in its rise and fall.—HOSMER.

On noiseless wing along that fair blue sea,
The halcyon flits.—LONGFELLOW.

As, when the kingfisher flits o'er his bay.—LOWELL.

The halcyon flutters in winter's track.—COATES (Stedman).

Let me lie here, far off from Zante's shore,
Where Susquehanna spreads her liquid miles;
To watch the circles from the dripping oar;
To see her halcyon dip, her eagle soar.—MIFFLIN.

Certain habits of the halcyon are signs whereby to judge the weather:

Non tepidum ad solem pinnas in litore pandunt
Dilectae Thetidi[2] alcyones.—VERG., *Geor.* I, 398.

Vergil's simple observation of the halcyon's habits and his freedom from the traditions of metamorphosis, etc., mark a characteristic which makes him the greatest Roman nature-poet.

Cf. also Prop. III, 7, 61: A miser alcyonum scopulis affligar acutis.

---

[1]Cf. the explanation of Varro, *L. L.* VII, 88: Haec enim avis graece dicitur ἀλκυών, nostri nunc alcedo: haec hieme quod pullos dicitur tranquillo mari facere, eos dies Alcyonios appellant. Quod est in versu 'alcyonis ritu,' id est eius instituto.

[2]Cf. Neri., op. cit.: Era sacro a Teti perchè dicevasi covasse sulle acque e fra le canne, e perchè Alcione, figlia di Eolo, essendo inconsolabile per la morte del suo sposo Ceice, figlio di Lucifero, perito in un naufragio, essendosi gettata in mare, fu dagli Dei, per ricompensa, trasformata col suo sposo in un uccello, che da lei si nomò. Gli antichi riguardarono questo uccello come simbolo di pace.

Propertius calls upon the halcyons to lull the fury of a gale:

Et merito, quoniam potui fugisse puellam!
Nunc ego desertas[1] alloquor alcyonas.
—Prop. I, 17, 1.

On the morning of Cynthia's birthday the poet prays that no suggestion of sorrow may cross his way, not even the plaintive songs of halcyon and nightingale:

Aspiciam nullos hodierna luce dolentes,
Et Niobae lacrimas supprimat ipse lapis,
Alcyonum[2] positis requiescant ora querelis,
Increpet absumptum nec sua mater Itym.
—Prop. III, 10, 7.

Ceyx is lost at sea. His wife Alcyone, finding his dead body, is filled with inordinate grief, so that both are metamorphosed into birds:

Insilit (Alcyone) huc; mirumque fuit potuisse; volabat,
Percutiensque levem modo natis aëra pennis
Stringebat summas ales miserabilis undas.
Dumque volat, maesto similem plenumque querelae
Ora dedere sonum tenui crepitantia rostro.
Ut vero tetigit mutum et sine sanguine corpus,
Dilectos artus amplexa recentibus alis,
Frigida nequiquam duro dedit oscula rostro.
Senserit hoc Ceyx, an vultum motibus undae
Tollere sit visus, populus dubitabat. At ille
Senserat, et tandem, superis miserantibus, ambo
Alite mutantur. Fatis obnoxius isdem
Tunc quoque mansit amor, nec coniugiale solutum
Foedus in alitibus. Coeunt fiuntque parentes;
Perque dies placidos hiberno tempore septem

---

[1]The adjective *desertas* is a true description of the halcyons (cf. Ov., *Her.* 17, 81: Alcyones solae), and is also a transferred epithet with a touch of the pathetic fallacy, suggestive of the love-lorn poet's own heart:

Cf. And when he heaved a sigh profound
The sympathetic swallow swept the ground.—Emerson.

The summer-bird his sorrow heard.—Emerson.

Passing the song of the hermit-bird and the tallying
song of my soul.—Whitman.

[2]To take *alcyonum* here and elsewhere in Propertius with Butler as 'merely seabirds' is to ignore the metamorphosis of the bird, which is the underlying cause of the tone of sorrow.

Incubat Alcyone pendentibus aequore nidis.
Tunc iacet unda maris: ventos custodit et arcet
Aeolus egressu praestatque nepotibus aequor.
Hos aliquis senior iunctim freta lata volantes
Spectat et ad finem servatos laudat amores.
—Ov., *Met.* XI, 731.

A song that is sad as the lone sea-bird's
When it seeks its mate with plaintive words.—STRONG.

For another tradition of the metamorphosis of Alcyone, cf. Ov., *Met.* VII, 401; Serv., in Verg., *Geor.* I, 399.

For Alcyone, the Pleiad, who shared the couch of Neptune, cf. Ov. *F.* IV, 172; Id., *Her.* XIX, 133.

Halcyon heavenly blue;
Lone contur, nighest to the star of day
Ranging, of winged life.—BAILEY.

For a passing reference to the sons of Alcyoneus, who threw themselves into the sea and were metamorphosed into halcyons, cf. Claud., *Rapt. Pros.* 185.

With the above compare these unique American accounts of metamorphosis:

And he heard the kingfisher
Who from his God escaped with crumpled crest
And the white medal hanging on his breast.
—BAYARD TAYLOR.

"Go! Thou shalt fish for minnows all thy life!"
Wrathful, the King the magic sentence heard;
He strove to answer, but he only *chirr-r-ed;*
His royal robe was changed to wings of blue,
His crown a ruby crest,—away he flew!
So every summer day along the stream
The vain king-fisher darts, an azure gleam,
And scolds the angler with a mocking scream.
—HENRY VAN DYKE.

It is deadly sorrow which causes the plaintive songs of Progne and Alcyone. Ovid seeks the same method of relief:

Est aliquid, fatale malum per verba levare:
Hoc querulam Prognen Alcyonemque facit.
—Ov., *Trist.* V, 1, 59.

The plaintive notes of the lonely halcyons seem sweet to the ears of Leander as he crosses the strait:

Alcyones solae, memores Ceycis amati,
Nescio quid visae sunt mihi dulce queri.
—Ov., *Her.* XVIII, 81.

The laments of Livia over her dead son are like complaints of the halcyons to the unheeding waters:

Alcyonum tales ventosa per aequora questus
Ad surdas tenui voce sonantur aquas.
—*Cons. ad Liv.* 107.

The halcyons come to Andromeda and with sympathetic songs of sorrow and with shadowing wings, seek to comfort and protect her:

Te circum Alcyones pennis planxere volantes
Fleveruntque tuos miserando carmine casus
Et tibi contextas umbram fecere per alas.
—MANIL., *Astron.* V, 558.

Octavia bids her laments to exceed those of halcyon, nightingale and swallow, for her grief is greater than theirs:

Age, tot tantis onerata malis,
Repete assuetos iam tibi questus
Atque aequoreas vince Alcyonas,
Vince et volucres Pandionias
Gravior namque his fortuna tua est.
—SEN., *Oct.* 5.

In a chorus to Cassandra advising lamentation as a relief to sorrow, the halcyon—with some description of its nest and young—is placed among the four great song-birds of antiquity. As usual, sorrow and grief are thought of as the essential qualities in their songs:

Non quae verno mobile carmen
Ramo cantat tristis aedon
Ityn in varios modulata sonos,
Non quae tectis Bistonis ales
Residens summis impia diri
Furta mariti garrula narrat,
Lugere tuam potuit digne
Conquesta domum. Licet ipse velit
Clarus niveos inter olores
Histrum cycnus Tanainque colens
Extrema loqui, licet alcyones

Ceyca suum fluctu leviter
Plangente sonent, cum tranquillo
Male confisae credunt iterum
Pelago audaces fetusque suos
Nido pavidae si titubante fovent.
—SEN., *Ag.* 670.

The idea of sorrow associated with the halcyon and other metamorphotic birds, is maintained even in speaking of the nest and in depicting scenes of general bird-life:

Addita de querulo volucrum medicamina nido
Ore fugant maculas, Alcyonea vocant.
—Ov., *De Med. Fac.* 77.

Vid. Hor., *Epod.* 11, 26: *Queruntur* in silvis aves, and cf. the wide use of the adjective *querulus* as a bird epithet. The scholiast to Horace tells us that *queror,* etc. was originally applied to the voices of all animals, but he cites only Verg., *Geor.* 1, 378 (*ranae*) and *Geor.* 3, 328 (*cicadae*). Vid. Porphyr. ad loc.

Contrast the above with these American descriptions of the kingfisher's note and habits:

When pacing through the oaks he heard
The rattle of the kingfisher.—EMERSON.

His are resplendent eyes;
His mien is kingliwise;
And down the May wind rides he like a king,
With more than royal purple on his wing.
—MAURICE THOMPSON.

Over the river, loud-chattering, aloft in the air, the king-fisher,
Hung, ere he dropped, like a bolt in the water beneath him.
—HOWELLS-PIATT.

Thy voice is like in sound
The twirling of a watchman's rattle loud.—HOSMER.

He laughs by the summer stream
Where the lilies nod and dream,
As through the sheen of water cool and clear
He sees the chub and sunfish cutting sheer.
—MAURICE THOMPSON.

The kingfisher watches, where o'er him his foe,
The fierce hawk, sails circling, each moment more low.
—STREET.

The kingfisher flies with a crack-cr-r-r-ack and a limping or flitting flight.—THOREAU, op. cit., p. 192.

The halcyon follows her nest and young when set adrift by the waves and bemoans their loss:

> Fluctus ab undisoni ceu forte crepidine saxi
> Cum rapit halcyones miserae fetumque laremque,
> It super aegra parens queriturque tumentibus undis
> Certa sequi, quocumque ferant, audetque pavetque,
> Icta fatiscit aquis donec domus haustaque fluctu est;
> Illa dolens vocem dedit et se sustulit alis.
> —VAL. FLACC. IV, 44.

Another similar situation of bird mother-love is portrayed:

> Fluctivagam sic saepe domum madidosque penates
> Alcyone deserta gemit, cum pignora saevus
> Auster et algentes rapuit Thetis invida nidos.
> Mergitur orba iterum, penitusque occulta sub undis
> Limite non uno, liquidum qua subter eunti
> Lucet inter, miseri nequidquam funera nati
> Vestigat, plangitque tamen.—STAT., *Theb.* IX, 360.

Vid. also Stat., *Silv.* III, 5, 57.

For a very curious conception (apparently allegorical) of the halcyon, with nest and young, vid. *Anth. Lat.* 383.

The more truly traditional conception of the halcyon, with nest and young unharrassed by storms, is portrayed in the following lines:

> Cum sonat alcyones cantu, nidosque natantes
> Immota gestat, sopitis fluctibus, unda.
> —SIL. ITAL. XIV, 275.

In a metrical inscription, three of the traditional song-birds, including the halcyon, are portrayed as joining in laments with a father for his dead wife and son:

> Cum te, nate, fleo, planctus dabit Attica aedo
> Et comes ad lachrimas veniet pro coniuge Siren
> Semper et Alcyone flebit te voce suprema
> Et tristis mecum resonabet carmen et Echo
> Oebaliusque dabit mecum tibi murmura cycnus.
> —C. I. L. VI, 25063.

The words *voce suprema* seem to suggest a confused reminiscence of the swan's death song.

Throned on a limb, lit by the sun's soft beam,
A lone kingfisher sat, as if in a dream.—WALLACE.

I know not, but the Past,
When I behold thee, bird, her face unveils,
And back on busy recollection, fast
Crowd old, romantic tales.—HOSMER.

ANAS. Νῆττα. Duck.

Hosmer: *The Wood-duck.*

Like several other bird names, the diminutive is used as a term of endearment:

Dic igitur med aneticulam, columbam vel catellum
Hirundinem, monerulam, passerculum putillum.
—PLAUT., *Asin.* 693.

My little love!
My duck! my dove!—FESSENDEN.

Jackdaws, ducks and quails are the pets of patrician children. A pun:

Nam ubi illo adveni, quasi patriciis pueris aut monerulae
Aut anites aut coturnices dantur, quicum lusitent,
Itidem haec mihi advenienti upupa qui me delectem datast.
—PLAUT., *Capt.* 1002.

Exposure is nothing to a duck. Proverbial:

Utinam fortuna nunc anetina uterer,
Ut quom exiissem ex aqua, arerem tamen.
—PLAUT., *Rud.* 533.

Some description of the wild duck and its pursuit by night:

Neque qua vagipennis anates remipedas buxeirostris pecudes paludibus nocte nigra ad lumina lampadis sequeris.
(*Sexagesis.*) —VARRO, *Men. Reliq.* 5.

The wild duck alert on the stream.—STEAD.

Where 'mid the river's rustling reeds
The water fowl to plumpness feeds.—ARLO BATES.

In their early flight,
Towards the creek or muddy sedge, the ducks
Oft coast along the wood.—M'KINNON.

For the wild duck, *fluvialis anas,* pursued by the hawk, vid. supra, s. v. ACCIPITER; also Ov., *Met.* XI, 771.

The duck as a basis of comparison:

> Et anatis habeas orthopygium macrae.
> —MART. III, 93, 12.

How ducks were served on the table:

> Tota quidem ponatur anas; sed pectore tantum
> Et cervice sapit: cetera redde coco.
> —MART. XIII, 52.

> Aside, twin ducks a savoury sage exhale.—M'KINNON.

> What first I want is daily bread,
> And canvass-backs and wine.—JOHN QUINCY ADAMS.

> His grace, the Canvas-back, My Lord
> *Anas* and *Anser*—both served up by dozens
> At Boston's Rocher, half-way to Nahant.—HOLMES.

> Ducks bursting with pistachio nuts.—BAYARD TAYLOR.

A gift of ducks sent to a friend by Ausonius. Some description of their characteristics and markings:

> Tum, quas vicinae suggessit praeda lacunae,
> Anates maritas iunximus,
> Remipedes, lato populantes caerula rostro
> Et crure rubras Punico.
> Iricolor vario pinxit quas pluma colore,
> Collum columbis aemulas.
> Defrudata meae non sunt haec fercula mensae.
> Vescente te, fruimur magis.
> Vale bene, ut valeam.
> —AUS., *Ep.* III, 11.

> A duck, beside an isle of wood,
> Within a watery streak was steering,
> Dipping his green head in the flood,
> When, quick his bill of yellow rearing,
> With a loud whiz he flew away.—STREET.

> And from yon nook of clustered water-plants,
> The wood-duck, shaking its rich purple neck,
> Skims forth, displaying through the liquid glass
> Its yellow feet, as if upborne in air.—STREET.

> Or crested wood-duck, rich in all the dies
> That tinge the fleecy robes of vernal skies.—ALSOP.

The far-famed canvass-backs at once we know,
Their broad flat bodies wrapt in pencilled snow;
The burnished chestnut o'er their necks that shone,
Spread deepening round each breast a sable zone.
(*The Foresters.*) —ALEXANDER WILSON.

Ducks, when leaving the sea, foretell the coming of storms:

Latipedemque anatem cernes excedere ponto
Saepius et summa nebulas se tendere rupe
Inde etiam ventos mox adfore praemonet usus.
—AVIEN., 1685.

A bit of observation as to the duck's note:

Pausitat arborea clamans de fronde palumbes
In fluviisque natans forte tetrinnit anas.
—*Anth. Lat.* 762, 21.

Cf. Suet., *Reliq.* 161: "Anatum (vox est) tetrissitare."
Cf. also Wackernagel, op. cit., p. 49.

Among the reeds the ducklings cry.—BURNS.

And gabbling in sequestered cove,
The black duck oiled her breast, and dove.—HOSMER.

The silver scream
Of wild duck startled from their marshy bed.—VALENTINE.

The wild duck from his reedy bed
Summons his fellow.—CARMAN-HOVEY.

It rang out over the marshes,
And the army of ducks was still.—BALLARD.

The ducks and geese are riotous, an' strainin' hard to sing.
What's the reason?
Oh, the reason's cause it's gittin' spring.—BEN KING.

ANSER. Χήν. Goose.

Cf. especially Thompson, op. cit., s. v.; Keller, op. cit., p. 288.
American parallels: Wild goose, brant.
Roberts: *The Flight of the Geese.*
Thaxter: *Wild Geese.*
Sigourney: *To a Goose.*
Field: *Gosling Stew.*

In a simile, reference is made to the driving away of geese from fields of grain:

Sed est huic unus servos violentissumus,
Qui ubi quamque nostrarum videt prope hasce aedis adgrediri
Item ut de frumento anseres, clamore apsterret, abigit.
—PLAUT., *Truc.* 250.

Cf. Avien., *Arat.* 1758: Gramina si carpit semensa anser.

Here, leave the geese, Carlo, to nibble their grass.—STREET.

Cf. also *Priap.* 61, 10.

Improbus anser
Strymoniaeque grues et amaris intiba fibris
Officiunt aut umbra nocet.—VERG., *Geor.* I, 119.

A proverbial reference to the softness of goose marrow:

Cinaede Thalle, mollior cuniculi capillo
Vel anseris medullula vel imula oricilla.
—CAT. XXV, 1.

Cf. *Priap.* 64: Quidam mollior anseris medulla.

Their sense of smell is very keen. Thus they saved the Roman citadel.

Et humanum longe presentit odorem
Romulidarum arcis servator candidus anser.
—LUCR. IV, 683.

Cf. Isid., *Orig.* XII, 7: Nullum animal ita odorem hominis sentit ut anser.

Other references to the same incident, which often recurs in the Roman writers:

In summo custos Tarpeiae Manlius arcis
Stabat pro templo et Capitolia celsa tenebat,
Romuleoque recens horrebat regia culmo.
Atque hic auratis volitans argenteus anser
Porticibus Gallos in limine adesse canebat.
—VERG., *Aen.* VIII, 652.

Anseris et tutum voce fuisse Iovem.
—PROP. IV, 4, 12.

Haec servavit avis Tarpeia templa Tonantis.
—MART. XIII, 74.

Nec servaturis vigili Capitolia voce
Cederet anseribus nec amanti flumina cycno.
—OV., *Met.* II, 137.

Sed reppulit unus
Tum quoque totam aciem, Senones dum garrulus anser
Nuntiat et vigilat vestrum sine milite fatum.
—SEDUL. V, 83.

Do those worthies know
That when old Rome had let the ruffian Gauls
Tread on her threshold of vitality,
And all her sentinels were comatose,
Thy clarion-call did save her? Mighty strange
To call *thee* fool!—SIGOURNEY.

By cackling, as their sires saved Rome.—HALLECK.

Geese are as guards more wise than dogs. A description of the abode of sleep:

Non vigil ales ibi cristati cantibus oris
Evocat Auroram, nec voce silentia rumpunt
Sollicitive canes canibusque sagacior [1] anser.
—Ov., *Met.* XI, 597.

The feathers of the goose and various other birds were used in making decoys:

Dat tibi pennarum terrentia millia vultur,
Dantque grues, cycnique senes et candidus anser.
—NEMES., *Cyn.* 312.

In one of the most appreciative passages of bird life in the Latin poets, Ovid gives the reasons for the destruction of birds, viz., that they reveal the purposes of the gods. The Capitoline geese are forgotten:

Intactae fueratis aves, solacia ruris,
  Adsuetum silvis, innocuumque genus;
Quae facitis nidos, quae plumis ora fovetis,
  Et facili dulces editis ore modos.
Sed nihil ista iuvant, quia linguae crimen habetis,
  Dique putant mentes vos aperire suas.
Nec tamen id falsum: nam, dis ut proxima quaeque,
  Nunc penna veras, nunc datis ore notas.
Tuta diu volucrum proles, tunc denique caesa est,
  Iuveruntque deos indicis exta sui.
Ergo saepe suo coniunx abducta marito
  Uritur Idaliis alba columba focis.
Nec defensa iuvant Capitolia, quo minus anser
  Det iecur in lances, Inachi lauta, tuas,
Nocte deae Nocti cristatus caeditur ales,
  Quod tepidum vigili provocet ore diem.
—Ov., *Fast.* I, 441.

[1] The modern proverbial 'stupid as a goose' was unknown in antiquity.—KELLER.

For punning references to *Anser* the poet vid. s. v. CYCNUS, and cf. Verg., *Ecl.* IX, 35; Ov., *Trist.* II, 435; Prop. II, 34, 83.

Cf. for something of the same tone:

Come, let me lead thee o'er this "*second Rome!*"
Where tribunes rule, where dusky Davi bow,
And what was *Goose-Creek* once is Tiber now.
(*Poems relating to America. From the City of Washington.*) —THOMAS MOORE.

The cackling or hissing note of geese:

Caccabat hinc perdix et graccitat improbus anser.
—*Anth. Lat.* 762, 19.

Dum miluus iugilat, trinnit tunc improbus anser.
—*Anth. Lat.* 733, 11.

Cf. *Argutus anser,* Mart. III, 68, 13; and *argutus olor,* Verg., *Ecl.* IX, 36; "With regular anserine clangor," Thoreau, op. cit., p. 51; Wackernagel, op. cit., p. 50.

Around the ducks their gabbling frolicks play'd,
While o'er the stream the aged gander sway'd,
The saucy monarch of the mimic main,
With num'rous plumy subjects in his train:
And oft he scar'd the ling'ring truant boys
Along the banks, with fearful hissing noise.—CHATTERTON.

The fowls loud cackling swarm about the yard;
The snowy geese harangue their numerous brood.
(*The Foresters.*) —ALEXANDER WILSON.

Philemon and Baucis attempt to kill their only goose for the entertainment of their guests Jupiter and Mercury. The goose flies to the gods for protection and is saved:

Unicus anser erat, minimae custodia villae,
Quem dis hospitibus domini mactare parabant.
Ille celer penna tardos aetate fatigat
Eluditque diu; tandemque est visus ad ipsos
Confugisse deos. Superi vetuere necari.
—Ov., *Met.* VIII, 684.

Pâtes de foie gras:

Deinde secuti
Mazonomo pueri magno discerpta ferentes
Membra gruis, sparsi sale multo non sine farre,
Pinguibus et ficis pastum iecur anseris albae.
—HOR., *Sat.* II, 8, 91.

Aspice, quam tumeat magno iecur ansere maius!
Miratus dices, 'Hoc, rogo, crevit ubi?'
—MART. XIII, 58.

Cf. Juv. V, 114; Pers. IV, 71; Stat., *Silv.* IV, 6, 9; Pet., *Sat.* 65; Mart. XIII, 73, et al.

But he could cook a goose as brown
As any man that set foot on
The mist-kissed shores of Oregon.—MILLER.

A goose was vowed to Mars by Velius. When the god demanded its fulfillment, the goose gladly hastened to the altar. A silver statue of the goose, with tokens, commemorates the deed:

Ipse suas anser properavit laetus ad aras
Et cecidit sanctis hostia parva focis.
Octo vides patulo pendere numismata rostro
Alitis? Haec extis condita nuper erant
Quae litat argento pro te, non sanguine, caesa.
Victima iam ferro non opus esse docet.
—MART. IX, 31, 5.

The goose was sacred also to Isis and Osiris.

Cf. Juv. 6, 540; *Anth. Lat.* 395, 43.

Jupiter as the consort of Leda, is referred to once as the 'Amyclaeus anser':

Ciris Amyclaeo formosior ansere Ledae.[1]
—VERG., *Ciris* 489.

You tell me, with a little scorn,
That all my swans are veriest geese.—COOLIDGE.
(*Optimism.*)

A resumé of the usefulness of the Roman goose:

Aedibus in nostris volitans argenteus anser,
Dulcisono strepitu colla canora levat.
Ales grata bono duplici; nam fercula mensae
Conplet et adservat nocte silente domum.
Solus Tarpeia canibus in rupe quietis
Eripuit Gallis Romula tecta vigil.
(*De Ansere.*) —*Anth. Lat.* 106.

[1]This may be the original form of the myth. The swan was substituted in a later and more aesthetic age. Cf. Keller, op. cit., p. 228 and 455. Buckland, *Mythological Birds Ethnologically Considered. Anthrop. Jour.* 4, 277. See this important article also for illuminating discussion of the mythology of the dove, eagle, hawk, owl, peacock and phoenix.

Meantime, the worthy and hard-working goose
Hath rear'd up goslings, fed us with her flesh,
Lull'd us to sleep upon her softest down,
And with her quills maintain'd the lover's love,
And saved the tinsel of the poet's brain.—SIGOURNEY.

For the Fable of the Stork, Goose and Hawk vid. s. v. ACCIPITER.

For the Fable of the Goose that laid the golden egg vid. Avianus, *Fab.* 33.

I move the owl
Be straightway swept from the usurper's seat,
And thou forthwith be voted for, to fill
Minerva's arms.—SIGOURNEY.

AQUILA. 'Αετός. Eagle.

For the best discussion of identifications and astronomic lore vid. Thompson, op. cit., s. v. 'Αετός; Harting, op. cit., chap. I; Boraston, *The Birds of Homer. Jour. of Hell. Studies,* vol. 31.

For the eagle in mythology and ancient art vid. Keller, op. cit., s. v.

In the American poets the eagle is mentioned more often than any other bird.

Neal (Kettell): *The Eagle.*

Percival: *To the Eagle.*

Street: *The Gray Forest Eagle.*

Melville (Stedman): *The Eagle of the Blue.*

Simms: *The Slain Eagle.*

Epithets. Characteristics:

Fulva aquila, Verg., *Aen.* XI, 751; *Nuntia fulva Iovis,* Cic., *Carm. frag.* 18; *Ales fulva Iovis,* Sil. Ital. XII, 56; *Fulvus Iovis ales,* Verg., *Aen.* XII, 247; Av., *Arat.* 1007, et passim; *Iovis pinnata satelles,* Cic., *Mar.* Bücheler, P. M., p. 305; *Aquila minore pinna,* Mart. X, 19, 10; keen-sighted, Hor., *Sat.* I, 3, 27; *Densis pinnis,* Enn., *Ann.* 149; *Praedator,* Ov., *Met.* VI, 516; *Improbus,* Verg., *Aen.* XII, 250; *Aquilis coruscis, Ciris* 529; *Ferox aquila,* Hor., *Carm.* IV, 4, 31; *Tremebundis pennis,* Cic., *Arat.* 329, et al.

As the bird of Jupiter:

Satelles Iovis, Cic., *ex Aes.* Bücheler, P. M., p. 309; *Famulae Iovis,* Juv. XIV, 81; *Iovis ales,* Ov., *Met.* VI, 516; Verg., *Aen.* I, 394, et passim; *Armiger Iovis,* Ov., *Met.* XV, 386; Sil. Ital. X, 108, et passim; *Iovis praepes,* Ov., *Met.* IV, 714; Verg., *Aen.* V, 254; *Flammiger ales,*

Stat., *Theb.* VIII, 675; *Fulminis ales,* Hor., *Carm.* IV, 4, 1; *Volucrum regina,* Mart. V, 55; *Avis regis,* Mart. X, 19; *Regia ales.* Ov., *Met.* IV, 362; *divum gratissima regi,* Ov., *Met.* XII, 561, et passim.

The nimble messenger of Jove
On earth alights not from above
With step so light as theirs.—HOPKINSON.
(*The British Light Infantry.* 1778.)

And Jove's swift eagles soared above the vales.—PROCTOR.

O pine tree! Jove sends down his word to you
By his own eagle from the heights of heaven.—VALENTINE.

An Eagle, soaring in his pride of place,
Was seen, the head of Japheth hovering o'er;
A thunderbolt the pluming stranger bore.
—ALLEN (Duyckinck).

And looked the fable of the Greek—
The bird with thunder in his beak.
(*The Bird of Washington.*)—WARFIELD-LEE (Griswold).

Thou with the gods upon Olympus dwelt,
The emblem and the favorite bird of Jove—
And godlike power in thy broad wings hast felt
Since first they spread o'er land and sea to rove.
(*To the Eagle.*) —KINNEY (Griswold).

Speak! speak! Through this dark cloud
The eyes of Zeus's eagle cannot pierce.—MOODY.

Sounds. Clangor:
Sil. Ital. XVII, 55; *Anth. Lat.* 762, 27.

And above him wheeled and clamored
The Keneu, the great war-eagle.—LONGFELLOW.

Nesting habits and young:

Non aliter, quam cum pedibus praedator obuncis
Deposuit nido leporem Iovis ales in alto.
—Ov., *Met.* VI, 516.

Aquila in sublimi quercu nidum fecerat.
—PHAED. II, 4, 1.

Cf. also Verg., *Aen.* IX, 563; Sil. Ital. IV, 55; XII, 55, et al.

The eagle from Bellona's eyrie.—STEDMAN.

Like eagle's nest built in the air.—MILLER.

The youthful Drusus, in a splendid simile, is likened to the eagle's young that are driven from the nest to seek their prey:

Hor., *Carm.* IV, 4. Cf. Schmid, *De aquila, quae apud Horatium Carm.*, IV, 4.

But like the fledgling eaglet leave the nest.—SILL.

A reference to the eagle-stone, *lapis aëtites.* Cf. Plin. X, 3, 4:

Quaeque sonant feta tepefacta sub alite saxa.
—LUC. VI, 673.

Dicuntur quidam lapides inveniri in Armenia, qui praegnantes vocantur, eo, quod habent lapillos intra se, et prosunt partui, quos et aquilae sub se ponunt cum ovis, ne incendantur ipsius (aquilae) calore.—*Schol. ap. Oud.*, Weber, C. P. L., p. 719.

The callow young are tried by the sun test:

Utque Iovis volucer, calido cum protulit ovo
Implumes natos, solis convertit ad ortus:
Qui potuere pati radios, et lumine recto
Sustinuere diem caeli, servantur in usus:
Qui Phoebo cessere, iacent.—LUC. IX, 900.

Armiger haud aliter magni Iovis, anxia nido
Cum dignos nutrit gestanda ad fulmina fetus,
Observam spectans ora ad Phaethontia prolem,
Explorat dubios Phoebea lampade natos.
—SIL. ITAL. X, 108.

The eagle and the sun in the American poets:

Thro' the far clouds, the eagle cleft his way,
And soar'd, and wanton'd in the flames of day.
(*Creation.*) —TIMOTHY DWIGHT.

The eagle eye that mocks the God of day.—PAULDING.
(*The Backwoodsmen.*)

Go climb the fields of air, the heights explore,
Beyond where even eagles dare to soar.—ALLEN (Kettell).

The eagle was always the friend of the sun.—HOLMES.

The bird, whose pinion courts the sunbeam's fire.
—SPRAGUE (Griswold).

(Apollo) thou in whose bright
And hottest rays the eagle fills his eye
With quenchless fire, and far, far up on high
Screams out his joy to thee.—GEN. ALBERT PIKE.

Your eagle climbing to the sun
Keeps not the straightest course in sight.—MILLER.

To soar like eagles in the blaze of noon,
Above the gaping crowd of friends and foes.—HALLECK.

Still, like the eaglet on its new-fledged wing,
Her spirit-glance bespoke the daughter of a king.
—SIGOURNEY.

A sun-bent eagle stricken
From his high soaring down.—WILLIS.

What! soar'd the old eagle to die at the sun!
Lies he stiff with spread wings at the goal he had won!
—WILLIS.

Hither the eagles fly, and lay their eggs;
Then bring their young ones forth out of those crags,
And force them to behold Sol's majesty,
In mid-noon glory, with a steady eye.—ROGER WOLCOTT.
(*Connecticut River.*)

How the eagle sharpens his beak:

Here the old eagle his long beak belays
Upon a rock, till he renews his days.—ROGER WOLCOTT.
(*Connecticut River.*)

Whilst now and then the eagle gray
Pointed his beak and soared away.—STREET.

Flight. The grandeur in the spectacle of a soaring eagle was felt by the Roman poets:

Utque volans alte raptum cum fulva draconem
Fert aquila, implicuit pedes, atque unguibus haesit;
Saucius at serpens sinuosa volumina versat,
Arrectisque horret squamis, et sibilat ore,
Arduus insurgens; illa haud minus urget obunco
Luctantem rostro, simul aethera verberat alis.
—VERG., *Aen.* XI, 751.

Qualis ubi aut leporem aut candenti corpore cycnum
Sustulit alta petens pedibus Iovis armiger uncis.
—VERG., *Aen.* IX, 560.

The death of Periclymenus, and his metamorphosis into a soaring eagle:

> Tendit in hunc nimium certos Tirynthius arcus,
> Atque inter nubes sublimia membra ferentem,
> Pendentemque ferit, lateri qua iungitur ala.
> —Ov., *Met.* XII, 564.

Cf. Fronto, 146, 17n: Aquilarum maiestate volare.
Apul., *Flor.* 8: Paene eodem loco pendula circumtuetur.
Cf. Beneath a tilted hawk is balancing.—SILL.

> The lofty Eagle, and the Stork fly low,
> The Peacock and the Ostrich, share in woe.
> —ANNE BRADSTREET.

> To wastes
> O'er which the eagle hovered.—BRYANT.

> Skies where desert eagle wheels and screams.—BRYANT.

> Gloriously the morning breaks,
> And the eagle's on his cloud.—LONGFELLOW.

> The hawk sailing where men have not yet sailed.
> —WHITMAN.

The eagle and his prey. The swan:

> Namque volans rubra fulvus Iovis ales in aethra
> Litoreas agitabat aves turbamque sonantem
> Agminis aligeri: subito cum lapsus ad undas
> Cycnum excellentem pedibus rapit improbus uncis.
> —VERG., *Aen.* XII, 247.

Cf. Verg., *Aen.* I, 394; IX, 563; Stat., *Theb.* III, 524; VIII, 674; IX, 858, et al.

The dove. The proverbial prey also of the hawk. Cf. Sil. Ital. IV, 114.

> Sic aquilam penna fugiunt trepidante columbae.
> —Ov., *Met.* I, 506.

> Ut fugiunt aquilam, timidissima turba, columbae.
> —Ov., *Ars. Amat.* I, 117.

> Sed carmina tantum
> Nostra valent, Lycida, tela inter Martia, quantum
> Chaonias dicunt aquila veniente columbas.
> —VERG., *Ecl.* IX, 11.

Birds in general:

Et Iovis in multas devolat ales aves.
—Ov., *Ars Amat.*, III, 420.

Master of all fowls and feathers.—LONGFELLOW.

Pursues him like audacious eagle
In quest of plover, snipe or sea-gull.—FESSENDEN.

Not for this
Did great Columbus tame his eagle soul
To jostle with daws that perch in courts.—LOWELL.

The hare:

Aut dumis subit, albenti si sensit in aethra
Librantem nisus aquilam, lepus ore citato.
—SIL. ITAL. V, 283.

Cf. Verg., *Aen.* IX, 560; Ov., *Met.* VI, 517; Phaed., *Fab.* I, 9; Juv. XIV, 81.

With darting haste, behold her ample size,
Full to th' enjoy'd, though distant victim hies,
Couch'd horrid now she nimbly hovers o'er
Her untorn prey, in raptures at its gore.
Back to her nest she shapes her upward flight,
Her young suck up the blood, with dire delight.
—DEVENS (Kettell).

The lamb. Excitement of shepherds and dogs:

Vid. *The Eagle and the Lamb.* (Painting by Audubon.) *Journal,* vol. I, p. 242 and p. 299.

Talia constanti laevum Iovis armiger aethra
Advenit, et validis fixam erigit unguibus agnam.
At procul e stabulis trepidi clamore sequuntur
Pastores fremitusque canum; citus occupat auras
Raptor, et Aegaei super effugit alta profundi.
Accipit augurium Aesonides, laetusque superbi
Tecta petit Peliae. —VAL. FLACC. I, 156.

Hooh! hooh! how the eagle screams,
As the blood of the fawn from his talons streams!—STREET.

Serpents. The most striking picture perhaps is the battle between an eagle and serpent in midair:

Verg., *Aen.* XI, 751. Vid. supra. Almost equally vivid are the following descriptions:

> Denique nitentem contra, elabique volentem
> Implicat, ut serpens, quam regia sustinet ales,
> Sublimemque rapit: pendens caput illa pedesque
> Alligat, et cauda spatiantes implicat ales.
> —Ov., *Met.* IV, 361.

> Utque Iovis praepes, vacuo cum vidit in arvo
> Praebentem Phoebo liventia terga draconem,
> Occupat aversum, neu saeva retorqueat ora,
> Squamigeris avidos figit cervicibus ungues.
> —Ov., *Met.* IV, 714.

> Haud secus, occubuit saxi quos vertice fetus
> Ales fulva Iovis, tacito si ad culmina nisu
> Evasit serpens, terretque propinquus hiatu:
> Illa, hostem rostro atque assuetis fulmina ferre
> Unguibus incessens, nidi circumvolat orbem.
> —Sil. Ital. XII, 55.

For other prey:

Cf. Phaed. I, 28: *Vulpi catuli*; Id. II, 6: *Testudinem*; Id. II, 4, 15. *Porcelli;* Juv. XIV, 81: *Capream;* Hor., *Carm.* IV, 4, 9: *In ovilia.*

For Prometheus and an eagle instead of a vulture. Cf. Cic., *Ex Aes.* (*Tusc. Dis.* II, X). This confusion is common in Greek. Vid. Thompson, op. cit., p. 3.

On the eagle in augury int. al. cf. the following:

Cic., *De Div.* I, 47, 106; Verg., *Aen.* I, 393; Id. XII, 244; Val. Flacc. I, 156; Sil. Ital. IV, 104.

For the eagle with Ganymede portrayed in the arts as described by the poets, cf. int. al. Plaut., *Men.* 143; Verg., *Aen.* V, 250; Mart. V, 50; Id. X, 19; Val. Flacc. II, 408; Stat., *Theb.* I, 548; Sil. Ital. XV, 421.

> As Ganymede by the eagle was snatched up.—Lowell.

> Recall that sound as of a lute,
> When from the empyrean deep,
> We saw the eagle downward sweep,
> And, as we gazed in wonder mute,
> Bear up a lad from 'mid his sheep,
> Who dropped a shepherd's flute.—Mifflin.
> (*The Slopes of Helicon.*)

For an attempt to rationalize the Ganymede myth vid. Keller, op. cit. p. 439.

Cf. Margaret Fuller, *Ganymede to his Eagle.* (Suggested by a work of Thorwaldsen's.)

Fables:

The Eagle, Crow, and Tortoise: Phaed. II, 6. The Eagle, Cat, and Sow: Id. II, 4. The Eagle's strength is a gift from the Fates: Id. III, 18. The Eagle and Kite wedded: *Aes. Fab.* XXXIV.

Various proverbial associations:

> 'Nil' narras? Visa verost, quod dici solet,
> Aquilae senectus. —TER., *Heaut.* 520.

> Tam dispar aquilae columba non est.
> —MART. X, 65, 12.

> Quid congregare cum leonibus vulpes
> Aquilisque similes facere noctuas quaeris?
> —MART. X, 100, 3.

References to the eagle as a military standard. Maximus Cotta is addressed by Ovid:

> Vos eritis nostrae portus et ara fugae
> Vos ego complector, Geticis si cingar ab armis.
> Utque meas aquilas, vos mea signa sequar.
> —Ov., *Ex Pont.* II, 8, 68.

The conquered eagles of Crassus:

> Signa, decus belli, Parthus Romana tenebat,
> Romanaeque aquilae signifer hostis erat.
> —Ov., *Fast.* V, 585.

> These are they whose fathers carried the conquering eagles,
> Over all Gaul and across the sea to Ultima Thule.
> —JOHNSON (Stedman).

> For it was Trajan that carried the battle-flushed eagles to
> Dacia.—HAY.

Cf. The condor, frowning from a southern plain,
Borne on a standard, leads a numerous train.—BARLOW.
(*Columbiad.*)

Cf. Turn from the eagles; woo the dove,
For it will glad the angels more
If you will train a vine above
A lowly cottage door.—WATERMAN.
(*Peace on Earth.*)

> Who bides at home, nor looks abroad,
> He carries the eagles—he masters the sword.—EMERSON.

A battle scene with graphic details:

Gallus at, in castris dum credita signa tuetur,
Concidit ante aquilae rostra cruenta suae.
—PROP. V, 1, 95.

The splendid devotion of a dying standard-bearer. The finest touch of patriotic war verse in Latin literature:

Inde honor ac sacrae custodia Marte sub omni
Alitis: hinc causam nutrivit gloria leti.
Namque, necis certus, captae prohibere nequiret
Cum Poenos aquilae, postquam subsidere fata
Viderat, et magna pugnam inclinare ruina,
Occulere interdum et terrae mandare parabat:
Sed, subitis victus telis, labentia membra
Prostravit super atque iniecta morte tegebat.
Verum ubi lux nocte e Stygia miseroque sopore
Reddita, vicini de strage cadaveris hasta
Erigitur, soloque vigens conamine, late
Stagnantem caede et facilem discedere terram
Ense fodit, clausamque aquilae infelicis adorans
Effigiem, palmis languentibus aequat harenas.
Supremus fessi tenuis tum cessit in auras
Halitus, et magnam misit sub Tartara mentem.
—SIL. ITAL. VI, 25.

For thee they fought, for thee they fell,
And their oath was on thee laid;
To thee the clarions raised their swell,
And the dying warrior prayed.—PERCIVAL.

Emblem of Freedom, when thou cleav'st the air—
Emblem of Tyranny, when bathed in blood!
Thou wert the genius of Rome's sanguine wars:
Heroes have fought and freely bled for thee.
(*To the Eagle.*) —KINNEY (Griswold).

Our eagle's wing
Shall mount, our eagle shall be king!
And jackals shall be heard no more
When Freedom's monarch bird shall soar.—READ.

Then from his mansion in the sun
She called her eagle bearer down
And gave into his mighty hand
The symbol of her chosen land.—DRAKE.

Vid. also *The Conquered Banner*, Ryan: "The priest-Tyrtaeus of the South" (Sladen).

The eagle as a military standard was an object of worship and reverence. Cf. Sil. Ital. VI, 37, supra; Cic., *Cat.* I, 24; Val. Max. VI, 1, 11; Suet., *Cal.* 14.

Illa quidem faeno; sed erat reverentia faeno,
Quantam nunc aquilas cernis habere tuas.
—Ov., *Fast.* III, 115.

For the constellation *aquila* vid. int. al. Cic., *Arat.* 87, 294, 372; Ov., *Fast.* V, 732; VI, 196; Manil. I, 342, 620, 684; V, 487, 710.

The Swan and Eagle wing their silent flight;
And, from their spangled pinions, as they flew,
On Israel's vales of verdure shower the dew.—PIERPONT.
(*Airs of Palestine.*)

Once, could the Roman Eagle soar
Beyond the reach of human eye;
But now, she plumes her wing, no more,
No more invades the sky.—WILLIAM LAKE.
(*Columbia's Eagle.*)

ARDEA. Ἐρωδιός. Heron.
Various species are included in the generic *ardea*.
American parallels: Heron, egret.
Thompson: *The Death of the White Heron.*
Cawein: *The Heron;* Id.: *The Blue Heron.*

And boggy marges of the mere,
Whereon I see the heron stand,
Knee-deep in sable slush of sand.
—MAURICE THOMPSON.

Where tall blue herons stretch lithe necks, and lean
Over clear currents flowing cool and thin,
Through the clean furrows of the pebbly floor.
—MAURICE THOMPSON.

A solitary heron wings its way
Southward—save this no sound or touch of life.
—ALDRICH.

So silent is the air, so hushed, so mute,
That e'en the sentinel heron does not fear
But stands erect, nor drops his lifted foot.—MIFFLIN.

And near its edge, like some gray streak,
Stands gaunt the still fly-up-the-creek.—CAWEIN.
(*The Mill-water.*)

A heron[1] plume of snow hung o'er;
Memorial of that bird that swept
Its way to Hah-yoh-wont-hah dread,
And whose pure plumage long was kept
To deck the bravest warrior's head.—STREET.

While like the spirit of the coming night
The heron wings on high his sullen flight.—ARLO BATES.

Signs of approaching storm:

Iam sibi tum curvis male temperat unda carinis
Cum medio celeres revolant ex aequore mergi
Clamoremque ferunt ad litora cumque marinae
In sicco ludunt fulicae notasque paludis
Deserit atque altam supra volat ardea nubem.
—VERG., *Geor.* I, 360.

Cf. Luc. V, 555. *Anth. Lat.* 772, 37: Hinc super ardea nubes. Isid., *Orig.* 12, 7, 21: (Ardea) formidat enim imbres, et super nubes evolat, ut procellas nubium sentire non possit: cum autem altius volaverit, significat tempestatem.

When he leaves the seacoast, and traces on wing the courses of the creeks or rivers upwards, he is said to prognosticate rain; when downwards, dry weather.—ALEXANDER WILSON, op. cit., s. v. GREAT HERON.

The city of Ardea, where the bird *ardea* arose Phoenix-like from the ruins. Cf. Verg., *Aen.* VII, 411:

Cadit Ardea, Turno
Sospite dicta potens. Quam postquam Dardanus ignis
Abstulit et tepida latuerunt tecta favilla,
Congerie e media tum primum cognita praepes
Subvolat et cineres plausis everberat alis.
Et sonus et macies et pallor et omnia captam
Quae deceant urbem, nomen quoque mansit in illa
Urbis; et ipsa suis deplangitur ardea pennis.
—Ov., *Met.* XIV, 573.

The cry of the heron:

A flock of nearly a hundred blue herons alighted on a small island near us, Londoners', and made the air ring with their noise.—CELIA THAXTER (*Letters*, p. 175).

[1]In Seneca the heron is called Sah-dah-ga-ah, meaning 'the bird of the clouds.'—*Author's note.*

The Hern's hoarse clang, or Sea-gull's lonely cry.—ALSOP.

And the heron, the Shuh-shuh-gah,
From the melancholy moorlands,
Gave a cry of lamentations,
Gave a cry of pain and anguish.—LONGFELLOW.

No bird is heard; no throat to whistle awake
    The sleepy hush; to let its music leak
Fresh, bubble-like, through bloom-roofs of the brake:
    Only the green-blue heron, famine weak—
    Searching the stale pools of the minnowless creek,—
Utters its call. —CAWEIN.
  (*Drouth.*)

ATTAGENA (ATTAGEN). Ἀτταγήν. The Francolin. *Tetrao francolinus.*

American parallels: Partridge, prairie-hen, etc.

Francolins—delicious eating . . . uttered their grated calls near by.—ROOSEVELT, *African Game Trails,* p. 344.

The simplicity of early days:

Piscis adhuc illi populo sine fraude natabat,
    Ostreaque in conchis tuta suis.
Nec Latium norat, quam praebet Ionia dives,
    Nec quae Pygmaeo sanguine gaudet, avem;
Et praeter pinnas nihil in pavone placebat.
—OV., *Fast.* VI, 173.

The *attagena* is the finest of all game birds:

Inter sapores fertur alitum primus
Ionicarum gustus attagenarum.
—MART. XIII, 61.

Horace deprecates high living:

Non Afra avis descendat in ventrem meum,
    Non attagen Ionicus,
Iucundior quam lecta de pinguissimis
    Oliva ramis arborum, etc.
—HOR., *Epod* II, 54.

And men had better stomachs to religion
Than I to capon, turkey-cock or pigeon.
  (*New England's Crisis.*) —BENJAMIN TOMPSON.

BUBO. Βύας. Owl, eagle owl.

Strix bubo.

American parallel: Great-horned owl. *Bubo Virginianus.*

Proctor: *The Owl.*

Celia Thaxter: *The Great White Owl.*

The mournful notes of an owl on the roof-top add to the gloom of deserted Dido:

> Solaque culminibus ferali carmine bubo
> Saepe queri et longas in fletum ducere voces.
> —VERG., *Aen.* IV, 462.

Cf. [Hos. Get.] *Medea* 124 (*Anth. Lat.*, p. 66). *Bubo* is feminine only here in the Latin poets: vid. Serv. in loc.

> The tremulous sob of the complaining owl.—WORDSWORTH.

> There I hear the moping owl,
> His dismal whoopings roll,
> Upon the heavy ear of night,
> In sounds that would thy soul affright.—BIRTHA.

A charm to keep owls away, which has widely survived in modern lore and practice:

> Hinc Amythaonius, docuit quem plurima Chiron,
> Nocturnas crucibus volucres suspendit et altis
> Culminibus vetuit feralia carmina flere.
> —COL. X, 348.

Ascalaphus is metamorphosed into an owl. Some description of the bird and an interpretation of its note:

> Ingemuit regina Erebi testemque profanam
> Fecit avem, sparsumque caput Phlegethontide lympha
> In rostrum et plumas et grandia lumina vertit.
> Ille sibi ablatus fulvis amicitur in alis,
> Inque caput crescit, longosque reflectitur ungues,
> Vixque movet natas perinertia bracchia pennas:
> Foedaque fit volucris, venturi nuntia luctus,
> Ignavus bubo, dirum mortalibus omen.
> —OV., *Met.* V, 543.

Among other omens of woe to come, an owl was present at the marriage of Tereus and Progne:

> Eumenides stravere torum, tectoque profanus
> Incubuit bubo thalamique in culmine sedit.
> Hac ave coniuncti Progne Tereusque, parentes
> Hac ave sunt facti. —OV., *Met.* VI, 431.

The fateful note of the owl and other warnings did not prevent Myrrha from incestuous union with Conyras, her father:

> Ter pedis offensi signo est revocata, ter omen
> Funereus bubo letali carmine fecit.
> It tamen, et tenebrae minuunt, noxque atra pudorem.
> —Ov., *Met.* X, 452.

The gloomy calls of innumerable owls attend the death of Caesar:

> Tristia mille locis Stygius[1] dedit omnia bubo:
> Mille locis lacrimavit ebur, cantusque feruntur
> Auditi sanctis et verba minantia lucis.
> —Ov., *Met.* XV, 791.

Likewise, great numbers of owls frequented the ill-omened Roman camp at Cannae:

> Obseditque frequens castrorum limina bubo.
> —SIL. ITAL. VIII, 634.

The ill-boding notes of an owl were heard when Ibis was born:

> Sedit in adverso nocturnus culmine bubo
> Funereoque graves edidit ore sonos.
> Ov., *Ibis* 223.

Medea uses the heart of an owl in her incantations before the altar of Hecate. Cf. Ov., *Amor.* I, 12, 19.

> Mortifera carpit gramina ac serpentium
> Saniem exprimit miscetque et obscenas aves
> Maestique cor bubonis et raucae strigis
> Exsecta vivae viscera. —SEN., *Med.* 731.

Another incantation:

> Latratus habet illa canum gemitusque luporum
> Quod trepidus bubo, quod strix nocturna queruntur,
> Quod stridunt ululantque ferae, quod sibilant anguis.
> —LUC. VI, 686.

The owl with its gloomy note is one of the birds of Hades:

> Hic vultur, illic luctifer bubo gemit
> Omenque triste resonat infaustae strigis.
> —SEN., *Her. Fur.* 686.

---

[1]The epithet Stygius may be due to the metamorphosis association. Ascalaphus was the son of Styx. But vid. infra.

Hic dirae volucres pastusque cadavere vultur
Et multus bubo ac sparsis strix sanguine pennis.
—SIL. ITAL. XIII, 597.

In augury, the note of an owl from the left annuls the propitious notes of other birds:

Nec caelum servare licet: tonat augure surdo,
Et laetae iurantur aves bubone sinistro.
—LUC. V, 395.

For other augural references to owls:
Vid. Stat., *Theb.* III, 508; Claud., *In Eutrop.* II, 406.
Owls in proverbial comparisons, symbolizing the impossible:

Vocalem superet si dirus aedona bubo.
—CALP. VI, 8.

Praepes funereo cum vulture ludat hirundo,
Cum bubone gravi nunc philomela sonet.
—*Anth. Lat.* 390, 27.

And hawk and sparrow shared a nest.—LANIER.

In a simile a comparison is made with the notes of the owl:

Qualis et horrendus funesto carmine bubo
Conqueritur deflenda gemens dum tristia maestus
Funerea sub nocte canit, sic anxia nutrix
Ingemit et tremulas diffundit maesta querelas.
—DRAC. X, 307.

The *bubo* is associated with Pallas:

Pallada bubo vehit, sed eam rota nulla figurat.
—*Anth. Lat.* 939.

The onomatopoetic verb for the call of the owl—with its traditional interpretation:

Bubulat horrendum ferali murmure bubo
Humano generi tristia fata ferens.
—*Anth. Lat.* 762, 37.

Cf. Varr., *De L. L.* 5, 11; Isid., *Orig.* 12, 7, 39. Wackernagel, op. cit., p. 49.

And the hoarse owl, that now and then booms out
His harsh, unearthly, melancholy shout.—GEN. ALBERT PIKE.

And the solemn owl, with his dull "too-whoo,"
Settles down on the side of the old canoe.—EMILY R. PAGE.
(*The Old Canoe.*[1] *Poets of Vermont*, p. 419.)

BUTIO. 'Αστερίας. Bittern.
Ardea stellaris.
American parallel: Greater Bittern. *Butio mugitans.*
Vid. Endicott, *Bitterns. Am. Nat.* 3, 169.

The bittern slunk
Amongst the sedge—and lonely hern, that waits
His prey, oft stranded by the insidious ebb.—M'KINNON.

As the hawk whose glance of tawny fire
Is on the bittern's wing.—POLLOCK.

The dying thunders roll o'er dale and scar;
In the still pool the bittern sees the star.—MIFFLIN.

Naturally enough, neither Lucretia nor Margaret Davidson had any exact knowledge of bird life. But such errors as the following are comparatively rare in the American poets:

The woods echo round the bittern's shrill scream,
As he dips his black wing in the wave of the stream.
—LUCRETIA DAVIDSON.

The onomatopoetic call of the marsh frequenting bittern:

Ast ululant ululae lugubri voce canentes
Inque paludiferis butio butit aquis.
—*Anth. Lat.* 762, 41.

Vid. Newton, op. cit., p. 40: " 'Butter-bump' corrupted into 'Botley-bumb' and perhaps other uncouth forms, has reference to the booming or bellowing sound for which this species was famous." Cf. Germ. *Rohrdommel.* Wackernagel, op. cit., p. 57.

[1]This poem is printed in the last edition of General Pike's poems with the following note:

"While the authorship of this beautiful poem has been credited to General Pike, it has also been denied that he wrote it, and he himself is said to have stated that the honor did not belong to him but to a young lady whose name has never been mentioned to the knowledge of the editor of this volume. The verses were republished in the *Gazette* a few years ago with this reference: 'We do not know from what paper or magazine they were taken—but it was understood that Gen. Pike was the author.' " It is interesting to note that in its newspaper migration from Vermont to Arkansas—from Page to Pike—the little poem of fifty lines has suffered twenty-four textual variations.

And as a bitore bumbleth in the mire.—CHAUCER.

The bittern lone, that shakes the solid ground,
While thro' still midnight groans the hollow sound.
—ALEXANDER WILSON.

The bittern's boom.—EMERSON.

It is the bittern's solemn cry.—PETERSON (Stedman).

Making the solemn bittern stir
Like a half-wakened slumberer.—SLADEN.

Uprising from sedgy brink
The lonely bittern's cry will sink
Upon the startled ear.—HOFFMAN (Griswold).

Or, faintly heard, a bittern cries
Across the tasseled waterweeds.—STEIN.

When bitterns boom, and flapping fly.—STRONG.

Strange insects whir, and stalking bitterns boom.
—EMMA LAZARUS.

CASSITA. Κορύδαλος. Crested Lark. *Alauda cristata.*

The skylark (*Alauda arvensis*), so frequent in all modern literature, strangely enough seems to have made little impression upon the ancient poets. Cf. Theoc. VII, 141 and X, 50. Its song was apparently unnoted or ignored. Even Aristotle does not mention the ecstacy of the soaring bird.[1] This neglect is due to conditions of migration and to the fact that no great metamorphosis myth made the bird prominent in popular fancy. This in turn, I believe, is to be explained by the fact that the song is too joyous for the dramatic sorrows of metamorphosis. Dante (*Par.* XX, 73) responds to the later feeling:

Qual lodoletta, che in aere si spazia
Prima cantando, e poi tace contenta
Dell'ultima dolcezza che la sazia.

American literary parallels: Meadow lark, bobolink.

Vid. Burroughs, *Birds and Poets*, p. 17.

[1]In his delightful *'Idylls of Greece,'* Sutherland portrays the song of the lark with great charm—but the descriptions are neither Greek nor Roman. E. g.:

From the fields near-by a lark soar'd up and up
In measured flights with ever beating wing,
And trill'd its benediction o'er a world
Superlatively peaceful.

Sprague's Pipit (No doubt, destined to figure in the future poetical literature of the West.—BURROUGHS.) has not yet come into its manifest inheritance.

Low: *To a Lark.*

Hogg (Stedman): *The Lark.*

Piatt: *A Word with a Skylark.*

Thompson: *To an English Skylark.*

Garland: *The Meadow Lark.*

Dunbar: *The Meadow Lark.*

Matthews: *The Meadow Lark.*

Keeler: *Avila and Sturnellus. A myth of the meadow lark's song at dawn.*

When the bonny gray morning just peeps from the skies,
And the lark mounting, tunes her sweet lay;
With a mind unincumbered by care I arise.
(*Independent Farmer.*) —SUSANNA ROWSON.

The lark had called me at the birth of dawn,
My cheerful toils and rural sports to share.
—JOHN TRUMBULL.

In clouds th' embosom'd lark her matin sings.
(*Conquest of Canaan.*) —TIMOTHY DWIGHT.

Or see before us from the lawn
The lark go up to greet the dawn.—TIMROD.

Hear the new, golden flood of song
The lark pours to the blue.—HIGGINSON.

The meadow-lark at dawn that sings.—HIGGINSON.

Jolliest of our birds of singing,
Best he loved the Bob-o-link.—WHITTIER.

Of the glad bobolink, whose lyric throat
Pealed like a tangle of small bells afloat.—ROBERTS.

The linkèd bubblings of the bobolink.—ROBERTS.

Why, I'd give more for one live bobolink
Than a square mile o' larks in printer's ink.—LOWELL.

My colleague, Professor J. O. Snyder, reports having heard the bobolink several times this past summer (1913) in Nevada. The bird seems to be following the alfalfa and irrigation projects westward.

In the meads,
Shorn of their hay, the yellow-breasted larks
Melodious sung.—M'KINNON.

Gayly sings the meadow lark,
Bidding all the birds assemble.—SHERMAN (Sladen).

The lark and its young portrayed in a prose Fable from Aesop, the beauty of which as a type of its kind is fairly without a parallel in literature:

Avicula, inquit (Aesopus), est parva, nomen est cassita. Habitat nidulaturque in segetibus, id ferme temporis, ut appetat messis pullis iam plumantibus. Ea cassita in sementes forte congesserat tempestiviores; propterea frumentis flavescentibus pulli etiam tunc involucres erant. Dum igitur ipsa iret cibum pullis quaesitum monet eos, ut, si quid ibi rei novae fieret diceretur ve, animadverterent idque uti sibi, ubi redisset, nuntiarent. Dominus postea segetum illarum filium adolescentem vocat, et; 'Videsne,' inquit, 'haec ematurisse et manus iam postulare? Idcirco die crastini, ubi primum diluculabit, fac amicos adeas et roges, veniant operamque mutuam dent et messim hanc nobis adiuvent.' Haec ubi ille dixit, discessit. Atque, ubi redit cassita, pulli tremibundi, trepiduli circumstrepere orareque matrem, ut iam statim properet inque alium locum sese asportet: 'Nam dominus,' inquiunt, 'misit, qui amicos roget, uti luce oriente veniant et metant.' Mater iubet eos otioso animo esse: 'Si enim dominus,' inquit, 'messim ad amicos reiecit, crastino seges non metetur neque necessum est, hodie uti vos auferam.' Die, inquit, postero mater in pabulum volat. Dominus, quos rogaverat, opperitur. Sol fervit, et fit nihil. It dies, et amici nulli eunt. Tum ille rursum ad filium: 'Amici isti magnam partem,' inquit, 'cessatores sunt. Quin potius imus et cognatos adfinesque nostros oramus, ut adsint cras tempori ad metendum?' Itidem hoc pulli pavefacti matri nuntiant. Mater hortatur, ut tum quoque sine metu ac sine cura sint, cognatos adfinesque nullos ferme tam esse obsequibiles, ait, ut ad laborem capessendum nihil cunctentur et statim dicto oboediant. 'Vos modo,' inquit, 'advertite, si [modo] quid denuo dicetur.' Alia luce orta, avis in pastum profecta est. Cognati et adfines operam quam rogati sunt dare supersederunt. Ad postremum igitur dominus filio. 'Valeant,' inquit, 'amici cum propinquis. Afferes primo luci falcas duas: unam egomet mihi et tu tibi capies alteram, et frumentum nosmetipsi manibus nostris cras metemus.' Id ubi ex pullis dixisse dominum mater audivit. 'Tempus,' inquit, 'est cedendi et abeundi: fiet nunc dubio procul, quod futurum dixit. In ipso enim iam vertitur, cuia res est, non in alio, unde petitur.' Atque ita cassita nidum migravit, seges a domino demessa est. Hunc, Aesopi apologum Q. Ennius in satiris scite admodum et venuste versibus quadratis composuit. Quorum duo postremi isti sunt, quos habere cordi et memoriae operae pretium esse hercle puto:

Hóc erit tibi árgumentum sémper in promptú situm,
Néquid exspectés amicos, quód tute agere póssies.
—GELL. II, 29, 3.

The lark's keen joy was shed!
For what though the morning sulky was
And the punctual sun belated,
His nest was snug in the tufted grass,
Soft-lined and stoutly plaited,
And shine sun or stay away
Nests must be celebrated!—MOODY.

He rose, and singing passed from sight—
A shadow kindling with the sun,
His joy ecstatic flamed, till light
And heavenly song were one.—TABB.
(*The Lark.*)

Oh, Lark of Europe, downward fluttering near,
Like some spent leaf at best,
You'd never sing again if you could hear
My Blue-Bird of the West!—MRS. PIATT.

CAVANNUS. Κικκάβη, etc. An Owl (?).
Vid. s. v. PERDIX, *Anth. Lat.* 390, 29.

CEYX. Κῆϋξ. A mythical bird.

Vid. s. v. ALCEDO for the myth of Ceyx and Alcyone. *Ceyx* as a bird-name is probably the same as Κήξ (cf. Hom., *Od.* XV, 479), which has been identified by Netolicka, *Naturh. aus Homer,* p. 14, as the Great Crested Grebe, *Podiceps cristatus,* since the cry of this bird suggests the name Ceyx. The grebes, as is well known, build rude floating nests of aquatic plants. The observation of this fact and the mythical association of the *ceyx* and the *halcyon* may be the naturalistic basis of the myths concerning the floating nests of the halcyons. Cf. Plin. 32, 8, 27. For a reference to the floating nests of the *Podiceps cristatus* vid. Newton, op. cit., p. 630. Boraston, *The Birds of Homer, Jour. of Hell. Studies,* vol. 31, identifies the Κήξ from its note *kik!* as the Common Tern.

CICONIA. Πελαργός. Stork. *Ciconia alba.*
American literary parallels: Stork, crane.
Bayard Taylor: *The Village Stork.*
Field: *The Stork.*

Stands the well-sweep in the lane,
On its one leg, like a crane
    Long and gaunt.—TROWBRIDGE.

The stork in heaven knoweth
    Her own appointed time
And like an arrow goeth
    Back to our colder clime.—HOSMER.

As when autumnal storms awake their force
The storks[1] foreboding tempt their southern course,
From all the fields collecting throngs arise,
Mount on the wing and crowd along the skies.—BARLOW.
(*Columbiad.*)

The Praenestines shorten *ciconia* to *conea*:

As. Perii! 'rabonem'? Quam esse dicam hanc beluam?
Quin tu 'arrabonem' dicis? Tr. 'A,' facio lucri,
Ut Praenestinis *conea* est *ciconia*.
—PLAUT., *Truc*. 689.

In a simile, reference is made to falling storks—smitten in midair by lightning:

At nos caduci naufragi ut ciconiae,
Quarum bipinnis fulminis plumas vapor
Percussit, alte maesti in terram cecidimus.
—VARRO, *Sat. Men.* Bücheler, Petr. Sat., p. 190.

Vines are best planted when the stork (candida avis) arrives, as a harbinger of spring:

Optuma vinetis satio, cum vere rubenti
Candida venit avis longis invisa colubris.
—VERG., *Geor.* II, 319.

Cf. Isid., *Orig.* XII, 7: Ciconiae veris nuntiae, societatis comites, serpentium hostes. Sid. II, 14, 2: Usque ad adventum hirundineum vel ciconinum Iani Numaeque ninguidos menses.

A certain Rufus brought into fashion the eating of young storks:

Tutus erat rhombus tutoque ciconia nido
Donec vos auctor docuit praetorius.
—HOR., *Sat.* II, 2, 49.

[1]Here Barlow clearly had in mind the Homeric and later classical epic similes referring to the fall migration of the crane. Vid. s. v. GRUS.

The crane (*grus*) later came into vogue, cf. Plin. X, 30, 3: Cornelius Nepos, qui Augusti principatu obiit, scribit ciconias magis placere, quam grues: cum haec nunc ales inter primas expetatur, illam nemo velit attigisse. Vid. s. v. GRUS.

This bird when fat is considered by many to be excellent eating.—ALEXANDER WILSON, op. cit., s. v. *American Bittern.*

The young are said to be excellent for the table, and even old birds, when in good order, and properly cooked, are esteemed by many.—ALEXANDER WILSON, op. cit., s. v. *Great Heron.*

The Rufus mentioned above was rejected and this epigram against him followed:

> Ciconiarum Rufus iste conditor
> Hic est duobus elegantior Plancis.
> Suffragiorum puncta non tulit septem.
> Ciconiarum populus ultus est mortem.
>
> —PORPHYR. in loc., Büch., P. L. M., p. 327.

Antigone, daughter of Laomedon, was metamorphosed into a stork:

> Pinxit et Antigonem, ausam contendere quondam
> Cum magni consorte Iovis, quam regia Iuno
> In volucrem vertit: nec profuit Ilion illi
> Laomedonve pater, sumptis quin candida pennis
> Ipsa sibi plaudat crepitante ciconia rostro.
>
> —OV., *Met.* VI, 93.

Cf. Serv. ad. *Aen.* I, 27: 'Spretae formae' referunt ad Antigonam, Laomedontis filiam, quam a Iunone propter formae adrogantiam in ciconiam constat esse conversam.

> And sacred stork, thought human soul disguised.—BAILEY.

A brief description of the habits of the stork, which is not a winter resident. The affection felt for the bird:

> Ciconia etiam grata peregrina hospita
> Pietaticultrix gracilipes crotalistria
> Avis, exul hiemis, titulus tepidi temporis,
> Nequitiae nidum in caccabo fecit modo.
>
> —PUB. SYR., Ribb. Com. Rom. Frag., p. 304.

Cf. Isid., *Orig.* XII, 7, 17: Eximia illis circa filios pietas; nam adeo nidos impensius fovent, ut assiduo in cubitu plumas exuant. Quantum autem temporis impenderint in foetibus educandis, tantum et ipsae invicem a pullis aluntur. Plin. X, 23, 32: Genetricum senectam invicem educant. Juv. I, 116: Quaeque salutatio crepitat Concordia nido.

And the sparrow finds her nest
In the temple's sacred rest.—TICHNOR.

My nest upon a temple stands.—BAYARD TAYLOR.

Did he give us the beautiful stork above
On the chimney top with its large round nest?
—LONGFELLOW.

Behind the back of Janus, no one imitating (with fingers) the clapping of the stork's bill, makes mockery of the god:

O Iane, a tergo quem nulla ciconia pinsit.
—PERS. I, 58.

Isid., *Orig.* 20, 15, 3: Ciconia levat ac deprimit rostrum dum clangit. The feeding habits of storks, young and old:

Serpente ciconia pullos
Nutrit et inventa per devia rura lacerta
Illi eadem sumptis quaerunt animalia pinnis.
—JUV. XIV, 74.

Plin. X, 24: Illis in Thessalia tantus honor serpentium exitio habitus est, ut ciconiam occidere capitale est, eadem legibus poena, qua in homicidas.

The Fable of the Fox and the Stork:

Ad coenam vulpis dicitur ciconiam
Prior invitasse, et illi in patina liquidam
Posuisse sorbitionem, quam nullo modo
Gustare esuriens potuerit ciconia.
Quae vulpem cum revocasset, intrito cibo
Plenam lagonam posuit: huic rostrum inserens
Satiatur ipsa et torquet convivam fame.
Quae cum lagonae collum frustra lamberet,
Peregrinam sic locutam volucrem accepimus:
'Sua quisque exempla debet aequo animo pati.'
—PHAED. I, 26.

Field: *The Cobbler and Stork.* The association of the stork with the beginnings of babyhood does not occur in ancient literature.

A folk-lore tale from Oppianus:

In Italia (inquit Oppianus), ut fertur, cum serpens quidam ad nidum prorepens ciconiarum pullos devorasset et alteram deinde sequentis anni foeturam sic iter perdidisset, ciconiae tertio demum anno reversae, novam quandam avem et prius non visam (quae brevior quidem ciconiis erat, sed rostrum magnum et acutum ensis instar a capite exerebat) secum adduxerunt, indicata nimirum ei foetus calamitate sui, sive pollicitationibus ullis sive verbis, ut opem ferret invitatam. Nam utrum aves et animantes aliae, suum inter se colloquium nobis ignotum misceant, in dubium vocari potest. Avis haec, nondum absoluto ciconarium foetu, coniuncta eis non erat: pullis vero iam exclusis cum parentes ad comparandum pullis avique custodi victum longius avolarent, ipsa nidum non deseruit, ut serpenti obsisteret. Serpens igitur paulo post progressus e latibulo, pullos aggreditur: et licet ab ave custode rostro impeteretur, non statim recessit, sed erectus corpore, caudaeque innitens, se opponebat, et secundo iam ictus spiris involere custodem frustra moliebatur, utcunque plurimis se flexibus insinuaret, nam facile evadebat avis in sublime se recipiens. Sic dum ille perdere, haec servare pullos annituntur, plurimis tandem ille vulneribus confossus iacuit: at non impune, avem enim in conflictu dentibus venerantis adeo laesit, ut omnes ei pennae defluerent. Cum vero revertendi tempus appetiisset, ac reliquae ciconiae, iam avolassent, parentes cum pullis servatis, ut beneficii memores se declararent, tantis permanserunt, donec novis ei pennis renatis simul avolarent.

—OPP., *Ixeut.*, Gesner, op. cit., p. 256.

The clattering note of the stork's bill:

Longoque ciconia collo
Glottorat et ranas grandi rapit improba rostro.
—*Anth. Lat.* 733, 7.

Glottorat immenso maerens ciconia rostro.
—*Anth. Lat.* 762, 29.

Vid. Wackernagel, op. cit. 75, 137; Isid., *Orig.* XII, 7. Ciconiae vocatae a sono, quo crepitant, quasi *cicaniae,* quem sonum oris potius esse constat, quam vocis, quia eum quatiente rostro faciunt.

Cf. supra, Pers. I, 58. Ov. *Met.* VI. 97 and Juv. I, 116; where *crepitare* is wrongly taken by Mayor, as it is also in the lexicons:

Mettendo i denti in nota di cicogna.—DANTE, *Inf.* XXXI, 36.

He just glanced downward
And snapped to his beak.—CHRISTINA G. ROSETTI.

Thus mused the stork, with snap of beak.—BAYARD TAYLOR.

COLUMBA. Περιστερά, *πέλεια*. Pigeon, dove. *Columba livia*. Blue-rock pigeon. Rock-dove.

Columba was the name usually applied to both the wild blue-rock pigeon and to its descendant, the domestic pigeon. *Columba* and *palumbes* were sometimes confused.

American parallels: Dove, pigeon, ring dove.

Newton, op. cit., p. 163. Fowler, op. cit. 219-223.

Lorrenz: *Die Taube im Alterthume.*

Thompson, op. cit., p. 132: Astronomic lore.

Philip Robinson: *The Poets' Birds. Atlantic* 49, 675.

Benjamin (Griswold): *The Dove's Errand.*

Willis: *The Belfry Pigeon.*

Mace: *The Two Doves.*

Some reflections on the relation of the dove to Venus, to whom the dove was sacred:

> Et Veneris dominae volucres, mea turba, columbae
> Tinguunt Gorgoneo punica rostra lacu.
> —PROP. III, 3, 27.

Punica is more accurate for the ring-dove (*palumbes*) than for the rock-dove (*columba*).

> See white winged swans, see red bill'd doves.—MILLER.

> To Venus' shrine no altars raised are,
> No venom'd shafts from painted quiver fly:
> Nor wanton Doves of Aphrodite's carr.
> —JOHN ROGERS (Kettell).

> The blue-eyed Aphrodite, whom the doves,
> White as her breasts, delight in following.—SUTHERLAND.

> Sed cape torquatae, Venus o regina, columbae
> Ob meritum ante tuos guttura secta focos.
> —PROP. IV, 5, 65.

Torquatae seems to point to the ring-dove, cf. Mart. XIII, 67, *Torquatus palumbus*.

> Nor the pigeon so glossy a ring on her throat.—ALICE CARY.

In *Aen*. VI, 190 ff. Vergil, I believe, had the ring-dove or wood-pigeon in mind, although he uses *columbae*. Cf. Morris, op. cit., vol. IV, p. 170: 'The rock-pigeon does not perch in trees.'

Necte comam myrto; maternas iunge columbas.
Qui deceat, currum vitricus ipse dabit:
Inque dato curru, populo clamante triumphum,
Stabis et adiunctas arte movebis aves.
—Ov., *Am.* I, 2, 23.

Ne violes teneras periuro dente columbas,
Tradita si Gnidiae sunt tibi sacra deae.
—MART. XIII, 66.

Hic iuvenum lapsus suaque aut externa revolvit
Vulnera, (pro! quanta est Paphii reverentia, mater,
Numinis!) hic nostrae deflevit fata columbae!
—STAT., *Silv.* I, 2, 100.

Cf. Mart. I, 7; VII, 14.

Why doves are dear to Venus:

Quae autem causa sit ficta, propter quam Venus columba delecta sit, talis est; quod Venus et Cupido, cum quodam tempore voluptatis gratia in quosdam nitentes descendissent campos, lasciva contentia certare coeperunt, qui plus sibi gemmates colligeret flores. Quorum Cupido adiutus mobilitate pennarum, postquam naturam corporis volatu superavit, victus est numero. Peristera enim nympha subito accurrit et adiuvando Venerem superiorem effecit cum poena sua. Cupido siquidem indignatus mutavit puellam in avem, quae a Graecis περιστερὰ appellatur. Sed poenam honor minuit. Venus namque consolatura puellae et innocentis transfigurationem, columbam in tutela sua esse mandavit.
—LACT., ad Stat. *Theb.* IV, 226.

In Euphratem flumen de coelo ovum mira magnitudine cecidisse dicitur, quod pisces ad ripam evoluerunt. Super quod columbae consederunt et excalfactum excludisse Venerem.
—HYG., *Fab.* 197.

Veneri consecratas, proper fetum frequentem et coitum.
—SERV., ad Verg. *Aen.* VI, 193.

Cf. also Ov., *Met.* XV, 389; Sil. Ital. IV, 106.

Take Venus, with her turtle doves.—FESSENDEN.

How doves were sacrified to Venus. Soothsaying:

Ergo saepe suo coniunx abducta marito
Uritur Idaliis alba columba focis.
—Ov., *Fast.* I, 451.

Cf. supra. Prop. IV, 5, 65.

Calidae pulmone columbae
Tractato Armenius vel Commagenus haruspex.
—JUV. VI, 549.

Lovers ever ran before the clock.
Oh, ten times faster Venus' pigeons fly.—SHAKESPEARE.

Pity thou,
And I will offer thee white doves, whose note
Sounds softer in the woods than hymning lutes.
—SUTHERLAND.

And since from Aphrodite's dove
The pattern of the fan was given
No wonder it breathes of Love.—HOLMES.

Even as, wafted by her doves,
She kissed the faces of the yearning waves.—STEDMAN.

Vid. also Gen. Albert Pike: *Hymn to Venus.*

Color and descriptive epithets applied to the dove:

Alba, albulus, albiplumen, niveo, sine labe, pulchra, torquatae, aeriae, praecipites, sublimem in nube, timidus, timidissima, trepidas, pavidae, placida, trepidante penna, teneras, castus, blanda, sine felle, molles, Argoa.

Love to her
Was whiter than the foam-white doves that warmed
The rosy feet of Venus.—SUTHERLAND.

In the east
The sky is like the bosom of a dove,
All gray and crimson.—SUTHERLAND.

How the oracles of Zeus at Dodona and in Libya were occasioned by two doves from Thebes:

Nam cui dona Iovi non divulgata per orbem,
In gremio Thebes geminas sedisse columbas?
Quarum, Chaonias pennis quae contigit oras,
Implet fatidico Dodonida murmure quercum.
At quae, Carpathium super aequor vecta, per
Auras in Libyen niveis tranavit concolor alis,
Hanc sedem templo Cythereïa condidit ales;
Hic, ubi nunc aram lucosque videtis opacos,
Ductore electo gregis, admirabile dictu,
Lanigeri capitis media inter cornua perstans,
Marmaricis ales populis responsa canebat.
—SIL. ITAL. III, 677.

The air with birds they flocked; oracular dove,
Thrice holy in tradition from the egg,
Hid by Aturian turtle, and the flood,
To Jordan's sacred streamlet.—BAILEY.

Where once the mighty voice of Jove
Rang through Dodona's haunted grove,
No more the dove with sable plumes
Swept through the forest's georgeous glooms.
—SARAH HELEN WHITMAN.

Cf. Herod. II, 55.

For a discussion of the doves at Dodona, vid. Jebb, Soph., *Trach.* 1166. Appendix; Serv. ad. Verg., *Aen.* III, 466.

For doves in Palestine, vid. Tib. I, 7, 17; Hyg. 197.

White dove-cots were preferred. Other references to dove-cots.

Totus autem locus et ipsae columbarum cellae poliri debent albo tectorio, quoniam eo colore praecipue delectatur hoc genus avium. Colum. 8, 8.

Aspicis, ut veniant ad candida tecta columbae,
Accipiat nullas sordida turris aves?
—Ov., *Trist.* I, 9, 7.

God! if I might in this white dove-cote dwell.—HIGGINSON.

A poor soiled dove of this dear St. Mark.—MILLER.

Cf. Gould, *The Dove on the Chimney.*

Quaeque gerit similes candida turris aves,
Munera sunt dominae.
—MART. XII, 31, 6.

Quasque colat turres, Chaonis ales habet.
—Ov., *A. A.* II, 150.

Nam prius incipient turres vitare columbae,
Antra ferae, pecudes gramina, mergus aquas;
Quam male se praestat veteri Graecinus amico.
—Ov., *Ex Pont.* I, 6, 51.

Sonantque turres plausibus columbarum.
—MART. III, 58, 18.

And hear, from their high perch along the eaves,
The bright-necked pigeons call.—ELIZABETH A. ALLEN.

Qualiter Idaliae volucres, ubi mollia frangunt
Nubila, iam longum coeloque domoque gregatae,
Si iunxit pennas diversoque hospita tractu
Venit avis, cunctae primum mirantur et horrent:
Mox propius propiusque volant, atque aere in ipso
Paulatim fecere suam, plausuque secundo
Circueunt hilares et ad alta cubilia ducunt.
—STAT., *Ach.* I, 372.

The epithet *hilares* is almost unique as applied to bird life among the Roman poets. The note of joy is the prevailing modern concept, save where the ancient tradition is followed. Vid. s. v. LUSCINIA and Note IV, RUSCINIA.

Sic ubi perspicuae scandentem limina turris
Idaliae volucres fulvum adspexere draconem,
Intus agunt natos et feta cubilia vallant
Unguibus, imbellesque citant ad proelia pennas.
Mox ruerit licet ille retro, tamen aera nudum
Candida turba timet, tandemque ingressa volatus
Horret et a mediis etiamnum respicit astris.
—STAT., *Theb.* XII, 15.

There too the dove-cot stood, with its meek and innocent inmates
Murmuring ever of love.—LONGFELLOW.

There must have been a dove-cote too, I know,
Where white-winged birds like Spirits come and go.
—STEDMAN.

Cf. also Varr., *R. R.* III, 7; Juv. III, 200.

The metamorphosis of Dercetis and her daughter Semiramis:

Illa, quid e multis referat (nam plurima norat),
Cogitat et dubia est, de te, Babylonia, narret,
Derceti, quam versa squamis velantibus artus
Stagna Palaestini credunt motasse figura
An magis, ut sumptis illius filia pennis
Extremos albis in turribus egerit annos.
—OV., *Met.* IV, 44.

But all agree that from no lawful bed,
This great renowned empress issued.
For which she was obscurely nourished,
Whence rose that fable, she by birds was fed.
(*Semiramis.*) —ANNE BRADSTREET.

The poets feign'd her turn'd into a dove,
Leaving the world to Venus soar'd above.
(*Semiramis.*) —ANNE BRADSTREET.

Medea passes over the city of Alcidamas, whose daughter was transformed into a dove:

Transit et antiquae Cartheia moenia Ceae,
Qua pater Alcidamas placidam de corpore natae
Miratus erat nasci potuisse columbam.
—OV., *Met.* VII, 368.

Tenderly her dove-eyes glistened.—MORRIS.

And then a dove, dear nunlike dove
With eyes all tenderness.—MILLER.

Now what is thy secret, serene gray dove?—MILLER.

How the daughters of Anius were changed into doves:

Nec qua ratione figuram
Perdiderint, potui scire aut nunc dicere possum:
Summa mali nota est: pennas sumpsere tuaeque
Coniugis in volucres, niveas abiere columbas.
—Ov., *Met.* XIII, 672.

Where, transform'd to sacred doves,
Many a blessed Indian roves
Through the air on wing, as white
As those wond'rous stones of light.—THOMAS MOORE.
(*Poems relating to America.*)

Daedalion, metamorphosed into a hawk, preys upon the Thisbean doves:

Illius virtus reges gentesque subegit,
Quae nunc Thisbaeas agitat mutata columbas.
—Ov., *Met.* XI, 299.

Cf. Hom., *Il.* II, 502; Stat., *Theb.* VII, 261. Doves are still found in enormous numbers at Kokosi, on the site of ancient Thisbe, and from this fact Chandler identified the site. Vid. Frazer, *Paus.*, vol. V, p. 160.

References to the Argo, Symplegades and Dove:

Tuque tuo Colchum propellas remige Phasim,
Peliacaeque trabis totum iter ipse legas,
Qua rudis Argoa natat inter saxa columba
In faciem prorae pinus adacta novae.
—PROP. III, 22, 11.

Et qui movistis duo litora, cum ratis Argo
Dux erat ignoto missa columba mari.
—PROP. II, 16, 39.

Qualis et ille fuit, quo praecipiente columba
Est data Palladiae praevia duxque rati.
—Ov., *Ib.* 265.

How a dove (possibly a carrier-pigeon—cf. Thompson, op. cit., p. 143) came to Aretulla:

Aëra per tacitum delapsa sedentis in ipsos
    Fluxit Aretullae blanda columba sinus.
Luserat hoc casus, nisi inobservata maneret
    Permissaque sibi nollet abire fuga.
Si meliora piae fas est sperare sorori
    Et dominum mundi flectere vota valent,
Haec a Sardois tibi forsitan exulis oris
    Fratre reversuro, nuntia venit avis.
—MART. VIII, 32.

Bear gently, Ocean's carrier-dove,
Thy errands to and fro.—WHITTIER.

True as the homing-bird flies with its message.
—WARD (Stedman).

Like homeward pigeon with uncaged wing.—LAMPMAN.

But nightly, like white courier doves
    They all come home to rest.—HIGGINSON.

As some stray carrier-pigeon onward hies
    O'er alien spire, and dim cathedral dome,
    With weakening pinions, that reluctant roam
    Athwart the high, inhospitable skies;
Famished and faint, with eager, yearning eyes,
    Whirled by the winds above the wild sea's foam,
    Till, at the last, outworn, he gains his home,
    Falls at his mistress's feet, content, and dies.—MIFFLIN.

Medea flees to Jason even as a dove flees when seeing the shadow of a hawk:

Ecce autem pavidae virgo de more columbae,
Quae super ingenti circumdata praepetis umbra
In quemcumque tremens hominem cadit: haud secus illa
Acta timore gravi mediam se immisit.
—VAL. FLACC. VIII, 32.

But fly all helpless here to me
A fluttered dove that night of dread.—MILLER.

Like shadows by a brilliant day
Cast down from falcons on their prey.
—PINKNEY (Duyckinck).

Whose omen flits
Across thy heart as o'er a troop of doves
The fearful shadow of the kite.—LOWELL.

Seest thou shadows sailing by
As the dove with startled eye
Sees the falcon's shadow fly?—LONGFELLOW.

For *columba* used as a term of endearment, vid. Plaut., *Asin.* 693; *Cas.* 138. This use is by no means 'very frequent' (cf. Thompson, op. cit., p. 142).

Very likely the poor chick sheds copious tears.—FIELD.

I kissed him and called him my little bird
O' th' woods, my dove, my darling.—ALICE CARY.

Poor little dove! Thou tremblest like a leaf.—LONGFELLOW.

Cruel death!
To take away my dove, my lamb, my darling.—LONGFELLOW.

My sad, sweet dove.—MILLER.

A Christian use of *columba* from the grave of an unknown pope:

Quam domino fuerant devota mente parentes,
Qui confessorem talem genuere potentem
Adque sacerdotem sanctum, sine felle columbam,
Divinae legis sincero corde magistrum.
—BÜCH., *Carm. Epig.* 787.

The Holy Dove of Peace, the promised guest,
Folded its fragrant pinions on my breast.
—SARAH HELEN WHITMAN.

With patient hand Jesus in clay once wrought,
And made a snowy dove that upward flew.
(*Jesus and the Dove.*) —MARIA LOWELL (Griswold).

Go then, my Dove, but now no longer mine!
Leave Earth and now in Heavenly Glory shine.
(*Epitaph of Abigail, his wife,* 1703.)—COTTON MATHER.

So with the wings of Faith and Love,
And feathers of an Holy Dove,
She bid this wretched world adieu
And swiftly up to Heaven flew.—NOYES.
(*A consolatory poem, addressed to Cotton Mather upon the death of his wife.* 1703.)

A soft dove gray that shrouds the dead.—MILLER.

As regards color, white doves are most common:

Et ille nunc superbus et superfluens
Perambulabit omnium cubilia
Ut albulus columbus aut Adoneus?
—CAT. XXIX, 6.

Nec tantum niveo gavisast ulla columbo
Compar, quae multo dicitur improbius
Oscula mordenti semper decerpere rostro.
Quam quae praecipue multivolast mulier.
—CAT. LXVIII, 124.

Nam fuit haec quondam niveis argentea pennis
Ales, ut aequaret totas sine labe columbas.
—Ov., *Met.* II, 536.

Et variis albae iunguntur saepe columbae.
—Ov., *Her.* XV, 37.

Lilia tu vincis ne adhuc delapsa ligustra,
Et Tiburtino monte quod albet ebur;
Spartanus tibi cedet olor Paphiaeque columbae,
Cedet Erythraeis eruta gemma vadis.
—MART. VIII, 28, 11.

Absit ut albiplumem valeat calcare columbam
Inter tot niveas rustica milvus avis.
—*Anth. Lat.*, 729, 3.

Ad iuga blanda sedet niveas moderata columbas,
Non satianda donis, divae soror alma.
—*Anth. Lat.* 941, 22.

It was white as whitest dove.—HIGGINSON.

The white doves filled the air,
Like white souls of the saints.—LONGFELLOW.

References to other colors:

Pluma columbarum quo pacto in sole videtur,
Quae sita cervices circum collumque coronat;
Namque alia fit uti claro sit rubro pyropo,
Inter dum quodam sensu fit uti videatur
Inter caeruleum viridis miscere zmaragdos.
—LUCR. II, 799.

Colla Cytheriacae splendent agitata columbae.
—BAEHRENS, *P. L. M.*, p. 368.

A white dove drowned in Tuscan wine.—MILLER.

And rows of doves that sit on beams,
With plump and glossy breasts.—ALICE CARY.

The reflections from their necks were very beautiful.—THOREAU, op. cit., p. 113.

Cf. Cic., *Acad.* II, 19, 79; Sen., *Nat. Quaest.* I, 5, 6; Aus., *Epist.* III, 15.

Notes on the nesting habits of the dove:

Qualis spelunca subito commota columba
Cui domus et dulces latebroso in pumice nidi
Fertur in arva volans, plausumque exterrita pennis
Dat tecto ingentem, mox aëre lapsa quieto
Radit iter liquidum, celeres neque commovet alas.
—Verg., *Aen.* V, 213.

This is one of the most exact descriptions of bird life in the Latin poets. *Columba* is here applied to the wild rock-dove, the progenitor of our domesticated pigeons. Cf. Shairp, op. cit., p. 165.

Piscium et summa genus haesit ulmo
Nota quae sedes fuerat columbis.
—Hor., *Od.* I, 2, 9.

The change to *palumbis* is, of course, better ornithology, but it is unnecessary, for while *columba* is usually applied to the rock-dove and the domesticated pigeon, and *palumbes* to the wood- or stock-dove (which Horace has in mind here), yet there existed at all times a slight mingling of names, habits, and mythological lore. Cf. especially *sine felle columbam* and *palumbes sine felle*. By Wordsworth the ring-dove is repeatedly called the stock-dove. Cf. Mackie, op. cit., p. 82.

True as the stock-dove to her shallow nest
And to the grove that holds it.—Wordsworth.

He went to her as goes the wild grey dove
Straight to its mate, though hills rise high, and hide
The brake where bides its loved one and their nest.
—Sutherland.

Pet name for a child. The mss. show the expected confusion of *columbo* and *palumbo*. The former is more likely correct:

At cur non potius, teneroque columbo,
Et similes regum pueris, poppare minutum
Poscis, et iratus mammae lallare recusas?
—Pers. III, 16.

Yet they contrived to rear their little dove,
And he repaid them with the tenderest love.—Timrod.

Doves feed their young by regurgitation. Some references and similes derived from this fact. The conjugal affection of doves was proverbial:

> Ubi quid dederam, quasi columbae pulli in ore ambae meo usque eratis. —PLAUT., *Asin.* 209.

> Sinuque amicam refice frigidam caldo
> Columbulatim labra conserens labris.
> —CN. MATIUS, BAEHRENS, *P. L. M.*, *p.* 282.

> Oscula dat cupido blanda columba mari.
> —OV., *Am.* II, 6, 56.

> Exemplo iunctae tibi sint in amore columbae.
> Masculus et totum femina coniugium.
> —PROP. II, 15, 27.

> Issa est purior osculo columbae.
> —MART. I, 109, 2.

> Basia me capiunt blandas imitata columbas.
> —MART. XI, 104, 9.

> Amplexa collum basioque tam longo
> Blandita, quam sunt nuptiae columbarum.
> Rogare coepit Phyllis amphoram vini.
> —MART. XII, 65, 8.

Cf. also Cat. LXVIII, 125 *supra*; Plin. X, 104.

> The loving turtle and his lovely spouse,
> From bough to bough, in deep affection move,
> And with chaste joy reciprocate their love.
> —ROGER WOLCOTT.

> The wail of an unmated dove.—MILLER.

> Far down the wood, a one-desiring dove.—LANIER.

> The righteous man that wandering dove received,
> And to her mate restored, who, with sad moans,
> Had wonder'd at her absence.—SIGOURNEY.

> The turtle on yon' withered bough
> Who lately moaned her murdered mate,
> Has found another partner now.—FRENEAU.

Monday Captain Hall called to speak to me about my paper on Pigeons; he complained that I expressed the belief that Pigeons were possessed of affection and tenderest love, and that this raised the brute species to a level with man.—AUDUBON, *Journal*, vol. I, p. 212.

A pun on the word *columbus*:

Ch. Isti capiti dicito.
Credo alium in aliam beluam hominem vortier:
Illic in columbum, credo, leno vortitur,
Nam in columbari collus hau multo post erit;
In nervuom ille hodie nidamenta congeret.
—PLAUT., *Rud*. 886.

'Stocks' and 'stock-dove' show the pun; but the tame pigeon, not the stock-dove, was probably in the poet's mind.

Cupid's wings compared to the ruffled back of a much handled dove:

Horrida pendebant molles super ora capilli,
Et visa est oculis horrida pinna meis;
Quolis in aeriae tergo solet esse columbae,
Tractantum multae quam tetigere manus.
—OV., *Ex Pont*. III, 3, 17.

The pet dove of Stella:

Stellae delicium mei columba,
Verona licet audiente dicam,
Vicit, Maxime, passerem Catulli.
Tanto Stella meus tuo Catullo,
Quanto passere maior est columba.
—MART. I, 7.

For the proverbial preying of eagles upon doves.

Cf. Verg., *Ecl*. IX, 13; Ov., *Met*. I, 506; *A. A*. I, 117; Mart. X, 65, 12, etc. Vid. s. v. AQUILA.

For the traditional preying of hawks upon doves.

Cf. Lucr. III, 752; Verg., *Aen*. XI, 721; Ov., *Met*. V, 605; VI, 529; *Fast*. II, 90; *Trist*. I, 1, 75; Hor., *Od*. I, 37, 17; Sil. Ital. V, 282, etc. Vid. s. v. ACCIPITER.

For the association of dove and kite, vid. Hor., *Ep*. XVI, 32; vid. s. v. MILVUS.

For the raven and dove, vid. Juv. II, 63, vid. s. v. CORVUS.

For the swan and dove, vid. *Anth. Lat*. 939, vid. s. v. CYCNUS.

References to the note of the dove:

Sonantque turres plausibus columbarum.
—MART. III, 58, 18.

Et castus turtur atque columba gemunt.
—*Anth. Lat*. 762, 20.

Ite agite, o iuvenes, et desudate medullis.
Omnibus inter vos! non murmura vestra columbae,
Brachia non hederae, non vincant oscula conchae.
—*Anth. Lat.* 711.

Cf. Wackernagel, op. cit., p. 59; Winteler, op. cit., p. 17.

He did not cease: but cooed and cooed:
And somewhat pensively he wooed.—WORDSWORTH.

Why the note of the dove is full of sadness:

But under Abel's date-palm trees
The dove forgot its tone,
And since, o'er other lands and seas,
It makes its plaintive moan;
Thus Deity hath marked the crime
For cycles passing round—
The blood that flowed in Adam's time
Is crying from the ground—
For this is why the dove declares
Its tearful, sad unrest.—STANTON.

For the dove as a target for archers, vid. Verg., *Aen.* V, 488.
For the dove on a cup as a work of art, vid. Mart. VIII, 6, 10.

The dove was hewn in Karnah stone
Before fair Jordan's banks were known.—MILLER.

For the Fable of the Kite and the Doves, vid. s. v. MILVUS.
A later myth. How pearls are polished:

As pearls, we're told, that fondling doves
Have play'd with, wear a smoother whiteness.
(*Poems relating to America.*)—THOMAS MOORE.

CORNICULA. Κολοιός. Jackdaw.
Corvus monedula, L.
American parallel: Blue-jay.

The *cornicula* who robbed birds of their plumage is reduced to ridicule:

Quid mihi Celsus agit? Monitus multumque monendus
Privatas ut quaerat opes et tangere vitet
Scripta, Palatinus quaecumque recepit Apollo;
Ne, si forte suas repetitum venerit olim
Grex avium plumas, moveat cornicula risum
Furtivis nudata coloribus? —HOR., *Ep.* I, 3, 15.

Cf. also Phaed. I, 3, s. v. GRACULUS.

To shine in borrowed plumes, with base design.—FRENEAU.

A jackdaw faith, mischievous, chatt'ring thing,
Dress'd in a plume of every heathen's wing.—CLIFFTON.

Who, jackdaws still, the peacock's pomp assume,
And strut in pride with half a pilfer'd plume.
—LINCOLN (Kettell).

CORNIX. Κορώνη. Crow. *Corvus corone.*
American parallels: Crow, raven.
Wilson (Stedman): *To a Crow.*
Trowbridge: *Watching the Crows.*
Hosmer: *The Crow.* Id.: *Origin of the Crow.*
Gardner: *A Flock of Mythological Crows.* *Pop. Sci. Mo.* 18, 43.
The long life of the crow is proverbial in the Latin poets:

Vivit et armiferae cornix invisa Minervae,
Illa quidem saeclis vix moritura novem.
—Ov., *Am.* II, 6, 35.

Cf. int. al. Lucr. V, 1083: cornicum ut saecla vetusta; Ov., *Met.* VII, 274: novem cornicis saecula passae; Hor., *Od.* III, 17, 9: annosa cornix; *Priap.* 61, 11: cornix anus; Aus., *Id.* XVIII, 3; *Anth. Lat.* 344, 2: Aut quantum cornix atque elefans superest.

A raven once an acorn took
From Bashan's strongest, stoutest tree;
He hid it near a murmuring brook,
And lived another oak to see.—FRENEAU.

The oldest crow that caws below
Recalls no sadder case.—TICHNOR.

The century living crow.—BRYANT.

The many-wintered crow.—TENNYSON.

And all noisy on the tree-tops cawed the rooks, that ancient race.
—LINEN.

Sed Cinarae breves
Annos fata dederunt,
Servatura diu parem
Cornicis vetulae temporibus Lycen.
—HOR., *Od.* IV, 13, 22.

Iam cornicibus omnibus superstes
Hoc tandem sita prurit in sepulchro
Calvo Plotia cum Melonthione.—MART. X, 67, 5.

Rex Pylius, magno si quidquam credis Homero,
Exemplum vitae fuit a cornice secundae.
—JUV. X, 247.

How the crow as a weather prophet foretells the coming of storms:

Et partim mutant cum tempestibus una
Raucisonos cantus cornicum et saecla vetusta
Corvorumque greges ubi aquam dicuntur et imbris
Poscere et interdum ventos aurasque vocare.
—LUCR. V, 1082.

Fuscaque non numquam cursans per litora cornix
Demersit caput et fluctum cervice recepit.
—CIC., *Prog.* 223.

Tum cornix plena pluviam vocat improba voce
Et sola in sicca secum spatiatur[1] arena.
—VERG., *Geor.* I, 388.

A comparison of the above lines from Verg., Cic., and Lucr. might seem to give some support for the genuineness of the marginal line found in mss. Med. and Gud. at Verg., *Geor.* I, 389: Aut caput obiectat querulum venientibus undis. The resemblance, however, to *Geor.* I, 386, is suspicious; furthermore, the epithet *querulus* as applied to the crow is unique, and is apparently due to the metamorphosis association. But cf.:

Who feeds the ravens, when the croaking brood
Raise hoarsely *querulous* their plaint to God?
—DEVENS (Kettell).

Quodque caput spargens undis, velut occupet imbrem,
Instabili gressu metitur litora cornix.
—LUC. V, 556.

Cras foliis nemus
Multis et alga litus inutili
Demissa tempestas ab Euro
Sternet, aquae nisi fallit augur
Annosa cornix. —HOR., *Od.* III, 17, 6.

[1]Cf. In there *stepped* a stately Raven of the saintly days of yore.—POE.

In the bare cornfield *stalked* the silent crow.—MIFFLIN.

Along the brim the lovely plover *stalks*
And to his visionary fellow talks.—KNAPP(?) (Duyckinck).
(*A New England Pond.*)

Antequam stantes repetat paludes
Imbrium divina avis imminentum,
Oscinem corvum prece suscitabo
Solis ab ortu. —HOR., *Od.* III, 27, 9.

Or gloom the strand, and croak the coming storm.
(*Conquest of Canaan.*) —DWIGHT.

Warned is the reaper of foul weather nigh,
When the prophetic creature, in its flight,
With changed note in its discordant cry,
Moves like a gliding kite.
While louder grows that wild, presageful call,
Sheaves are piled high upon the harvest wain,
And the stack neatly rounded ere the fall
Of hail, and driving rain.—HOSMER.

Cf. Cawein, *The Rain-Crow.* With us this name is most often applied to the cuckoo. Vid. Alexander Wilson, op. cit., s. v. YELLOW-BILLED CUCKOO.

How the crow appeared in omens and warnings:

Impetritum, inauguratumst: quovis admittunt aves,
Picus et cornix est ab laeva, corvus, parra ab dextera
Consuedent. —PLAUT., *Asin.* 259.

Quod nisi me quacumque novas incidere lites
Ante sinistra cava monuisset ab ilice cornix,
Nec tuus hic Moeris, nec viveret ipse Menalcas.
—VERG., *Ecl.* IX, 14.

From the second line is evidently made Verg., *Ecl.* I, 18:

Saepe sinistra cava praedixit ab ilice cornix.

Cf. And the ill-omened cawing of the crow.—LONGFELLOW.
Cf. Cic., *De Div.* I, 39; Hopf., op. cit., p. 115.

Sis licet felix, ubicumque mavis,
Et memor nostri, Galatea, vivas,
Teque nec laevus vetet ire picus.
Nec vaga cornix.—HOR., *Od.* III, 27, 13.

Heard with alarm the cawing of the crow,
That mingled with universal mirth,
Cassandra-like, prognosticating woe.—LONGFELLOW.

How the crow was used in incantations:

Cornicum immeritas eruit ungue genas,
Consuluitque striges nostro de sanguine, et in me
Hippomenes fetae semina legit equae.
—PROP. IV, 5, 13.

Nec defuit illic
Squamea Cinyphii tenuis membrana chelydri
Vivacisque iecur cervi; quibus insuper addit
Ora caputque novem cornicis saecula passae.
—Ov., *Met.* VII, 272.

How a crow tried to dissuade a raven, then the favorite bird of Apollo (and pure white), from revealing to the god the infidelity of the nymph Coronis. As a warning to the raven the crow tells her own story: how for tale-bearing (when she was yet the maiden Coronis) concerning the basket in which Erechthonius was concealed, she had been banished from the protection of Minerva and succeeded by the owl.

The first words of the crow to the raven:

Quem garrula motis
Consequitur pennis, scitetur ut omnia, cornix;
Auditaque viae causa, "Non utile carpis,"
Inquit, "iter. Ne sperne meae praesagia linguae."
—Ov., *Met.* II, 547.

For the garrulity of the crow cf.

And from the wood-top calls the crow through all the gloomy day.—BRYANT.

Shrieks the crow the live long day.—WHITTIER.

Whole flocks o' camp-meetin' crows
Shoutin' hallelujah.—DUNBAR.

How the crow saw the basket opened:

Abdita fronde levi densa spectabar ab ulmo,
Quid facerent. —Ov., *Met.* II, 557.

The crow moralizes upon her action and gives a warning to other birds:

Pro quo mihi gratia talis
Redditur, ut dicar tutela pulsa[1] Minervae,
Et ponar post noctis avem.[2] Mea poena volucres
Admonuisse potest, ne voce pericula quaerant.
—Ov., *Met.* II, 562.

[1]Cf. Ov., *Am.* II, 6, 35: Cornix invisa Minerva. [2]Cf. s. v. NOCTUA.

How Coronis was metamorphosed into a crow by Minerva to save her from the violence of Neptune:

Forma mihi nocuit. Nam cum per litora lentis
Passibus, ut soleo, summa spatiarer arena,
Vidit et incaluit pelagi deus; utque precando
Tempora cum blandis absumpsit inania verbis;
Vim parat et sequitur. Fugio, densumque relinquo
Litus, et in molli nequidquam lassor arena.
Inde deos hominesque voco: nec contigit ullum
Vox mea mortalem. Mota est pro virgine virgo,
Auxiliumque tulit. Tendebam brachia coelo:
Brachia coeperunt levibus nigrescere pennis.
Reicere ex humeris vestem molibar: at illa
Pluma erat, inque cutem radices egerat imas.
Plangere nuda meis conabar pectora palmis:
Sed neque iam palmas, nec pectora nuda gerebam.
Currebam: nec, ut ante, pedes retinebat arena
Sed summa tollebar humo; mox acta per auras
Evehor, et data sum comes inculpata Minervae.
Quid tamen hoc prodest, si diro facta volucris
Crimine Nyctimene nostro successit honori?
—Ov., *Met.* II, 572.

For the hostility of the crows and owls cf. int. al. Ov., *F.* II, 89: Et sine lite loquax cum Palladis alite cornix.

The Crow himself sometimes falls a prey to the superior strength and rapacity of the Great Owl, whose weapons of offense are by far the more formidable of the two.—ALEXANDER WILSON, op. cit., s. v. CROW.

Why the crows avoid the Acropolis of Athens and the regions near Cumae:

Is locus est Cumas aput, acri sulphure montes
Oppleti calidis ubi fumant fontibus aucti.
Est et Athenaeis in moenibus, arcis in ipso
Vertice, Palladis ad templum Tritonidis almae,
Quo numquam pennis appellunt corpora raucae
Cornices, non cum fumant altaria donis;
Usque adeo fugitant, non iras Palladis acris
Pervigili causa, Graium ut cecinere poetae;
Sed natura loci opus efficit ipsa suapte.
—LUCR. VI, 747.

Lapwing and reptile shun the curst abode,
And the foul dragon, now no more a god,
Trails off his train; the sickly raven flies;
A wide strong-stencht Avernus chokes the skies.—BARLOW.
(*Columbiad.*)

Cf. Leake, *Athens* I, p. 206. "As to the crow, the explanation seems to be that these birds, which are seen in great numbers around the rocks of the Acropolis, seldom rise to the summit."

For a dream in which a crow appears as symbolic of a trouble-causing procuress, cf. Ov., *Am.* III, 5.

For Tranio (as a crow) and two old men (as vultures), vid. Plaut., *Most.* 822 ff., s. v. VULTUR.

For proverbial reference to the crow and the acanthis vid. s. v. ACALANTHIS.

For a speaking crow vid. Suet., *Dom.* 23; Baehrens, *P. L. M.*, p. 370.

For the Fable of the Eagle, Crow and Tortoise, vid. s. v. AQUILA.

For the Fable of the Crane, Crow and Countryman, vid. s. v. GRUS.

For the Fable of the Crow and the Sheep, vid. Phaed., *Fab. Nov.* 24.

CORVUS. Κόραξ. Raven. *Corvus corax,* L.

The name *corvus* was applied also by Roman writers to both the crow and the rook.

For a discussion of *corvus* and *cornix* cf. Fowler: *A Year with the Birds,* p. 234 ff.

American parallels: Raven, crow.

Macdonald: *Consider the Ravens.*

Poe: *The Raven.*

The raven, originally white, was made black because of his tale-bearing to Apollo concerning the nymph Coronis.

Vid. the charming paraphrase by Saxe, *How the Raven Became Black.*

Di maris adnuerant: habili Saturnia curru
Ingreditur liquidum pavonibus aethera pictis,
Tam nuper pictis caeso pavonibus Argo,
Quam tu nuper eras, cum candidus ante fuisses,
Corve loquax, subito nigrantes versus in alas.
Nam fuit haec quondam niveis argentea pennis
Ales, ut aequaret totas sine labe columbas,
Nec servaturis vigili Capitolia voce
Cederet anseribus, nec amanti flumina cycno.
Lingua fuit damno; lingua faciente loquaci
Cui color albus erat, nunc est contrarius albo.
—Ov., *Met.* II, 531.

No raven's notes her sacred groves annoy.—R. T. PAINE.

How the raven was forbidden by Apollo to consort with white birds:

> Sperantemque sibi non falsae praemia linguae,
> Inter aves albas vetuit consistere corvum.
> —Ov., *Met.* II, 631.

The color of ravens in flight:

> Conveniebat enim, corvos quoque saepe volantis
> Ex albis album pennis iactare colorem.
> —LUCR. II, 820.

A plagiarized page suggests a raven among swans:

> Sic niger in ripis errat cum forte Caystri,
> Inter Ledaeos ridetur corvus olores.
> —MART. I, 53, 7.

An old man who dyed his hair black:

> Mentiris invenem tinctis, Lentine, capillis;
> Tam subito corvus, qui modo cygnus eras.
> —MART. III, 43, 1.

Cf. *Anth. Lat.* 182.

> When gay and raven-headed.—CARLTON.
>
> His locks are black as a raven.—LONGFELLOW.
>
> 'Tis not the hair like raven's plume.—TICHNOR.

M. Valerius won his cognomen *Corvinus* from the aid given him by a raven:

> Ex uno quidam celebres, aut torquis adempti,
> Aut corvi titulos auxiliaris habent.
> —Ov., *Fast.* I, 601.

> Atque hic, egregius linguae, nomenque superbum,
> Corvinus, Phoebea sedet cui casside fulva
> Ostentans ales proavitae insignia pugnae,
> Plenus et ipse deum, et socium terrente pavore,
> Immiscet precibus monita atque his vocibus infit.
> —SIL. ITAL. V, 77.

Cf. Prop. III, 11, 64: Est cui cognomen corvus habere; Liv. 7, 26: Conserenti iam manum Romano corvus repente in galea consedit in hostem versus. Cf. also Man., *Astr.* I, 778.

For the age of the *Corvi* vid. s. v. CORNIX.

Corvi as weather prophets:

Cf. Hor., *Od.* III, 27, 8.

Et e pastu decedens agmine magno
Corvorum increpuit densis exercitus alis.
—VERG., *Geor.* I, 381.

Cf. Lucr. V, 1084, s. v. CORNIX. *Class. Rev.* 1904, p. 280. Note by Mr. Powell: "Vergil's exact knowledge of rooks may be illustrated by 'corvorum exercitus,' which refers not merely to their numbers, but to their military precision and discipline." Cf. *Anth. Lat.* 772, 47: Corvus et agmina confert.

A beautiful picture of the return of the *corvi* to their nests and young after a storm:

Tum liquidas corvi presso ter gutture voces
Aut quater ingeminant, et saepe cubilibus altis,
Nescio qua praeter solitum dulcedine laeti,
Inter se in foliis strepitant; iuvat imbribus actis
Progeniem parvam dulcisque revisere nidos.
—VERG., *Geor.* I, 410.

The *corvi* here, as often, are probably rooks.

Cf. Fowler, op. cit., p. 143; Glover, op. cit., p. 112; Thompson, op. cit., s. v., p. 91.

'Presso gutture' means 'with clear, deep note.' Vid. Powell, *Cl. Rev.* 1904, p. 280.

Sweet throat, come back! O liquid, mellow throat.
—BROWN (Stedman).

In eager flights the birds wing to their nests.
—TILLEY (Stedman).

A raven on the left is a bad sign:

Cf. Cic., *De Div.* I, 39.

Non temere est quod corvos cantat mihi nunc ab laeva manu:
Semul radebat pedibus terram et voce crocibat sua.
—PLAUT., *Aul.* 624.

And heard the boding raven croak his song.—CHATTERTON.

That raven on yon left-hand oak
(Curse on his ill-betiding croak!)
Bodes me no good.—GAY.

With sympathetic wo, thy noontide ray,
Phoebus, suspend; ye clouds, obscure the day;
Her face let Cynthia veil,
Thick darkness spread her wing,
And the night-raven sing,
While Britons their sad fate bewail.—PIETAS ET GRATULATIO.

The boding raven e'en forgets to croak,
And nature seems in silent agony.—SUSANNA ROWSON.
(*Thunderstorm.*)

And she heard, in her ear, a death-bell toll,
And the raven croak on a blasted tree.
(*Crystalina, a Fairy Tale.*)—BY AN AMERICAN (Kettell).

Caw! Caw! the rooks are calling,
It is a sound of woe, a sound of woe.—LONGFELLOW.

An expression of gratitude to a raven for his timely warning:

Ni subvenisset corvus, periissem miser.
Nimis hercle ego illum corvom ad me veniat velim
Qui indicium fecit, ut ego illic aliquid boni
Dicam; nam quod edit tam duim quam perduim.
—PLAUT., *Aul.* 669.

A raven on the right is a good sign:

Plaut., *Asin.* 259. Vid. also s. v. CORNIX. Augury was a special gift to the raven from the fates: Phaed. III, 18 (vid. s. v. AQUILA).

Priapus makes a reference to ravens:

Mentior at si quid, merdis caput inquiner albis
Corvorum. —HOR., *Sat.* I, 8, 37.

The raven often says 'good-day' first:

Nunquam dicis Ave, sed reddis, Naevole, semper,
Quod prior et corvus dicere saepe solet.
—MART. III, 95, 1.

Cf. Mart. XIV, 74: Corve salutator. For an explanation of the obscene allusion in the next line cf. Arist., *De Gen.* III, 6, 756b; Plin. X, 15; Macr. II, 4.

Ravens as scavenger birds:

Atque ideo, postquam ad Cimbros stragemque volabant
Qui nunquam attigerant maiora cadavera corvi,
Nobilis ornatur lauro collega secunda.
—JUV. VIII, 251.

Non equidem dubito, quin primum inimica bonorum
Lingua execta avido sit data vulturio;
Effossos oculos voret atro gutture corvus,
Intestina canes, cetera membri lupi.
—CAT. CVIII, 3.

Mere trunks of ice, though limn'd like human frames,
And lately warmed with life's endearing flames,
They cannot taint the air, the world infest,
Nor can you tear one fibre from their breast.
No! from their visual sockets as they lie,
With beak and claws you cannot pluck an eye—
The frozen orb, preserving still its form,
Defies your talons as it braves the storm,
But stands and stares to God as if to know
In what curst hands he leaves his world below!
Fly then, or starve, though all the dreadful road
From Minsk to Moscow with their bodies strow'd
May count some myriads, yet they cannot suffice
To feed you more beneath these dreadful skies.—BARLOW.
(*Advice to a Raven in Russia.*)

These lines are from Barlow's last poem, which was written in Europe during Napoleon's retreat from Moscow. Vid. Duyckinck, op. cit., vol. I, p. 414.

For the mating of the raven and dove as symbolic of the impossible cf. *Anth. Lat.* 390, 30, s. v. COLUMBA.

The raven broods very late in the year:

Corvus maturis frugibus ova refert.
—*Anth. Lat.* 690, 2.

The breeding habits of the raven and crow were totally unnoted in antiquity.

Cf. Hudson, op. cit. p. 174: "The raven is the earliest bird to breed in England: the nest building begins in January and the eggs are laid in February and March."

The winter-fearless crow.—"JOHN PHILIP VARLEY."

How the raven appears in Latin proverbs:

"Non hominem occidi." Non pasces in cruce corvos.
—HOR., *Ep.* I, 16, 48.

Dat veniam corvis, vexat censura columbas.
—JUV. II, 63.

Felix ille tamen corvo quoque rarior albo.
—JUV. VII, 202.

An passim sequeris corvos testaque lutoque,
Securus quo pes ferat, atque ex tempore vivis?
—PERS. III, 61.

The last reference is the equivalent of the English, 'A wild goose chase.' Cf. Aes., *Ag.* 394, and Eur., *Auge*, Fr. 271, Nauck.

Ah! foolish man! that sets his heart upon
Such empty shadows, such wild Fowl as these.
—MICHAEL WIGGLESWORTH.

For ravens as poets vid. Pers., *Prol.* 12, s. v. PICA.

For the raven as the bird of Apollo cf. Ov., *Met.* V, 329: Delius in corvo; *Fast.* II, 250: 'I, mea,' dixit (Phoebus), 'avis'; *Met.* II, 545; Stat., *Silv.* II, 4, 17: Planga Phoebeius ales; Stat., *Theb.* III, 506: Comes obscurus tripodum; Petron., *Sat.* 122: Delphicus ales; Aus., *Idyll* XI, 1, 5: Phoebeius oscen; Cat. LXVI, 57: Famulum (vid. note by Ellis).

For the constellation of Corvus vid. Cic., *Arat.* 219, 292; Ov., *Fast.* II, 243.

For the Fable of the Fox and the Raven vid. Phaedr. I, 3; Hor., *Ep.* I, 17, 50; *Sat.* II, 5, 55. Cf. Carryl, *The Sycophantic Fox and the Gullible Raven.*

For the Fable of the Traveller and the Raven vid. Aes. Fab. XXI.

For the call of the raven cf. Wackernagel, op. cit., p. 43; *Anth. Lat.* 762, 28: Crocitat corvus.

The raven croaked.—EMERSON.

Crows and blackbirds, jays and ravens,
Clamorous on the dusky tree tops.—LONGFELLOW.

And de ole crow croak: 'Don' work, no, no.'—LANIER.

'Karock, karock,' the ravens cry.—STRONG.

COTURNIX. Ὄρτυξ. Quail. *Coturnix communis*, or *C. dactylisonans.*

L. L. *Quaquila;* O. Fr. *Quaille;* M. Fr. *Caille;* Ital. *Quaglia.*

American parallel: *O. Virginianus;* Quail, 'Bob-white', Colin. The last is given by Hernandez as the original old Mexican name.

Harris: *The Bonny Brown Quail.*

Johnson: *Bob-white.*

References to Delos, Ortygia, and the metamorphosis of Latona, etc. into quails do not occur in the Latin poets, but vid.:

From somewhere hidden in the dreamy dale—
Latona's sorrow yet within her note—
Reft of her comrades, o'er the stubbled oat
We heard the calling of the lonely quail.—MIFFLIN.

Coturnix used as a term of endearment:

Dic me igitur tuom passerculum, gallinam, coturnicem,
Agnellum, haedillum me tuom dic esse vel vitellum,
Prehende auriculis, compara labella cum labellis.
—PLAUT., *Asin.* 666.

Quails were given as pets to patrician lads:

Nam ubi illo adveni, quasi patriciis pueris aut monerulae
Aut anites aut coturnices dantur, quicum lusitent,
Itidem haec mihi advenienti upupa, qui me delectem, datast.
—PLAUT., *Capt.* 1002.

Quails fatten on hellebore:

Praeterea, nobis veratrum est acre venenum,
At capris adipes et coturnicibus auget.
—LUCR. IV, 640.

Cf. Plin. X, 197; X, 33; Thompson, op. cit., p. 125.

Quails live in constant strife and thereby become old:

Ecce, coturnices inter sua praelia vivunt,
Forsitan et fiant inde frequenter anus.
—OV., *Am.* II, 6, 27.

Cf. Newton, op. cit., p. 755: "During both migrations immense numbers are netted for the market. On capture they are placed in long, narrow, low cages, darkened to prevent the prisoners from fighting."

In a simile Martial likens himself to a parrot and an anonymous poet to a quail:

Credis hoc, Prisce,
Voce ut loquatur psittacus coturnicis,
Et concupiscat esse Canus ascaules?
—MART. X, 3, 7.

Quails are too worthless to offer in sacrifice:

Verum haec nimia est impensa, coturnix
Nulla umquam pro patre cadet.
—JUV. XII, 97.

Cf. also Phaed. I, 3, s. v. GRACULUS.

And clouds of quails, from every region driven,
Blacken'd the fields, and fill'd the bounds of heaven.
(*Conquest of Canaan.*) —TIMOTHY DWIGHT.

The call and flight of the quail:

Scar'd by the pond'rous mower starts the rail,
Or, whirring, flies the 'frighted, ominous quail.
—CHATTERTON.

When the quail all day
Pipe on the chaparral hill.—MILLER.

But the quail, whose quick whistle has lured me along,
No more will recall his stray'd mate with his song.
—STREET.

And, tilted on the ridered rails
Of deadnin' fences, "Old Bob White"
Whissels his name in high delight.—RILEY.

The bobwhite's liquid yodel, and the whir of sudden flight.
—RILEY.

CUCULUS. Κόκκυξ. Cuckoo. *Cuculus canorus.*

Cuculus is onomatopoetic. Cf. *Anth. Lat.* 762, 35: Et cuculi cuculant.

American literary parallels: Black-billed cuckoo, yellow-billed cuckoo, cow-bunting. The last named (after the manner of the European cuckoo) intrudes its eggs into the nests of other birds.

Hosmer: *The Cuckoo.*

Saxe (from Yriarte): *Fable of the Bee and the Cuckoo.*

Wordsworth: *Ode to the Cuckoo.*

Logan: *To the Cuckoo.*

Matthew Arnold: *Thyrsis.*

Cuculus used as a term of reproach, a usage probably first suggested by the vagabond habits of the bird:

. . . Immo es, ne nega, omnium (hominum) pol nequissumus
At enim cubat cuculus. Surge, amator, i domum.
—PLAUT., *Asin.* 923 (cf. 934).

Mocks married men: for thus sings he.
Cuckoo, cuckoo! O word of fear,
Unpleasing to a married ear.—SHAKESPEARE.

Hephaistos, the lame cuckold.—STEDMAN.

But indolence, like the cow-bird,
That's hatched in an alien nest.—TROWBRIDGE.

It can't build nests, for it's—the air!
I know a boy that knows!—MRS. PIATT.
(*His Views of the Cuckoo.*)

Cf. also Plaut., *Pseud.* 96; *Trin.* 245; *Pers.* 282 and possibly 173.

How Jupiter, in the form of a cuckoo, beguiled Juno on Mount Thomax. Vid. Pausan II, 17, 4, and Schol. ad Theocr. XV, 16:

Oft there came
Blest visions to his soul of forms divine;—
Of white-armed Juno, in that hour of love,
When, fondling close the cuckoo, tempest-chilled,
She all unconscious in that form did press
The mighty sire of the eternal gods
To her soft bosom.—GRACE GREENWOOD.

It was an insult to call a belated pruner a cuckoo. A hint from the spring migration and spring song of the bird:

Tum Praenestinus salso multoque fluenti
Expressa arbusto regerit convicia, durus
Vindemiator et invictus, cui saepe viator
Cessisset, magna compellans voce cuculum.
—HOR., *Sat.* I, 7, 28.

Or heard from branch of flowering thorn
The song of friendly cuckoo warn
The tardy-moving swain.—ALLSTON.

Cf. Plin. 18, 66, 249; Aus., *Idyll.* X, 167.

A cuckoo chuckles, half throttled on a neighboring tree.
—THOREAU, op. cit., p. 111.

And the cuckoo's shy, complaining note
Mocks the maidens in the corn.—BAYARD TAYLOR.

The cuckoo in American lore foretells the coming of rain:

"Here in this book," she said,—in faltering tones,
As sweet and sad as those the cuckoo frames,
Hid in her leafy covert, when the wind
Sighs from the east and clouds are set for rain.—PROCTOR.

The call of the cuckoo to its mates during the spring migration:

Nunc cuculus cantans socios[1] iter ire perurget.[2]
—*Anth. Lat.* 733, 13.

[1] Burmann; the ms. reading is unintelligible.

[2] Cf. Newton, op. cit., p. 119: "Its arrival is at once proclaimed by the peculiar and in nearly all languages onomatopoetic cry of the cock—a true song, since it is confined to the male sex and to the season of love."

Πρῶτος τῶν πτηνῶν ὑμῖν τὸ 'έαρ ἀγγέλλων: Dion., *De Avibus*, 1, 13.

The cuckoo told his name to all the hills.—TENNYSON.

Sure, he's arrived,
The tell-tale cuckoo; Spring's his confidant,
And he lets out her April purposes!—ROBERT BROWNING.

Hark how the jolly cuckoos sing
Cuckoo! to welcome in the spring.—JOHN LYLY.

The cuckoo's April call.—BAYARD TAYLOR.

I hear a cuckoo's silver call,
That stirs the slumberous solitude
With many a mellow rise and fall.—PROCTOR.

Again the year is at the prime
With flush of rose and cuckoo-croon.—SCOLLARD.

Thou hast no sorrow in thy song,
No winter in thy year.—LOGAN.

Cares the cuckoo for the woods
When the red leaves are down?—SILL.

And beyond the meadow the cuckoo lingers.—STRONG.

From that spot I heard a Cuckoo cry, for I do not, like the English, call it singing. Many people speak in raptures of the sweet voice of the Cuckoo, and the same people tell me in cold blood that we have no birds that can sing in America. I wish they had a chance to judge of the powers of the Mock-bird, the Red Thrush, the Cat-bird, the Oriole, the Indigo Bunting and even the Whip-poor-will.—AUDUBON, *Journal*, vol. I, p. 245.

Logan, whose "Cuckoo" will sing forever,
For a brief moment, my attention caught.—HOSMER.

CYCNUS and **OLOR**. Κύκνος. Swan. Mute swan, *Cygnus olor*. Whistling swan or whooper, *C. musicus*.

American parallels: Trumpeter swan and whistling swan.

Hosmer: *Address to the Swan*.

The exalted position of the swan in the ancient poets can be rationalized only by its connection with astronomical lore and myths of metamorphosis, whose inner meanings are for the most part veiled to us. (Cf. Thompson, op. cit. Preface and passim.) The widely attested belief in the swan's song, however, does, I believe, rest upon real observation, later expanded by the associations and influences mentioned above. In this connection the following testimony from Elliot. op. cit., p. 24, is of more than ordinary interest:

"The song of the dying swan has been the theme of poets for centuries, and is generally considered one of those pleasing myths that are handed down through the ages. I had killed many swan and never heard aught from them at any time, save the familiar notes that reach the ears of every one in their vicinity. But once, when shooting in Currituck Sound over water belonging to a club of which I am a member, in company with a friend, a number of swan passed over us at a considerable height. We fired at them, and one splendid bird was mortally hurt. On receiving his wound the wings became fixed and he commenced at once his song, which was continued until the water was reached, nearly half a mile away. I am perfectly familiar with every note a swan is accustomed to utter, but never before nor since have I heard any like those sung by this stricken bird. Most plaintive in character and musical in tone, it sounded at times like the soft running of the notes in an octave.

And now 'twas like all instruments,
Now like a lonely flute;
And now it is an angel's song
Which makes the heavens be mute.

and as the sound was borne to us, mellowed by the distance, we stood astonished, and could only exclaim,

'We have heard the song of the dying swan.' "

For the other side int. al. cf. Harting, op. cit., p. 201 ff. Neri, op. cit., p. 10. "Il canto dei cigni celebrato da tutti i poeti è pura finzione, emettendo anzi quest' animale un suono sgradevolissimo."

Ferrariae multos cygnos vidimus, sed cantores sane malos, neque melius ansere canere.—SCALIGER, quoted by Thompson (op. cit., p. 107), who is also a dissenter.

Epithets:

Albus, amans flumina, Amyclaeus, argutus, candens, candidus, canorus, cantans, Caystrius, Cyllenius, dulcis, flebilis, fluvialis,, flumineus, Idalius, innocuus, Ledaeus, loquax, lugubri voce, moribundus, niveus, plumeus, purpureus, Oebalius, raucus, Spartanus, senex.

The haunts of swans. The Minco, the Po, etc.:

Saltus et saturi petito longinqua Tarenti,
Et qualem infelix amisit Mantua campum,
Pascentem niveos herboso flumine cycnos.
—VERG., *Geor.* II, 197.

The swan, once familiar in the region of Mantua, is now rarely to be seen. This condition has been brought about by possible changes in the climate and by the drainage of swamps and marshes. Vid. Glover, op. cit., p. 112. Fowler, *Year with Birds*, pp. 143, 148, 153.

The wild swan swims the waters' azure breast
With graceful sweep, or, startled, soars away,
Cleaving with mounting wing the clear, bright air.
—ELLET (Griswold).

Then other swans wide-winged and white as snow,
Flew overhead and topp'd the timbered hills.—MILLER.

Speed thou upon thy white swans' wings.—FIELD.

Haud procul Hennaeis lacus est a moenibus altae,
Nomine Pergus, aquae. Non illo plura Caystros
Carmina cygnorum labentibus audit in undis.
—Ov., *Met.* V, 385.

Haud secus atque alto in luco cum forte catervae
Consedere avium, piscosove amne Padusae
Dant sonitum rauci per stagna loquacia cycni.
—VERG., *Aen.* XI, 456.

Rauci is almost unique as an epithet of real observation applied to the ordinary note of the swan, without the influence of the usual metamorphosis association. It is truly Vergilian.

Cf. Et canoras non tacere diva iussit alites.
Iam loquaces ore rauco stagna cycni perstrepunt.
—*Perv. Ven.* 85.

Guiltless swans frequent the Elysian fields of the birds:

Colle sub Elysio nigra nemus ilice frondens,
Udaque perpetuo gramine terra viret.
Si qua fides dubiis: volucrum locus ille piarum
Dicitur, obscenae quo prohibentur aves.
Illic innocui late pascuntur olores,
Et vivax Phoenix, unica semper avis.
—Ov., *Am.* II, 6, 49.

Ovid, in his sweetest verse,
Loved thy praises to rehearse;
Flaccus, in his polished lay,
Tribute unto thee did pay,
And in Plato's mighty tome
Ever wilt thou find a home.—HOSMER.

A swan soft floating tow'ds a magic strand.—LANIER.

Swans the prey of eagles:

> Namque volans rubra fulvus Iovis ales in aethra
> Litoreas agitabat aves turbamque sonantem
> Agminis aligeri; subito cum lapsus ad undas
> Cygnum excellentem pedibus rapit improbus uncis.
> —VERG., *Aen.* XII, 247.

> Qualis ubi aut leporem aut candenti corpore cygnum
> Sustulit alta petens pedibus Iovis armiger uncis.
> —VERG., *Aen.* IX, 560.

Vid. s. v. AQUILA. Cf. int. al. Verg., *Aen.* I, 392. Stat., *Theb.* III, 524; VIII, 674.

The swan was a good omen to sailors:

> Cygnus in auspiciis semper laetissimus ales,
> Hunc optant nautae, quia se non mergit in undas.
> —AEM. MAC., Baehrens, P. L. M., p. 344.

For the color of the swan vid. Epithets, supra, and cf. the following: Hor., *Od.* IV, 1, 10; Ov., *Met.* II, 536; Mart. I, 115, 2; VIII, 28, 13; Val. Flacc. VI, 102; Sil. Ital. XIII, 115; XIV, 190, et al.

> Throat as white as the throat of a swan
> And all as proudly graceful held.—CARLTON.

A perfect wife is as rare as a black swan. Proverbial.

> Rara avis in terris nigroque simillima cygno.
> —JUV. VI, 165.

> An honest treasure like a black-plumed swan,
> Not every day our eyes may look upon.—HOLMES.

> No *rara avis* was honest John
> (That's the Latin for "sable swan").—SAXE.

A negro slave's name:

> Nanum cuiusdam Atlanta vocamus:
> Aethiopem Cycnum parvam extortamque puellam
> Europen. —JUV. VIII, 33.

Ovid is now becoming old:

> Iam mea cycneas imitantur tempora plumas,
> Inficit et nigras alba senecta comas.
> —OV., *Tr.* IV, 8, 1.

For an old man who dyed his hair, cf. Mart. III, 43.

For the constellation vid. int. al. Thompson, op. cit., p. 107; Manil. *Astron.* I, 335; II, 31 et al.; Stat., *Theb.* VI, 521; *Anth. Lat.* 761, 9.

The swan in various comparisons of poets:

Lucretius (swallow) and Epicurus (swan), Lucr. III, 7; Horace (bee) and Pindar (swan), Hor., *Od.* IV, 2, 25; Fidentius (crow) and Martial (swan), Mart. I, 53, 7. For the goose and swan in this connection cf. Verg., *Ecl.* IX, 36; Prop. III, 26, 84 et al., and vid. s. v. ANSER.

Cf. Mifflin. Sonnet. *Milton* (Eagle).

Horace becomes a swan:

Iam iam residunt cruribus asperae
Pelles, et album mutor in alitem
Superne, nascunturque plumae.
Per digitos humerosque plumae.
—HOR., *Od.* II, 20, 9.

The transformation of the poet into a swan realistically portrayed before our eyes is a very bold treatment of the Roman poetic usage of the metamorphosis idea, and the Ode should be interpreted and estimated with this usage in mind. Cf. the more symbolical treatment of Eur., *Frag.* 903.

Well might the Roman Swan, along
The pleasing Tiber pour his song,
When bless'd with ease and quiet;
Oft did he grace Maecenas' board,
Who would for him throw by the lord,
And in Falernian riot.—EVANS (Kettell).

"Rare old Ben" could find no name
Worthy of a Shakespeare's fame
But thine own, majestic bird!
Now a consecrated word
With unmatched poetic love
Intertwined for evermore.—HOSMER.

Not every crow, nor croaking raven,
Can match the tuneful swan of Avon.—FESSENDEN.

When the Swan of sweet Avon touched hand to the lyre.
—MATTHEWS.

But again I ask'd,
"What nurtured Shakespeare?" The rejoicing birds
Wove a wild song, whose burden seem'd to be,
He was their pupil when he chose, and knew
Their secret maze of melody to wind,
Snatching its sweetness for his winged strain
With careless hand.—SIGOURNEY.

How often gazing where a bird reposes,
Rocked on wavelets, drifting with the tide,
I lose myself in strange metempsychosis
And float a sea-fowl at a sea-fowl's side.—HOWELLS.

From my window turning
I find myself a plumeless biped still;
No beak, no claws, no sign of wings discerning—
In fact with nothing birdlike but my quill.—HOWELLS.

My Calderon, my nightingale,
My Arab soul in Spanish feathers.—LOWELL.

New England's poet-laureate
Telling us spring has come again.—ALDRICH.
(*The Blue Bird.*)

Let Tennyson his Lilian sing
And lovely Oriana,
And scale the skies with tireless wing,
In praise of Mariana.—GEN. ALBERT PIKE.

Like his own sky-lark, up at Heaven's gate,
Above the earth and all its meaner things,
He sang, and soared higher than mortal ken.
(*Shelley.*) —GEN. ALBERT PIKE.

There, like her lark, gay Chaucer leads the day,
The matin carol of his country's day.—BARLOW.
(*Columbiad.*)

Swift I mount me on the plume
Of my Wakon-Bird, and fly.—THOMAS MOORE.
(*Poems Relating to America.*)

Why is't thus, this sylvan Petrarch
Pours all night his serenade?
'Tis for some proud woodland Laura,
His sad sonnets are all made!
But he changes now his measure—
Gladness bubbling from his mouth—
Jest, and gibe, and mimic pleasure—
Winged Anacreon of the South!
(*The Mocking Bird.*) —MEEK.

The metamorphosis of Cycnus (the son of Sthenelus and king of Liguria), into a swan, with a description of the process:

Adfuit huic monstro proles Stheneleïa Cycnus,
Qui tibi materno quamvis a sanguine iunctus,
Mente tamen, Phaëthon, propior fuit. Ille relicto,
(Nam Ligurum populos et magnas rexerat urbes)
Imperio ripas virides amnemque querelis
Eridanum implerat silvamque sororibus auctam,
Cum vox est tenuata viro, canaeque capillos
Dissimulant plumae, collumque e pectore longum
Porrigitur, digitosque ligat iunctura rubentes,
Penna latus velat, tenet os sine acumine rostrum.
Fit nova Cycnus avis nec se caeloque Iovique
Credit, ut iniuste missi memor ignis ab illo;
Stagna petit patulosque lacus, ignemque perosus
Quae colat, elegit contraria flumina flammis.

—Ov., *Met.* II, 367.

Namque ferunt luctu Cycnum Phaethontis amati,
Populeas inter frondes umbramque sororum
Dum canit et maestum Musa solatur amorem,
Canentem molli pluma duxisse senectam,
Linquentem terras et sidera voce sequentem.

—VERG., *Aen.* X, 189.

Cf. Thomas (Stedman), *The Tears of the Poplars.*

Vid. Hyg., *Fab.* 144: Cygnus autem rex Liguriae, qui fuit Phaethonti propinquus, dum deflet propinquum, in cygnum conversus est. Is quoque moriens flebile canit.

The story of Cycnus, the son of Apollo and Hyrie, who was metamorphosed into a swan. His mother, from grief, became thereupon the lake of Hyrie:

Inde lacus Hyries videt et Cycneïa tempe,
Quae subitus celebravit olor. Nam Phyllius illic
Imperio pueri volucresque ferumque leonem
Tradiderat domitos; taurum quoque vincere iussus
Vicerat, et, spreto totiens iratus amore
Praemia poscenti taurum suprema negabat.
Ille indignatus, 'cupies dare,' dixit, et alto
Desiluit saxo. Cuncti cecidisse putabant:
Factus olor niveis pendebat in aëre pennis.
At genetrix Hyrie, servati nescia, flendo
Delicuit stagnumque suo de nomine fecit.

—Ov., *Met.* VII, 371.

As some calm, still lake, whereon
Sinks the snowy-bosomed swan,
And the glistening water-rings
Circle round her moving wings.—WHITTIER.

For other associations for Apollo and the swan vid. Lucr. II, 503; *Anth. Lat.* 691, 5; Mart. IX, 43, 1, with which cf. Whitman:

Where the neck of the long lived swan is curving and winding.

The myth of Leda and the swan:

Qualis erat Leda, quam plumis aditus albis
Callidus in falsa lusit adulter ave.
—Ov., *Am.* I, 10, 3.

Dat mihi Leda Iovem cycno decepta parentem,
Quae falsam gremio credula fovit avem.
—Ov., *Her.* XVII, 55.

Non ego fluminei referam mendacia cycni
Nec querar in plumis delituisse Iovem.
—Ov., *Her.* VIII, 67.

Vid. also Ov., *Met.* VI, 109; *Her.* XVI, 249; *Am.* I, 3, 21; Verg., *Cat.* IX, 27; Sen., *Oct.* 204, 762; Manil., *Astron.* I, 337; Aet. 87; Mart. IX, 104, 2; Stat., *Theb.* X, 503; Val. Flacc. I, 431; *Carm. Epig.* 345, 1549, 23; *Anth. Lat.* 59; 141; 199, 93; 808, 46, et al. vid. s. v. ANSER.

And a swan
(Sire, by the light of Heaven's twin orbs, mis-told.)
—BAILEY.

Two stately snow-white swans are seen.
Whose every motion bears the trace
Of that majestic haughty grace
Jove left the fabled bird which gave
Its form from Juno's wrath to save.—CLARKE.

Yon snow-white cloud that sails sublime in ether
Is but the sovereign Zeus, who like a swan
Flies to fair-ankled Leda.—LONGFELLOW.
(*The Masque of Pandora.*)

The antique poetic records of the swan as a bird of Venus occur in the Latin poets only.

The goddess comes to stricken Adonis in a chariot drawn by swans:

Vecta levi curru medias Cytherea per auras
Cypron olorinis nondum pervenerat alis.
Agnovit longe gemitum morientis et albas
Flexit aves illuc. —Ov., *Met.* X, 717.

Venus borne by her swans with Amor as *auriga*:

Sic fata, levavit
Sidereos artus thalamique egressa superbum
Limen, Amyclaeos ad frena citavit olores,
Iungit Amor laetamque vehens per nubila matrem
Gemmato temone sedet. Iam Thybridis arces
Iliacae: pandit nitidos domus alta penates,
Claraque gaudentes plauserunt limia cycni.
—STAT., *Silv.* I, 2, 140.

Vid. also Hor., *Od.* III, 28, 14; Prop. IV, 3, 39; Ov., *Met.* X, 708; Stat., *Silv.* III, 4, 22; III, 4, 46; *Theb.* V, 63; Sil. Ital. VII, 440; *Anth. Lat.* 939, 2.

In silver traces fix'd unto her car,
Four snowy swans, proud of the imperial fair,
Wing'd lightly on, each in gay beauty dress'd,
Smooth'd the soft plumage that adorn'd her breast.
Sacred to her the lucent chariot drew,
Or whether wildly through the air she flew,
Or whether to the dreary shades of night,
Oppress'd with gloom she downward bent her flight,
Or proud aspiring sought the bless'd abodes,
And boldly shot among the assembled gods.
—GODFREY (Kettell).

Purer type the fabling mind
Grace to picture cannot find,
And when Art on canvas drew
Venus, born of ocean blue,
Yoked to chariot of the queen,
Swans, with arching neck, were seen.—HOSMER.

Beside them stood a chariot dazzling bright,
Yok'd with two beauteous swans of purest white.
—LUCRETIA DAVIDSON.

The song of swans as they return from their feeding grounds:

Ceu quondam nivei liquida inter nubilia cycni
Cum sese e pastu referunt et longa canoros
Dant per colla modos; sonat amnis et Asia longe
Pulsa palus. —VERG., *Aen.* VII, 699.

Drensare is the technical verb for the swan's song or note:

Grus gruit in gronnis, cygni prope flumina drensant.
—*Anth. Lat.* 762, 23.

The swan's song is contrasted with the trumpet's blare:

Nec simili penetrant aureis primordia forma,
Cum tuba depresso graviter sub murmure mugit
Et reboat raucum regio cita barbara bombum
Et validis cygni torrentibus ex Heliconis
Cum liquidam tollunt lugubri voce querelam.
—LUCR. IV, 544.

But, hark!—what sound—out of the dewy deep,
How like a far-off bugle's shrillest note
It sinks into the listening wilderness.
A Swan—I know her by the trumpet-tone.
(*To a Swan, flying by night on the Banks of the Huron.*) —NOBLE (Duyckinck).

Never listened mortal ear
To voice more full and clear,
Not unlike in depth of tone
Blast of conch-shell loudly blown,
Or a far-off trumpet wail
Modulated by the gale.—HOSMER.

According to Mr. Shields, the cry of the Trumpeter Swan resembles the tones of the French horn.—WHEELOCK: *Birds of California*, s. v.

Seebohm, who studied its habits in Siberia, says the notes of the whooper resemble those of a bass trombone.—KNOWLTON-RIDGWAY: *Birds of the World*, p. 173.

Cf. And the owl across the twilight
Trumpets to his gloomy fellow.—ROBERTS.

A long, low bugle-note
From the white-throated sparrow of the woods
Begins to swell and float.—MACE.

The joyous spring song of migrant swans:

Patriis concentibus audis
Exultare gregem, quales, cum pallida cedit
Bruma, renidentem deducunt Strymona cycni.
—STAT., *Theb.* VII, 285.

Sailing on the wind to northward,
Flying in great flocks, like arrows,
Like huge arrows shot through heaven,
Passed the swan, the Mahuahbezee,
Speaking almost as a man speaks.—LONGFELLOW.

At last I saw her watch the swan
Surge toward the north, surge on and on.—MILLER.

The short song of the swan excels that of migrating cranes:

Suavidicis potius quam multis versibus edam:
Parvus ut est cycni melior canor, ille gruum quam
Clamor in aetheriis dispersus nubibus austri.
—LUCR. IV, 180.

In song the swan is surpassed by the nightingale:

Iudice me cycnus et garrula cedat hirundo,
Cedat et inlustri psittacus ore tibi.
—*Anth. Lat.* 658, 19.

Here silver swans with nightingales set spells,
Which sweetly charm the traveller.
(*Mrs. Anne Bradstreet and her Poems.*)
—JOHN ROGERS.

The power of the muses:

O, testudinis aureae
Dulcem quae strepitum, Pieri, temperas,
O mutis quoque piscibus
Donatura cycni, si libeat, sonum.
—HOR., *Od.* IV, 3, 17.

For him, who sang like you his deathless songs,
O swans Strymonian, chaunt some dolorous dirge
Immortal and melodious as his own!—MIFFLIN.
(*The Lament for Bion.*)

The death song of the swan:

Sic ubi fata vocant, udis abiectus in herbis
Ad vada Maeandri concinit albus olor.
—OV., *Her.* VII, 1.

Reddidit icta suos pollice chorda sonos,
Flebilibus veluti numeris canentia dura
Traiectus penna tempora cantat olor.
—OV., *Fast.* II, 108.

Penna is here an arrow. Cf. Gesner, op. cit., p. 360: Moriturus flebilem cantum emittit, fixa prius in cerebro penna: quod miror Aristotelem ac Plinium vel ignorasse vel si sciverunt, non tradidisse. —PEROTTUS.

Dulcia defecta modulatur carmina lingua
  Cantator cycnus funeris ipsi sui.
—MART. XIII, 77.

Vid. also int. al. Ov., *Met.* XIV, 430; Sen., *Hippol.* 301; *Agam.* 680; Mart. V, 37, 1; Stat., *Silv.* II, 4, 10; V, 3, 80; Stat., *Theb.* V, 341; Sil. Ital. XI, 438; Lact., *De Phoen.* 49; Plin. X. 32, 1.

Still would I believer be
In the tale they tell of thee—
Breathing in the hour of death
Music with thy latest breath;
Tuning, with a failing tongue,
Strains the sweetest ever sung.—HOSMER.

Then shall come singers
Singing no swan song.—LOWELL.

Ovid, like a swan, is singing his own death song:

Utque iacens ripa deflere Caystrius ales
  Dicitur ore suam deficiente necem,
Sic ego, Sarmaticas longe proiectus in oras,
  Efficio, tacitum ne mihi funus eat.
—Ov., *Trist.* V, 1, 11.

Cf. Whittier, *The Swan Song of Parson Avery.*

How sweet the eloquence of dying men!
Hence poets feigned the music of the Swan,
When death upon her lays his icy hand,
She melts away in melancholy strains.
—THOMAS GODFREY (Duyckinck).

Nor Goethe sing with swan-like sweetness more.
(1832.) —ROSWELL PARK.

Where some lost maid wide chaplets wreathes,
And, swan-like, there her own dirge breathes.
—SPRAGUE (Griswold.)

He is floating down, by himself to die;
Death darkens his eye, and unplumes his wings,
Yet his sweetest song is the last he sings.
—DOANE (Griswold).

The swan's last song is sweetest.—HALLECK.

The pale swan in her watery nest
Begins the sad dirge of her certain ending.—SHAKESPEARE.

Above, fly cranes, geese, ducks, herons and teals;
And swans, which take such pleasure as they fly,
They sing their hymns oft long before they die.
(*Connecticut River.*) —ROGER WOLCOTT.

DIOMEDEAE AVES. *Ardea.* Ἐρωδιός. Heron.

Exact species indeterminant, but this general identification seems most in harmony with the myth, the tradition and the natural characteristics alluded to by Ovid and Vergil.

For a full treatment, especially of the Greek sources, of the myth and legend, vid. Thompson, op. cit., p. 59. Holland, *Herovögel in der Griechischen Mythologie.* Heyne, *Excursus;* Verg., *Aen.* XI, 271.

The Latin prose versions are of interest:

Hae aves hodieque Latine Diomedeae vocantur, Graeci eas ἐρωδιούς. Habitant autem in insula, quae est haud longe a Calabria, in conspectu Tarentinae civitatis. Quin etiam de his avibus dicitur quod Graecis navibus laetae occurrant, alienas vehementer fugiant, memores et originis suae et quod Diomedes ab Illyriis interemptus est.
—SERV. AD VERG., *Aen.* XI, 271.

Nam et Diomedem fecerunt deum (sc. Graeci), quem poena divinitus inrogata perhibent ad suos non revertissee; eiusque socios in volucres fuisse conversos non fabuloso poeticoque mendacio, sed historica attestatione confirmant; quibus nec deus ut putant factus humanam revocare naturam vel ipse potuit vel certe a Iove suo rege tamquam caelicola novicius impetravit. Quin etiam templum eius esse aiunt in insula Diomedea, non longe a monte Gargano, qui est in Apulia, et hoc templum circumvolare atque incolere has alites tam mirabili obsequio, ut aquam impleant et aspergant; et eo si Graeci venerint vel Graecorum stirpe prognati, non solum quietas esse, verum et insuper adulare; si autem alienigenas viderint, subvolare ad capita, tamque gravibus ictibus, ut etiam perimant, vulnerare. Nam duris et grandibus rostris satis ad haec proelia perhibentur armatae. —S. AUG., *De civ. Dei* XVIII, 16.

Cf. also Plin. X, 44, 61; Isid. 12, 7, 28.

The metamorphosis of the comrades of Diomedes:

Numerusque ex agmine maior
Subvolat et remos plausis circumvolat alis.
Si volucrum quae sit subitarum forma, requiris,
Ut non cycnorum, sic albis proxima cycnis.
—Ov., *Met.* XIV, 506.

Nunc etiam horribili visu portenta sequuntur,
Et socii amissi petierunt aethera pennis
Fluminibusque vagantur aves—heu dira meorum
Supplicia!—et scopulos lacrimosis[1] vocibus implent.
—VERG., *Aen.* XI, 271.

DROSCA. Song thrush. Vid. s. v. TURDUS.

EPOPS (UPUPA). Ἔποψ. Hoopoe.

Cf. Thompson, op. cit., p. 54; Newton, op. cit. s. v. Hoopoe.

Tereus metamorphosed into a hoopoe. A description of the bird in question:

Ille dolore suo poenaeque cupidine velox
Vertitur in volucrem, cui stant in vertice cristae
Prominet immodicum pro longa cupidine rostrum
Nomen epops volucri, facies armata videtur.
—Ov., *Met.* VI, 671.

For Tereus vid. Verg., *Ecl.* VI, 78; Aet. 585; Sen., *Thyest* 275; *Anth. Lat.* 199, 53; 808, 4; s. v. v. LUSCINIA, HIRUNDO, passim.

Cf. Verg., *Cul.* 253: Orbus epops maeret volucres evectus in auras. For the familiar pun on Upupa (Epops) vid. Plaut., *Capt.* 1004.

Cf. Go, borrow me a crow, a crow without feather.—SHAKESPEARE.

He knows a handsaw from a hawk whenever winds are southerly.
—FIELD.

When these young hands first closed upon a goose:
I have a scar upon my thimble finger.—HOLMES.

FICEDULA. Συκαλίς. Figeater.

A name given indiscriminately to many small birds which in the autumn frequent gardens. Cf. Newton, op. cit. s. v. FIG-EATER.

Motacilla ficedula or *Silvia hortensis.*

Thompson (op. cit., p. 163) thinks that the Black-cap Warbler (*Silvia atricapilla*) satisfies the prose statements better than any other species yet suggested.

American parallel: Reed-bird, (bobolink).

[1]Due to influence of metamorphosis association.

The 'reed-bird' of the Roman fable:

> Cerea quae patulo lucet ficedula lumbo,
> Cum tibi forte datur, si sapis, adde piper.
> —MART. XIII, 5.

> Cum me ficus alat, cum pascar dulcibus uvis,
> Cur potius nomen non dedit uva mihi?
> (*Ficedula.*) —MART. XIII, 49.

> Nec melius de se cuiquam sperare propinquo
> Concedet iuvenis, qui radere tubera terrae,
> Boletum condire et eodem iure natantes
> Mergere ficedulas didicit nebulone parente
> Et cana monstrante gula. —JUV. XIV, 6.

Vid. also Plaut., *Capt.* 163; Lucil. 726; Baehrens, *P. L. M.* 529; Petr. 33.

> There the hunter stealthily lurks for the hare or the pheasant,
> Or for the birds in the twigs at the great feast of the fruit.
> (*Greek Idyl. In the Olives.*)—SNIDER.

FRINGILLUS. Σπίνος. Chaffinch(?).
Fringilla coelebs.
American parallels: Finch, indigo-bird, linnet.
The spring song of the *fringilli*:

> Nunc sturnos inopes fringillorumque querelas
> Audit, et arguto passere vernat ager.
> —MART. IX, 55, 7.

Σπίνος, Arat. 1024, is translated by Avienus with *fringilla,* in a passage where the morning song of the bird is said to be prophetic of approaching storms. *Querelas* above is an echo of the traditional Roman attitude toward the song of birds. Here it is notably false according to modern feeling, if the equation *Fringillus* = chaffinch is true. Cf. Hudson, op. cit., p. 135: "It is a loud song and a joyous sound; 'Gay as a chaffinch,' is a proverbial saying of the French."

> And early linnets hail the purple spring.—R. T. PAINE.

> The yellow finches perched and sang
> Their few notes sweet and loud.—HIGGINSON.

FULICA. Φαλαρίς. Coot(?).
Fulica atra. Exact identification impossible.
American parallel: Coot, 'mud-hen,' 'marsh-hen.'

As the marsh-hen secretly builds on the watery sod,
Behold, I will build me a nest on the greatness of God.
—LANIER.

The wanton coot the water skims.—BURNS.

I come from haunts of coot and hern.—TENNYSON.

The mud-hen's whistle from the marsh at morn.—LAMPMAN.

The *fulix* (*fulica*) portends the coming of a storm:

Cana fulix itidem fugiens e gurgite ponti
Nuntiat horribilis clamans instare procellas
Haud modicos tremulo fundens gutture cantus.
—CIC., *Prog.* 183.

Cicero has confused the *fulix* with the ἐρωδιός (heron) of Aratus. The epithet *cana* (if *fulix* = coot) is hardly possible, and the habits described seem best to fall in with the traditional treatment of the heron, vid. s. v. ARDEA.

Iam sibi tum curvis male temperat unda carinis
Cum medio celeres revolant ex aequore mergi
Clamoremque ferunt ad litora, cumque marinae
In sicco ludunt fulicae notasque paludes
Deserit atque altam supra volat ardea nubem.
—VERG., *Geor.* I, 360.

In Vergil there is another confusion. *Fulica* is here applied to the αἴθυια of Aratus, which according to Plin. X, 91, is the *mergus*. The latter was also a foreteller of storms. Cf. Plin. XVIII, 362. Vid. also Luc. V, 555; *Anth. Lat.* 772, 37.

The haunts of the *fulicae*:

Haud procul hinc stagnum est, tellus habitalis olim,
Nunc celebres mergis fulicisque palustribus undae.
—OV., *Met.* VIII, 624.

The black ducks gather, with plumes so rich,
And the coots in twinkling lines.—CELIA THAXTER.

The verges and islets of the lagoon were elegantly embellished with flowering plants and shrubs; the laughing coots with wings half spread were tripping over little coves, and hiding themselves in the tufts of grass.—JOHN BARTRAM.

GALBULUS. Ἴκτερος. Golden Oriole(?). *Oriolus galbulus.*

The Oriole (Baltimore and Orchard) is a favorite bird in all the American poets. The bobolink on its fall migration, when known as the 'reed-bird,' is a parallel to the unique reference below:

Alexander Wilson: *The Baltimore Bird.*
Field: *The Fire-Hangbird's Nest.*
Emily Dickinson: *The Oriole's Secret.*
Arlo Bates: *The Oriole.*
Chadwick: *The Golden-Robin's Nest.*
Maurice Thompson: *Spring's Torch-bearer.*

A golden oriole with midnight wings
Dreamed in the city's topmost elm and sang
Of endless summer and undying fog.—LAMPMAN.

'Twixt cypresses and slim palmetto trees,
Like to the golden oriole's hanging nest,
Her airy hammock swings.—EMMA LAZARUS.

Gay Columbine, orioles are chanting
Your trumpet-note, loud on the gale.—LARCOM.

And there within the emerald twilight, which
Defied the mid-day sun, from bough to bough
A torch of downy flame—the oriole
Passed to his nest, to feed the censer-fires
Which Love had lit for Airs of Heaven to swing.
—HOLLAND.

I never thought that Jason sought
For any golden fleece;
But then I am a rural man,
With thoughts that make for peace.

But if there were a Jason,
Tradition suffer me
Behold his lost emolument
Upon the apple tree.
(*The Oriole.*) —EMILY DICKINSON.

The bird that wears the bright attire,
The down of fire-grained Nessean woof,
Burned like a phoenix on her pyre.—WRIGHT.

The *galbulus* (lemma) or *galbina ales* (text), is caught with reeds and nets, while the grapes are yet unripe:

Galbina decipitur calamis et retibus ales,
Turget adhuc viridi cum rudis uva mero.
(*Galbulus.*) —MART. XIII, 68.

Cf. Plin. XXX, 94. Avis icterus vocatur a colore, hanc puto Latine vocari *galgulum* (Sillig, Detlefsen), *galbulum* (Jan.).

GALLINULA. Πορφυρίων. Purple gallinule(?).
Porphyrio hyacinthus.

The purple gallinule, a rare straggler in the Northern States, is a parallel.

And rasping notes of joy were heard
From gallinule and crying-bird.—MAURICE THOMPSON.

A sign of approaching storm:

Pectora cum curvo gallinula rostro.
—AVIEN, 1713.

Curvo seems to point tc some other bird, possibly the curlew.
The call of the curlew in the American poets:

And heard afar the curlew call.—WHITTIER.

That was a curlew calling overhead,
That fine, clear whistle shaken from the clouds.
See! hovering o'er the swamp with wings outspread,
He sinks.—CELIA THAXTER.

GRACULUS. Κολοιός. Jackdaw.
Corvus monedula. Vid. s. v. v. CORNICULA, MONEDULA.
American literary parallels: Black-bird, bronzed grackle, jay.
The *graculus* as a weather prophet:

Vivit edax vultur ducensque per aera gyros
Milvus et pluviae graculus auctor aquae.
—Ov., *Am.* II, 6, 33.

Note the following American birds which foretell the coming of rain:

And long-bill'd snipe that knows approaching rain.
—ALEXANDER WILSON.

When in his slender treble, far and clear,
Reiterates the rain-bird (the cuckoo) his complaint.
—ROBERTS.

The blackcaps pipe among the reeds,
And there'll be rain to follow.—TROUBETSKOY (Stedman).

For days before, the wild dove cooed for rain.
—BAYARD TAYLOR.

Still, still I hear the robins sing
With raindrops in their throats.—HIGGINSON.

The hills, orange-misted and blue,
Are touched with the voice of the rain-bird
Unsullied and new.—CARMAN-HOVEY.

The *graculus* as a basis for a comparison in color:

Quaedam me cupit—invide—, Procille!
Loto candidior puella cycno,
Argento, nive, lilio, ligustro.
Iam suspendia saeva cogitabis.
Sed quandam volo nocte nigriorem,
Formica, pice, graculo, cicada,
Si novi bene te, Procille, vives.
—MART. I, 115, 1.

For the thieving *graculus* and statue of Priapus, *Priap.* LXI, 10, vid. s. v. CORNIX.

The Fable of the Graculus, who donned the plumage of a Peacock:

Tumens inani graculus superbia.
Pennas, pavoni quae deciderant, sustulit,
Seque exornavit: deinde contemnens suos
Formoso se pavonum immiscuit gregi.
Illi impudenti pennas eripuit avi,
Fugantque rostris. Male mulcatus graculus
Redire maerens coepit ad proprium genus.
A quo repulsus tristem sustinuit notam.
Tum quidam ex illis, quos prius despexerat:
Contentus nostris si fuisses sedibus,
Et, quod natura dederat, voluisses pati,
Nec illam expertus esses contumeliam,
Nec hanc repulsam tua sentiret calamitas.
—PHAED. I, 3.

Cf. Hor., *Epist.* I, 3, 14, s. v. CORNICULA.

Carryl: *The patrician Peacocks and the overweening Jay.*

The note of the *graculus*:

Dum clangunt aquilae, vultur pulpare probatur,
Et crocitat corvus, fringulit et graculus.
—*Anth. Lat.* 762, 27.

And the jay in the woods never studied the gamut, yet trills
pretty well to me.—WHITMAN.

The grackles bicker in the alder-boughs.—ROBERTS.

Here a grackle chirping low.—MAURICE THOMPSON.

And the querulous, leering jay
How he clamours for a fray.—MAURICE THOMPSON.

Mr. Bluejay, full of sass.—RILEY.

Sounds the musical jargon of bluejay and grackle.
—TROWBRIDGE.

GRUS. Γέρανος. Crane.

Ardea grus. Grus cinerea.

American literary parallels: Sand-hill crane, whooping crane.

Garland: *The Herald Crane.*

Lazarus: *The Cranes of Ibycus.*

Cranes in high flight to sheltering valleys announce the coming of rain. Vid. s. v. ARDEA.

Numquam inprudentibus imber
Obfuit: aut illum surgentem vallibus imis
Aëriae fugere grues.—VERG., *Geor.* I, 373.

Vid. also Avien. 1746, 1768, 1799.

Cf. *Anth. Lat.* 772, 45: Vallibus effugit hinc grus.

Cf. Then a white pair of herons trailing,
Flapped inland.—LOWELL.

And his vessels, like a troop
Of cranes in file, had spread their wings for home.
—STEDMAN.

Floating upward from the green
Young willow wands, with sunny sheen
On pearly breast, and wings outspread,
A white crane journeys overhead.—STEIN.

The winter hunting of a Roman husbandman:

Tum gruibus pedicas et retia ponere cervis,
Auritosque sequi lepores: tum figere dammas,
Stuppea torquentem Balearis verbera fundae,
Cum nix alta iacet, glaciem cum flumina trudunt.
—VERG., *Geor.* I, 307.

At cum tonantis annus hibernus Iovis
Imbres nivesque comparat,
Aut trudit acres hinc et hinc multa cane
Apros in obstantes plagas,
Aut amite levi rara tendit retia,
Turdis edacibus dolos,
Pavidumque leporem et advenam laqueo gruem
Iucunda captat praemia.—HOR., *Epod.* II, 29.

With subtle arts, his traps, and nets,
To catch the tender thrush, he sets;
Lays for the crane, some stouter snare,
Or takes, delicious treat! the hare.—DOANE (Duyckinck).
(*From the Latin of Horace.*)

Cf. And the *exiled* bird of some far-off shore,
As she plumes her drooping wing.—POLLOCK.

Cf. At quem caeruleus nodo constringit amictus
Quique paludicolam prendere gaudet avem.
(*Februarius.*) —*Anth. Lat.* 395, 5.

Ah miseri! Quos nosse iuvat, quid Phasidis ales
Distet ab hiberna Rhodopes grue.
—STAT., *Silv.* IV, 6, 8.

And small wild-hens in reed-snares caught
From the banks of Sondagardee brought.—WHITTIER.

Or potting the crane in the rushes.—STEAD.

Two methods of capturing cranes:

Grues cum aliis modis, tum ita capiuntur. Cucurbita sicca et decollata excavatur, visco intus illinitur, iniicitur scarabaeus, qui exitum quaerens immurmurabit, eo sonitu excitata grus accurret, et capite inserto, captoque scarabaeo, ipsum etiam cucurbitae vas oculis, capitique agglutinabit, ut eo pennis haerente iam neque visu neque progressu uti valeat, sed uno in loco consistat, donec ab ancupe manibus capiatur. Se desit scarabaeus, cepae folium iniecisse in alvum cucurbitae sat fuerit.

Laqueis etiam facile capietur, si quis arundinem sectam utrinque perforet, et exiles festucas imponat, ac per foratum lapidem ab arundine suspendat, in media autem arundine ferreum acum figat, et fabam ei inserat, quam grus respiciens laqueo caput insinuet. Hac arrepta, iam retractura caput, collum illaqueatum sentiet: perceptoque dolo, sursum evolare nitetur: sed lapidis pondus obsistet, donec ab accurente aucupe comprehendatur.—(OPP., *De Aucupio.*) GESNER, op. cit., p. 513.

The manner of cooking and serving the crane:

Deinde secuti
Mazonomo pueri magno discerpta ferentes
Membra gruis sparsi sale multo, non sine farre.
—HOR., *Sat.* II, 8, 86.

Their flesh is said to be well tasted, nowise savoring of fish.—ALEXANDER WILSON, op. cit., s. v. Whooping Crane.

This is not a *goûter* with friend Bourgeat on the Flat Lake, roasting the orange-fleshed Ibis, and a few sun-perch.—AUDUBON, *Journal,* vol. I, p. 162.

Cf. s. v. CICONIA. The crane became more fashionable fifty years later.

A picture of earlier simplicity:

Nec Latium norat [attagen], quam praebet Ionia dives,
Nec, quae Pygmaeo sanguine gaudet, avem.
—Ov., *Fast.* VI, 175.

The hurtling of weapons and the cries of battle are likened to the noisy flight of cranes:

Clamorem ad sidera tollunt
Dardanidae e muris; spes addita suscitat iras;
Tela manu iaciunt; quales sub nubibus atris
Strymoniae dant signa grues, atque aethera tranant
Cum sonitu, fugiuntque Notos clamore secundo.
—VERG., *Aen.* X, 263.

Vergil is probably thinking of the northward migration of the cranes.

In Lucr. IV, 181, the flight call of the crane is compared, to its disadvantage, with the shorter song of the swan.

While passing crane, with slender neck outstretched,
Of that wild band will be the trumpeter.—HOSMER.

They crossed the desert's burning line,
And heard the palm-trees' rustling fan,
The Nile-birds' cry, the low of kine,
And voice of man.—WHITTIER.

A whooping crane erects his skeleton form,
And shrieks in flight.—SIMMS.

The clamorous cranes go singing through the night.
—LONGFELLOW.

The stork, the heron and the crane through the clear realms
of azure drift.—LONGFELLOW.

The joyous spring migration of cranes and swans:

Tellus iam pulvere primo
Crescit, et armorum transmittunt fulgura silvae.
Qualia trans pontum Phariis defensa serenis
Rauca Paraetonio decedunt agmina Nilo,
Cum fera ponit hiemps: illae clangore fugaci,
Umbra fretis arvisque volant, sonat avius aether,
Iam Borean imbresque pati, iam nare solutis
Amnibus et nudo iuvat aestivare sub Haemo.
—STAT., *Theb.* V, 9.

The fall migration of cranes to Egypt, with some description of their flight:

Strymona sic gelidum, bruma pellente, relinquunt
Poturae te, Nile, grues primoque volatu
Effingunt varias, casu monstrante, figuras;
Mox ubi percussit tensas Notus altior alas,
Confusos temere immixtae glomerantur in orbes,
Et turbata perit dispersis littera pennis.
—LUC. V, 711.

Faint from the upper air is heard the weird cry of the
blue-crane,
That sad and plaintive refrain, a warning of winter's
privations. —MCKEEVER.

And through the misty air
Passed like the mournful cry
Of sunward sailing cranes.—LONGFELLOW.

The same, with a picture of the joy felt by the cranes at their arrival:

Ceu patrio super alta grues Aquilone fugatae
Cum videre Pharon, tunc aethera latius implent,
Tunc hilari clangore sonant; iuvat orbe sereno
Contempsisse nives et frigora solvere Nilo.
—STAT., *Theb.* XII, 515.

Above is the blue sky,
Empty, save for the sudden crane-flight, with
Its *clangor, f*rom the marshes and the sea.—COX.

As when some grey November morn the files,
In marching order spread, of long-necked cranes.
—MATTHEW ARNOLD.

And the crane flies back over sea.—ROBERTS.

The same, with allusions to the Pygmies and the letters formed by the cranes in their flight:

Pendula ceu parvis moturae bella colonis
Ingenti clamore grues aestiva relinquunt
Thracia, cum tepido permutant Strymona Nilo:
Ordinibus variis per nubila texitur ales
Littera, pennarumque notis inscribitur aer.
—CLAUD., *De Bell. Gild.* 474.

A reference on a web, woven by Minerva, to the myth of Gerana, who was metamorphosed, through envy, by Juno into a crane (γέρανος) and condemned to eternal warfare with her own people, the Pygmies.

Altera Pygmaeae fatum miserabile matris
Pars habet; hanc Iuno victam certamine iussit
Esse gruem, populisque suis indicere bellum.
—OV., *Met.* VI, 90.

A description of a Pygmaean battle with comments:

Ad subitas Thracum volucres nubemque sonoram
Pygmaeus parvis currit bellator in armis,
Mox inpar hosti raptusque per aera curvis
Unguibus a saeva fertur grue. Si videas hoc
Gentibus in nostris, risu quatiare: sed illic,
Quamquam eadem adsidue spectentur proelia, ridet
Nemo, ubi tota cohors pede non est altior uno.
—JUV. XIII, 167.

For an opinion on the credibility of this myth, cf. Namat. I, 291. Cosa by tradition had been abandoned because of mice. Namatianus ridicules the story and adds:

Credere maluerim Pygmaeae damna cohortis,
Et coniuratas in sua bella grues.

Other references to the myth:

Pygmaeo brevior gruem timente.
—*Priap.* 46, 3.

Anguibus Alcides et caesa languidus hydra
Non chortes timuit, grus homicida, tuas.
—*Anth. Lat.* 931, 133.

Extas longis Pygmaeus in armis,
Ne te deprensum grus peregrina voret.
(*De Bumbulo.*) —*Anth. Lat.* 190.

Cranes in flight form the letter "V," which suggests *ver* and the Greek ἔαρ, hence these verses in praise of Earinus:

Nomen habes, teneri quod tempora nuncupat anni,
Cum breve Cecropiae ver populantur apes:

Quod penna scribente grues ad sidera tollant.
—MART. IX, 13.

Cf. Cic., *De D. N.* II, 49: Grues, cum loca calidiora petentes maria transmittunt, trianguli efficere formam.

Cf. On which the wild-geese ink themselves, a far triangled train.
—CAWEIN.

Day after day, the flying flocks go south,
In living lines, which write along the sky
The prophecy of winter's sure approach.—READ.

Angles of water-fowl winnowed the purple sky,
Clanging their trumpet-notes
As if from brazen throats.—MAURICE THOMPSON.

Ah! say you so, bold sailor
In the sunlit deeps of sky!
Doest thou so soon the seed-time tell?—GARLAND.

Hoarse trumpeters are in the sky,
From which a dripping rain is shed—
Onward in wedge-like form they fly,
By leader piloted.
A flourish of the feathered band
Announces that they seek a land
Of sunniness and flowers—
Blue waters, edged by golden sand,
Flashing through tropic bowers.—HOSMER.
(*November.*)

Other references to the flight of cranes, which are also called the birds of Palamedes:

Turbabis versus nec littera tota volabit,
Unam perdideris si Palamedis avem.
—MART. XIII, 75.

Ausonius compares a crane in flight to the letter Φ. Cf. Lucil., Baehrens, *P. L. M.*, 137.

Haec gruis effigies Palamedica porrigitur Φ.
(*De litteris.*) —AUS., *Idyll.* XII, 25.

Littera sum caeli pinna perscripta volanti,
Bella cruenta gerens volucri discrimine Martis.
Nec vereor pugnas, dum non sit longior hostis.
—*Anth. Lat.* 286, XXVI.

E come i gru van cantando lor lai
Facendo in aer di se lunga riga.—DANTE, *Inf.* V, 46.

The crane-flock leaves no trace of passage there.
—WHITTIER.

How cranes avenged the death of Ibycus:

Ibycus ut periit, vindex fuit altivolans grus.
(*De historiis.*) —AUS., *Idyll.* XII, 12.

[Ibyci grues, Graecis in proverbiam abierunt, quod dici consuevit, quotiens sceleribus novo quodam et improviso casu proditis, scelesti poenas dant eis quos laeserunt. Id ex huiusmodi quodam eventu natum memorant.] Ibycus, poeta quidam, cum in latrones incidisset iam occidendus, grues forte supervolantes obtestatus est. Aliquando post tempore cum eidem latrones in foro sederunt, rursumque grues supervolarent, per iocum inter se susurrabant in aurem: adsunt Ibyci ultores. Eum sermonem assidentes in suspicionem rapuerunt, maxime desiderato iampridem Ibyco. Rogati quidnam sibi vellet ea oratio, haesitanter atque inconstanter responderunt. Subiecti tormentis facinus confessi sunt, atque ita velut gruum indicio poenas Ibyco dederunt, aut potius suo ipsorum indicio, ut dicitur, perierunt.
—PLUT., *De Garrul.* GESNER, op. cit., p. 520.

Cf. Stat., *Silv.* V. 3, 153: Volucrumque precator Ibycus. Vid. Suid. s. v. Ἴβυκος. Welcher, *Die Kraniche des Ibykos. Rh. Mus.* I, p. 401.

Call to him herons as slowly you pass.—LONGFELLOW.

Or Hermes who interpreted
What the sage cranes of Nilus said.—WHITTIER.

The Fable of the Wolf and the Crane:

Os devoratum fauce cum haereret lupi,
Magno dolore victus coepit singulos
Inlicere pretio, ut illud extraherent malum.
Tandem persuasa est iureiurando gruis,
Gulaeque credens colli longitudinem
Periculosam fecit medicinam lupo.
Pro quo cum pactum flagitaret praemium,
'Ingrata es,' inquit, 'ore quae nostro caput,
Incolume abstuleris et mercedem postules.'
—PHAED. I, VIII, 4.

The Fable of the Crane and the Peacock:

Threiciam volucrem fertur Iunonius ales
    Communi sociam continuasse cibo.
Namque inter varias fuerat discordia formas,
    Magnaque de facili iurgia lite trahunt:
Quod sibi multimodo fulgerent membra decore,
    Caeruleam facerent livida terga gruem.
Et simul erectae circumdans tegmina caudae
    Sparserat arcanum rursus in astra iubar.
Illa licet nullo pennarum certet honore,
    His tamen insultans vocibus usa datur.
Quamvis innumerus plumas variaverit ordo,
    Mersus humi semper florida terga geris.
Ast ego deformi sublimis in aëra penna,
    Proxima sideribus numinibusque feror.

—AVIAN. XV.

The Fable of the Crane, the Crow and the Countryman:

Foedus iuratae grus et cornix iunxerant,
Cornicem grus ab avibus ut defenderet,
Gruique cornix futura ut praediceret.
Quae cum frequenter ad cuiusdam rustici
Agrum volarent atque evellerent sata
Radicibus, agri dominus vidit, et dolens:
'Puer, saxum da,' clamat, 'quo feriam gruem.'
Cornix ut audit, ilico gruem monet,
Sibi quae cavit. Alia dein die audiens
Cornix petentem saxum, commonuit gruem
Iterum, ut vitaret sedulo periculum.
Avem divinam suspicatus rusticus
Audire iussa puero: 'Si,' inquit, 'dixero,
Offam da, lapidem tu mihi clam porrige.'
Grus venit: ille puerum offam iussit dare.
At hic porrexit lapidem, quo gruem ferit
Et crura frangit. Vulnerata grus ait:
'Divina cornix, ubi nunc auspicia tua?
Cur non monere sociam, quod iuraveras,
Properasti, tale ne mihi veniret malum?'
Respondit illa: 'Non meretur ars mea
Culpari; sed dolosa sunt bilinguium
Consilia, qui aliud dicunt atque aliud agunt.'

—*Aes. Fab.* X.

Cf. Verg., *Geor.* I, 119. Vid. s. v. ANSER. These seem to be the only references in Latin poetry to the crane as an enemy of the farmer.

The onomatopoetic call of the crane:

Grus gruit in gronnis, cygni prope flumina drensant.
—*Anth. Lat.* 762, 23.

Cf. Wackernagel, op. cit., p. 53.

No sound
Of higher life is heard in the profound
And melancholy forest, than the harsh
Cry of the blue-crane rising from the marsh.—MATTHEWS.

Slow, solemn cranes, with drowsy eyes,
Nod in the shallow surf, breast-high.—M'KINLEY.

HALIAEETOS. Ἁλιάετος. Sea-eagle. Osprey.

Ossifraga is the native Latin designation, Lucr. V, 1099. *Haliaëtos albicilla. Pandion haliaëtos.* The latter is the traditional identification from Aristotle (*H. A.* IX. 32, 619) to modern times.

American parallels: Sea-eagle, osprey.

Alexander Wilson: *The Fisherman's Hymn.*

For a discussion of the myth of Nisus, Scylla and Ciris and of the poem *Ciris,* vid. Thompson, op. cit., p. 27; Keller, op. cit., p. 259; Siecke, *De Niso et Scylla in aves mutatis;* Sudhaus, *Die Klage der Ciris*; *Rh. Mus.* 61, p. 28.

The above believe that we have here an elaborated sun (Nisus) and moon (Scylla) myth. The kinship of Nisus and the Hebrew *nesher,* (eagle), and the relation of this myth to the Sampson-legend has been noted time after time. Keller attempts to explain the myth in its beginnings, as a reflection of the warfare between the sea-eagle and the osprey, or of the fighting for their common prey between the young and old of the latter. (Cf. Lucr. V, 1077.) This rationalization, however, does not clear away the accumulations of astronomic lore, which, as in so many of the bird myths, seems to present a barrier, beyond which we can get only disappointing half-lights. The whole poem, with its obscure references to bird myths, has as yet never been adequately interpreted.

Not fleeter pouncing eagle flies
To rob the fish-hawk of his prize.—HOSMER.

His lordly stomach gorged with prey
From screaming sea-hawk snatched away.—LUNT.

The metamorphosis of Scylla into the bird *Ciris,* with some description of its appearance and habits. This metamorphosis is given in full detail in the characteristic Roman manner. The identification of the *Ciris* is impossible. Cf. Sieke, op. cit., p. 14.

Et patulae frontis species concrescere in unum
Coepere et gracili mentum producere rostro.
Tum qua se medium capitis discrimen agebat,
Ecce repente, velut patrios imitatus honores,
Puniceam concussit apex in vertice cristam,
At mollis varios intexens pluma colores
Marmoreum volucri vestivit tegmine corpus,
Lentaque perpetuas fuderunt brachia pennas.
Inde alias partes minioque infecta rubenti
Crura nova maciesque obduxit squalida pelli,
Et pedibus teneris ungues adfixit acutos.
—*Ciris*, 497.

Quae simul ut sese cano de gurgite velox
Cum sonitu ad caelum stridentibus extulit alis
Et multum late dispersit in aequora rorem.
Infelix virgo nequiquam a morte recepta
Incultum solis in rupibus exigit aevum,
Rupibus et scopulis et litoribus desertis.
—*Ciris*, 514.

The *haliaetos* is mentioned passim throughout the poem.

Another version of the metamorphosis of Nisus into the *haliaetos* and of Scylla into the bird called *Ciris*:

Vix dixerat; insilit undis,
Consequiturque rates, faciente Cupidine vires,
Gnosiacaeque haeret comes invidiosa carinae.
Quam pater ut vidit, nam iam pendebat in auras,
Et modo factus erat fulvis haliaeetos alis;
Ibat, ut haerentem rostro laceraret adunco.
Illa metu puppim dimittit; at aura cadentem
Sustinuisse levis, ne tangeret aequora, visa est.
Pluma fuit; plumis in avem mutata vocatur
Ciris; et a tonso est hoc nomen adepta capillo.
—Ov., *Met*. VIII, 143.

Cf. Prop. IV, 18, 26; Hyg., *Fab*. 98. Nisus autem dum filiam persequitur, in avem haliaeeton, id est aquilam marinam conversus est, Scylla filia in piscem, cirim quem vocant.

The enmity of Nisus and Scylla in terms of bird life:

Quacumque illa levem fugiens secat aethera pennis,
Ecce inimicus, atrox, magno stridore per auras
Insequitur Nisus; qua se fert Nisus ad auras,
Illa levem fugiens raptim secat aethera pinnis.
—Verg., *Geor*. I, 406.

The human side of bird life, due to the metamorphosis idea, is, on the other hand, reflected in the following line from Namat. II, 54:

> Nisaeum crinem flere putantur aves.

> Above the eagle flew, the ospreys screamed.—EMERSON.

> Like birds that, stooping from the far cliff, ride
> A moment on the billow, shriek and rise
> With loaded talons, wheeling to the skies.—NEAL.

> She brings us fish—she brings us spring,
> Good times, fair weather, warmth and plenty.
> "God bless the fish-hawk and the fisher."
> (*The Fisherman's Hymn.*)—ALEXANDER WILSON.

HIRUNDO. Χελιδών. Swallow.

Chimney swallow: *H. rustica;* House martin: *H. urbica;* Sand martin: *H. riparia.*

American parallels: Barn swallow, purple martin, bank swallow.

Sprague (Stedman): *The Winged Worshippers.*

French (Duyckinck): *To the Swallow.*

Wilcox: *Spring in New England.*

Hosmer: *The Swallow.*

Celia Thaxter: *The Swallow.*

Stedman: *The Swallow.*

Wyatt: *To a City Swallow.*

Stoddard: *The Chimney Swallow's Idol.*

Tabb: *Swallow.*

Arlo Bates: *The Swallow.*

> The use of *hirundo* and *passer*:
> All this you will probe to the pith.—CARMAN-HOVEY.

In the swallow we have another of the four great song-birds of the ancients. The domestic habits of the bird, its early appearance as a harbinger of spring, and the fact that a great metamorphosis myth was early attached to it, account in great part for its antique preeminence.

He is the constant destroyer of insects—the friend of man; and, with the stork and ibis, may be regarded as a sacred bird.—SIR HUMPHREY DAVY.

Beyond all others the swallow is the bird of spring:

Ver blandum viget arvis, et adest hospes hirundo.
—VARR., *Sat. Men.* 579.

Horace will visit Maecenas when the warm winds come and the first swallow appears:

Te, dulcis amice, reviset
Cum Zephyris, si concedes, et hirundine prima.
—HOR., *Epist.* I, 7, 12.

A description of the charms of spring. The swallow and her nest:

Omnia tunc florent; tunc est nova temporis aetas,
Et nova de gravido palmite gemma tumet,
Et modo formatis operitur frondibus arbor,
Prodit et in summum seminis herba solum,
Et tepidum volucres concentibus aera mulcent,
Ludit et in pratis luxuriatque pecus.
Tum blandi soles, ignotaque prodit hirundo
Et luteum celsa sub trabe figit opus.
—OV., *Fast.* I, 151.

The restless swallow building in the eaves.—LONGFELLOW.

Yes, it was a swallow's nest,
Built of clay and hair of horses.—LONGFELLOW.

The swallows, startled from their nests
By pain's discordant sound,
Among the rafters bare and brown
Went circling round and round.—SIGOURNEY.

The swallow dips beneath the eaves,
And flirts his plumes and folds his wings.—RILEY.

Where sang the noisy masons of the eaves.—READ.

Swingeth the swallow to his old home under
The unforgotten eaves.—TICHNOR.

The swallow at times returns too early in the spring. Cf. Swinburne, *Had I wist.*

Fallimur, an veris praenuntia venit hirundo
Nec metuit, ne qua versa recurrat hiemps?
Saepe tamen, Progne, nimium properasse quereris,
Virque tuo Tereus frigore laetus erit.
—OV., *Fast.* II, 853.

Cf. *Anth. Lat.* 235, 17. *De Adventu Veris.*

Nota tigilla linit iam garrula voce chelidon:
Dum recolit nidos, nota tigilla linit.

Varr., *Sat. Men.* 526. Ut hirundines culmis oblitis luto tegulas fingebant.

Cf. Mart. XI, 18, 19, where *seges* is given as a material in the swallow's nest.

The black swift swallow gathers moss
And builds in peace above his head.—MILLER.

When low about her clay-built nest.—ALICE CARY.

The swallow comes with its bit of clay,
When the busy Spring is here,
And twittering bears the moistened gift
A nest on the eaves to rear.
—OAKES-SMITH (Griswold).

In the Autumn, when the hollows
All are filled with flying leaves,
And the colonies of swallows
Long have quit the stuccoed eaves.—TROWBRIDGE.

I envy nests of *sparrows*[1]
That dot His distant eaves.
—EMILY DICKINSON.

For the traditional reason of the Progne's grief, cf. Ov., *Trist.* V, 1, 60, s. v. ALCEDO.

A folk-lore date:

Vere novo, cum iam tinnire volucres
Incipient nidosque reversa lutabit hirundo,
Protinus hiberno pecus omne movebis ovili.
—CALP. V, 16.

Plastering our swallow nests on the awful cast.
—LOWELL.

[1]The ornithologist would emend the text to 'swallows.' Indeed the ms. may show this reading. Miss Dickinson, however, never mentions the swallows either in her poems or her letters, while the sparrows of her garden were favorite birds. Here, I venture to believe, she had in mind the biblical references to the latter bird. Cf. *Letters*, vol. I, p. 227.

The same. Another folk-lore date:

Post ubi Riphaeae torpentia frigora brumae
Candidus aprica Zephyrus regelaverit aura
Sidereoque polo cedet Lyra mersa profundo,
Veris et adventum nidis cantabit hirundo.
—Colum. X, 77.

Warble me now the joy of lilac time,
Bluebird and darling swallow.—Whitman.

The swallow and nightingale return in March:

Tempus vernum aedus petulans et garrula hirundo
Indicat et sinus lactis et herba vivens.
(*Martius.*) —*Anth. Lat.* 395.

Cf. Colum. XI, 2, 22. Sid., *Ep.* II, 14, 2, s. v. ciconia.

The martins, white-breasted swallows, came promptly the first day of April.

Yesterday [May 2nd] appeared the barn swallows.—Celia Thaxter (*Letters*, pp. 175-176).

For another reference to the nest of the swallow cf. Plaut., *Rud.* 598.

Juturna in her wild flight with Turnus is likened to a swallow, flitting about the atrium of a Roman villa:

Nigra velut magnas cum divitis aedes
Pervolat et pennis alta atria lustrat hirundo,
Pabula parva legens nidisque loquacibus escas;
Et nunc porticibus vacuis, nunc umida circum
Stagna sonat. —Verg., *Aen.* XII, 473.

By homesteads old, with wide-flung barns
Swept through and through by swallows.—Whittier.

Of swallows flying in and out.—Alice Cary.

He like some swallow
O'er a lake the morning smites.—Cawein.

Like a swallow that stoops to lave
Its burnished bosom in the wave,
Just tipping with its airy breast
The enamoured billows eager crest.—Read.

Yet as the unharm'd swallow skims his way,
And lightly drops his pinions in thy spray.
(*Connecticut River.*) —Brainard (Kettell).

While flocks of swallows o'er the surface throng,
Just dip the wing, and twittering, skim along.—ALSOP.

As the gentle dip of the swallow's wing
    Breaks the bubbles of the sea.—HALLECK.

While our bark-canoes the river
    Skim like swallows on the wing.—MORRIS.

1ne swallow went down where the dew-drops were clinging,
    And sipped from the grass, as she skimmed o'er the vale.
—GOULD.

Along the surface of the winding stream,
Pursuing every turn, gay swallows skim;
Or around the borders of the spacious lawn
Fly in repeated circles, rising o'er
Hillock and fence, with motion serpentine,
Easy and light. One snatches from the ground
A downy feather, and then upward springs,
Followed by others, but oft drops it soon,
In playful mood, or from too slight a hold,
When all at once dart at the falling prize.—WILCOX.

I come, but as the swallow dips
Just touching with her feather tips
The shining wave below.—HOLMES.

Though its bliss on my lips were fleeter
Than a swallow's dip to the stream.—LOWELL.

Homeward shoots the arrowy swallow.—LONGFELLOW.

And down like swallows that dip to the sea.—MILLER.

The silent swallow swoops, a flash
Of light, and leaves, with dainty plash,
A ring of ripples, in her wake.—AVERILL.

Across the river's shadow-haunted floor,
The paths of skimming swallows interlace.—LAMPMAN.

At the silent eventide,
When the flocking swallows glide,
Lazily, mazily glide and swim
Through the warm air waxing dim.—POLLOCK.

A morning scene at a swallow's nest:

Incipit ardentes Phoebus producere flammas,
Spargier et rubicunda dies: iam tristis hirundo
Argutis reditura cibos immittere nidis
Incipit et molli partitos ore ministrat.
—JUL. MONTANUS, Baehrens, *P. L. M.*, p. 355.

Cf. Maestaque sub tecto sua murmuret acta chelidon.
—*Anth. Lat.* 199, 55.

Cf. also Verg., *Aen.* VIII, 455, where the swallow too was in the poet's mind:

Evandrum ex humili tecto lux suscitat alma
Et matutini volucrum sub culmine cantus.

The hill-born rustick, hale and gay,
Ere prattling swallows sally,
Or ere the pine-top spies the day,
Sings cheerly through his valley.—R. T. PAINE.
(*Green Mountain Farmer.*)

And sorrow in the twitter of the swallers round the shed.
—RILEY.

From their nest beneath the rafters sang the swallows wild and high.—LONGFELLOW.

And how the swallows' liquid notes
Are in the eaves at dawn.—HIGGINSON.

And, singing with the early birds, her daily task begins.
—WHITTIER.

The swallows, twittering from the tower,
Salute the rosy morn.—SARAH HELEN WHITMAN.

In a simile, reference is made to the fasting mother bird feeding her eager young:

Ipse ad conspectum cenae diducere rictum
Suetus hiat tantum ceu pullus hirundinis, ad quem
Ore volat pleno, mater ieiuna.
—JUV. X, 230.

Ovid dreads the land of the Getae as much as swallows do the coming of winter. Fall migration:

Gramina cultus ager, frigus minus odit hirundo,
Proxima Marticolis quam loca Naso Getis.
—OV., *Ex Pont.* IV, 14, 13.

In autumn, ere the waters freeze,
The swallows fly across the seas.—CHRISTINA G. ROSSETTI.

And millions of warblers, that charmed us before,
Have fled in the train of the sun-seeking swallows.
—ALEXANDER WILSON.

Smiling at the airy ease
Of southward flying swallow.—CARLTON.

For a discussion of the supposed hibernation of birds vid. Note III, HIBERNATION.

The story of the swallow that stayed behind:

Hibernos peterent solito cum more recessus
Atthides, in nidis una remansit avis.
Deprendere nefas ad tempora verna reversae
Et profugam volucres diripuere suae.
Sero dedit poenas: discerpi noxia mater
Debuerat, sed tunc cum laceravit Ityn.
—MART. V, 67.

These are the days when birds come back,
A very few, a bird or two,
To take a backward look.—EMILY DICKINSON.
(*Indian Summer.*)

In the gray of the hollow
Still lingers the swallow.
(*An Open Winter.*) —MATTHEWS.

For the swallow as a weather prophet vid. Verg., *Geor.*, I, 377; P. Ter. Varr. Atac., Baehrens, *P. L. M.*, p. 336; *Anth. Lat.* 772, 46; Avien. 1701.

Cf. Swallow that skims the gale.—CRANDALL.

The big drops scatter from the leaves,
And the wet swallow wheeling past,
Sails home to brood beneath the eaves.—GOODWIN.

The swallows alone take the storm on their wing,
And, taunting the tree-sheltered labourers, sing.—READ.

The myth of the Χελιδονία (Plin. XI, 79, XXXVII, 56), the 'swallow-stone' as a cure for blindness, does not occur in the Latin poets. But cf. Longfellow, *Evangeline.*

Seeking with eager eyes that wondrous stone, which the swallow
Brings from the shore of the sea to restore the sight of its fledglings.
Lucky was he who found that stone in the nest of the swallow.

See Preface for a brief discussion of the above.

For the myth of Tereus, Philomela and Progne vid. s. v. LUSCINIA, Note IV, RUSCINIA.

Say now, thou twit'ring swallow, say,
How shall I punish thee? Which way?
Say, shall I rather clip thy wing,
Or tongue, that thou no more mayst sing?
As cruel Tereus once is said
T'have done, while yet thou wert a maid.
(*To a Swallow.*) —FRENCH (Duyckinck).

The swallow is an enemy of bees, which they feed to their young.

Absint et picti squalentia terga lacerti,
Pinguibus a stabulis, meropesque aliaeque volucres,
Et manibus Progne pectus signata cruentis;
Omnia nam late vastant ipsasque volantis
Ore ferunt dulcem nidis immitibus escam.
—VERG., *Geor.* IV, 13.

The swallow, mordrer of the beēs small.—CHAUCER.

Cf. Did wasps or king-birds bring dismay.
(*Honey Bee.*) —FRENEAU.

For her repast he bears along the lea
The bloated gad-fly and the balmy bee.
(*The King-bird.*) —ALEXANDER WILSON.

Color of the swallow's breast:

Altera [Progne] tecta subit, neque adhuc de pectore caedis
Excessere notae, signataque sanguine pluma est.
—Ov., *Met.* VI, 669.

Altera dira parens haec est, quam cernis, hirundo;
Adspice, signatum sanguine pectus habet.
—Ov., *A. A.* II, 383.

The myth of Progne as material for tragedy:

Grande locuturi nebulas Helicone legunto
Si quibus aut Prognes, aut si quibus olla Thyestae
Fervebit, saepe insulso coenanda Glyconi.
—PERS. V, 7.

Credamus tragicis, quidquid de Colchide torva
Dicitur et Progne. —JUV. VI, 644.

(Cf. also Juv. VII, 12 and 92.)

Ne pueros coram populo Medea trucidet,
Aut humana palam coquat exta nefarius Atreus,
Aut in avem Progne vertatur, Cadmus in anguem.
—HOR., *A.P.* 185.

The Fable of the Birds and the Swallow and why the latter frequents the abodes of men:

Aves in unum cum devenissent locum,
Viderunt hominem seminantem linum agro.
Quod ut pro nihilo habere hirundo intellegit,
Sic convocatas allocuta traditur:
Hinc nobis instat omnibus periclum,
Si semen ad maturitatem venerit.
Aves risere. Deinde, ut fruticavit seges,
Hirundo rursus: "Instat pernicies," ait,
"Adeste, germen eruamus noxium,
Ne, si mox crescat, inde fiant retia,
Et nos possimus artibus humanis capi."
Ridere pergunt verba aves hirundinis
Consilium et spernunt stulte prudentissimum.
At illa cauta ad homines se mox contulit,
Sub eorum tectis tuta posthac ut foret.
Sed, quae salubre monitum respuerant aves,
De lino factis captae pereunt retibus.
—*Aes. Fab.* XII.

Why farmers love the swallow:

The winter-fearless crow, and all the tribe
Of termagant jays, and epauletted starlings,
That over-shriek your head in hot mid-summer,
Are nought to me; the drab-dressed wren may seek
Some other cornice than mine, and singing robins,
That gabble loudly in the sleepy dawn,
Mad-drunk with dew among my breezy poplars,
May choose another home, and nought be said;
So that the swallow when from the south he comes,
May not forget to build within my barn,
And twitter gently underneath my eaves.
For where he breeds, the new-mown sweating hay
Will not take fire; and every grain of wheat
In any field o'er which his lucky flight
Has skimmed, grows fat; he brings prosperity;
And I, when I can hear him in the morn,
Talking his swallow-tongue beneath the rafters,
Always take it as a blessing to the fields.
(*The Farmer's Prayer.*) —"JOHN PHILIP VARLEY."

Where sang the noisy masons of the eaves,
The busy swallows circling ever near,
Foreboding, as the rustic mind believes,
An early harvest and a plenteous year.—READ.

And I thought of homely proverbs, that on simple lips had
 birth,
How, where'er the swallow builded under human roofs her
 nest,
Something holier, purer, higher, in the house became a guest.
 (*Higher Tenants.*) —PIATT.

Barns that they haunt no thunder-bolt can shatter,
 Full many a hind believes;
No showers that bring a blighting mildew patter
 Upon the golden sheaves.
Taught were our fathers that a curse would follow,
 Beyond expression dread,
The cruel farmer who destroyed the swallow
 That builded in his shed.—HOSMER.

The proprietor of the barn last mentioned, a German, assured me that if a man permitted the swallows to be shot his cows would give bloody milk, and also that no barn where swallows frequented would ever be struck by lightning.—ALEXANDER WILSON. (Op cit., s.v. Barn swallow.)

Cf. J. G. Fraser, *Swallows in the House*. *Cl. Rev.* 1891, I.

The injunction of Pythagoras—χελιδόνα οἰκίᾳ μὴ δέχου—and the suggestion that the swallow was ever an ill-boding bird, are unknown in the American tradition. Vid. s. v. LUSCINIA.

Cf. At caret insidiis hominum, quia mitis, hirundo.
—Ov., *A. A.* II, 149.

Cf. also *Cl. Rev.*, 1891, p. 230.

In the popular *versos* and *coplas* of the New Mexicans, collected by my colleague Professor A. M. Espinosa and by him kindly placed at my disposal, I had hoped to find many survivals from Latin times. These folk poets, however, appear to know but only a very few of our native birds, and the traditions of the European birds seem to be almost wholly lost among them. My friend called attention to the lines below, which are of interest as types of Christian folk-lore reminiscence. They appear in a very wide range of modern literature.

En el monte Calvario las golondrinas
Le arrancaron Cristo diez mil espinas.
—*Bib. Tr. Popul.* IV, 90.

Cf. also:

Los gilgueritos
Le quitaron a Cristo
Los tres clavitos.—RODRIG., Marin. IV, 43.

Cf. Why the robin's breast is red:

'Twas but one thorn I might untwine
From all that agony.
Yet I shall wear the rosy sign,
The red-cross of his smile divine,
Upon me till I die.—TICHNOR.
(*Redbreast at Calvary.*)

LEGEND OF THE SWALLOW

In the hush of the summer morning
The children silent stood,
While a swallow over the sunny eaves
Was feeding her early brood.

Five little bright-eyed brownies
Fearlessly poised and hung
On the edge of the roof, while the mother bird
Over them circled and sung.

And we all kept watchful silence
Till the dear bird stooped to rest,
And called their fledglings home again
To the shelter of the nest.

When the blessed Son of Mary
On the cross of sorrow hung,
One little brave bird, faithful still,
Over him fluttered and swung.

All other birds were silent
And dumb in the fearful shade,
For even the winds were hushed in grief,
And the waters were afraid.

But she called, "Console, console Him!"
And at last the branches stirred,
And forth with tremulous note of woe
Came many a pitying bird.

The stork cried, "Strengthen, strengthen Him!"
The dove could only wail
The name of the dear Lord, "Kyrie!"
The cross-bill plucked at a nail!

Then the eyes of the Son of Mary
Grew soft with a dying light,
And a look of eternal blessing fell
On the birds as His soul took flight.

And now are these winged ones sacred,
The swallow, the stork, the dove,
And the cross-bill that bears on his blood-red beak
The sign of the Savior's love.

But the bird of consolation
Is the swallow, and he may well
Rejoice, on whose roof in the summer days
The swallow may choose to dwell.

For that blessed glance makes sunlight
In the nest beneath the eaves,
And comfort falls in heavenly dew
If one in that household grieves.

—MACE.

Cf. And there, when pulsing sadly, stood
The robin by the slain,
His plumage caught from Abel's blood
Its never-fading stain.—STANTON.

Vid. also Whittier, *The Robin.*

But cf.

No blackbird bates his jargoning
For passing Calvary.—EMILY DICKINSON.
(*Two Worlds.*)

Cf. Gales, *Birds in Christian Legend and Symbolism. Liv. Age,* 256, 416. Vid. also Longfellow, *The Legend of the Crossbill.*

For *hirundo* as a term of affection vid. s. v. ANAS. Plaut., *Asin.* 694.

The song of the swallow. Cf. Wackernagel, op. cit., p. 58.

Pulpulat et pavo, trissat hirundo vaga.
—*Anth. Lat.* 762, 26.

Garrula versifico tignis mihi trissat hirundo.
—*Anth. Lat.* 733, 5.

Iudice me cycnus et garrula cedat hirundo,
Cedat et inlustri psittacus ore tibi.
(*Carmen filomelaicum.*) —*Anth. Lat.* 658, 19.

Cf. Lucr. III, 6; Stat., *Theb.* XII, 478; *Anth. Lat.* 390, 27; 199, 55.

The mother swallow thrills.—ALICE CARY.

I wish the twittering swallow had
A finer song to sing.—ALICE CARY.

And the gossip of swallows through all the day.—BRYANT.

But up and down the chimney stack
The swallows moaned and stirred.—WHITTIER.

And his talk a sweeter twitter
Than the swallow understands.—RILEY.

Or chimney-swallows come anew,
And talking in the sooty cavern.—READ.

IBIS. **Ἶβις.** **Ibis.**

Tantalus ibis, Ibis religiosa, White or Sacred Ibis. *Plegades falcinellus,* Glossy or Black Ibis. Vid. Thompson, op. cit. s. v. for a particularly good discussion and bibliography of this interesting bird.

American parallels: Scarlet Ibis, which name is wrongly applied in Liddell and Scott to the second species, mentioned above. White-faced glossy Ibis.

Butterworth (Sladen): *The Florida Ibis.*

No snowy heron, no rose-colored ibis ever is seen here, wild and charming.—AUDUBON, *Journal* (England), vol. I, p. 113.

The sacred ibis. Flight and service:

> Tum sacrae veniunt altis ex nubibus ibes.
> Auxilium sacrae veniunt cultoribus ibes.
> —AEM. MAC., Baehrens, *P. L. M.*, p. 344.

Cf. Cic., *N. D.* I, 36; *Tusc.* V. 27.

Cf. But why grant such honors to the wild, harmless and apparently useless ibis? It is perfectly well proved at this day that the ibis is as useless as it is inoffensive.—ALEXANDER WILSON. (Op. cit., s. v. Glossy Ibis.)

Wilson's whole discussion is of interest as a commentary upon the treatment of the ibis by Herodotus, Aelian, Cicero and Pliny.

> Soon will the sacred ibis her weird flight
> Wing from the fens where shore and river merge.—ROBERTS.

The ibis uses its bill as a clyster pipe:

> Et quibus exiguo volucris devota libello est,
> Corpora proiecta quae sua purgat aqua.
> —OV., *Ib.* 449.

Cf. Cic., *N. D.* II, 50; Plin. VIII, 41, X, 68.

The gods in order to escape the giants assume various shapes. Mercury takes the form of an ibis:

> "Duxque gregis," dixit, "fit Iuppiter. Unde recurvis
> Nunc quoque formatus Libys est cum cornibus Ammon:
> Delius in corvo, proles Semeleïa capro,
> Fele soror Phoebi, nivea Saturnia vacca,
> Pisce Venus latuit, Cyllenius ibidis alis."
> —OV., *Met.* V, 327.

O Ibis, Ibis, bird of Hermes bold.
—BUTTERWORTH (Sladen).

Or Hermes who interpreted
What the sage cranes of Nilus said.—WHITTIER.

The ibis was worshipped in Egypt:

Quis nescit, Volusi Bithynice, qualia demens
Aegyptus portenta colat? Crocodilon adorat
Pars haec, illa pavet saturam serpentibus ibin.
—JUV. XV, 1.

Cf. Cic., *N. D.* I, 101; Plin. X, 75.

Ibis, destroyer of sin's viperous brood.—BAILEY.

The ibis stands in this tomb of lands,
As if in a pallor of woe,
On the banks of the Nile, the sacred Nile,
The Nile of ages ago.—BEN KING.

The tide that loosens the temple's stones,
And scatters the sacred ibis-bones.—WHITTIER.

Thou look'st in vain for Egypt's mystic strand;
The holy ibis never comes anear,
Nor bannered Bedouins in their spangled gear.—MIFFLIN.
(*The Obelisk, in New York.*)

LAGOIS. Λαγώπους. Ptarmigan(?).

L. Alpinus. The *lagois* and *lagopus* (Plin. X, 68), are probably the same.

American literary parallels: Partridge, grouse.

The exotic *lagois* on the Roman table:

Tu pulmentaria quaere
Sudando: pinguem vitiis albumque neque ostrea
Nec scarus aut poterit peregrina iuvare lagois.
—HOR., *Sat.* II, 2, 20.

Cf. Schol. Porphyr.: Avis leporini coloris. Plin. X, 68: Alpium peculiaris avis est lagopus, praecipuo sapore: pedes leporino villo nomen ei hoc dedere, cetero candidae, columbarum magnitudine.

The *lagopode* (*glaucopide, lagalopece*) of Mart. VII, 87, 1, may possibly refer also to the *lagois* or *lagopus,* although the epithet *aurita* is against this identification.

LUSCINIA, (AEDON, PHILOMELA). **'Αηδών.** Nightingale.

Motacilla luscinia, L., Daulias luscinia.

American literary parallels: Mocking-bird, brown thrush, whip-poor-will.

> I—who, though born where not a vale
> Hath ever nursed a nightingale,
> Have fed my muse with English song
> Until her feeble wing grew strong.—TIMROD.

Cf. Billson, *Nightingales and Poets. Liv. Age,* 156, 756; Burroughs, *A Hunt for the Nightingale. Cent.* 5, 774.

Vid. int. al.:

Matthew Arnold: *Philomela.*
Barnefield: *Philomel.*
Bridges: *Nightingales.*
Drummond of Hawthorne: *To the Nightingale.*
Milton: *To the Nightingale.*
Sidney: *Philomela.*
Swinburne: *Itylus.*
Allston: *The Angel and the Nightingale.*
Kemble (Stedman): *Lament of the Mocking-bird.*
Hayes: *The Mocking-bird.*
Lanier: *To our Mocking-bird.*
Morris: *The Whip-poor-will.*
Machar (Sladen): *The Whip-poor-will.*
Van Dyke: *The Whip-poor-will.*
Pike: *To a Mocking-bird.*
Stanton (Stedman): *The Mocking-bird.*
Stedman: *Le jour du Rossignol, Music at home* (*Catbird*).
Stockard (Stedman): *The Mocking-bird.*
Wilde (Stedman): *To the Mocking-bird.*
Van Dyke: *The Mocking-bird.*
W. H. Timrod: *The Mocking-bird.*
Carman-Hovey: *The Mocking-bird.*
Tabb: *The Mocking-bird.*

> Hic avis est quaedam dulci celeberrima voce,
> Quae variare sonos usque canendo solet.
> (*Descriptio Pennsylvaniae,* anno 1729.) —THOMAS MAKIN.

Translation:

> 'Tis here the mocking-bird extends his throat,
> And imitates the birds of every note.—PROUD.
> (*History of Pennsylvania,* vol. II, p. 365.)

The lonely whip-poor-will, our bird of night,
Ever unseen, yet ever seeming near.
(*The Backwoodsman.*) —PAULDING.

And from the woods the late resounding note
Issued of the loquacious whip-poor-will.—FRENEAU.

Lone whip-poor-will,
There is much sweetness in thy fitful hymn
Heard in the drowsy watches of the night.
—McLELLAN (Griswold).

The Bird of sorrow[1] wak'd her funeral song.—ALSOP.

The plaint of the wailing whip-poor-will,
Who moans unseen, and ceaseless sings
Ever a note of wail and woe,
Till Morning spreads her rosy rings,
And earth and sky in her glances glow.—DRAKE.

Why dost thou come at set of sun,
Those pensive words to say?
Why whip poor *Will?* What has he done?
And who is *Will,* I pray?—MORRIS.

In the grove the whip-poor-will
Forgot his story, and sat still.—READ.

The hand of sorrow touched me,
And made my senses thrill
With all the pain that haunts the strain
Of mournful whip-poor-will.
"Whippoorwill! whippoorwill!"
Sad and shrill,—*"whippoorwill!"*—HENRY VAN DYKE.

Hic avis est repetens, *whip-whip-will,* voce jocosa;
Quae tota verno tempore nocte canit.—THOMAS MAKIN.
(*Descriptio Pennsylvaniae,* anno 1729.)

Translation:

Here's Whip-per-will; a bird, whose fanci'd name
From its nocturnal note imagin'd came.—PROUD.
(*History of Pennsylvania,* vol. II, p. 360.)

[1] By this appellation I have thought proper to designate the Whipperwill, a species of goatsucker, whose mournfully monotonous and funeral note appears to me to justify the term.—*Author's Note.*

Nor screams of night bird rend the twilight air,
Excepting him who, when the groves are still,
Hums am'rous tunes and whispers *whip-poor-will;*
To hear whose carol elves in circles trip,
And lovers' hearts within their bosoms leap.
(*A New England Pond.*) —KNAPP(?) (Duyckinck).

And the lone *muk-a-wiss*[1] was heard,
That solemn and prophetic bird,
Outpouring a melodious hymn
Beneath the shade of leaf and limb.—HOSMER.

For a discussion of *Luscinia* vid. Note IV, RUSCINIA.

The myth of Philomela, Progne and Tereus:

Progne and Philomela were the daughters of Pandion, king of Attica. Tereus, king of Thrace, married Progne, and at her request went to Athens to bring Philomela to see her sister, and, having ravished her on the way, he cut out her tongue. Of this Progne was informed by a robe which Philomela sent her, on which was described the conduct of Tereus. Progne, on this, killed Itys, the son of Tereus, and served him to his father. Tereus would have slain her, but the gods changed him into a hoopoe, Progne into a swallow, and Philomela into a nightingale.

Cf. Ov., *Met.* VI, 412, int. al.

So Philomel bewailed sad Isis'[2] fate,
And mournful accents still her woes relate.—AQUILA ROSE.

The later myth of the nightingale immolating herself, in sorrow, upon a thorn, does not occur in the ancient poets, but cf. inter al. the following:

Sings out her woes, a thorn her song-book making.—SIDNEY.

She, poor bird, as all forlorn
Leaned her breast up-till a thorn,
And there sung the dolefullest ditty,
That to hear it was a great pity.
Fie, fie, fie! now would she cry,
Tereu, Tereu! by and by.—BARNEFIELD.

---

[1] Indian name for the whip-poor-will. The Indians and some of the inhabitants of the back settlements think if this bird alights upon any house, that it betokens some mishap to the inhabitants of it.—CARVER.

[2] Thus printed by Stedman and Hutchinson, op. cit., p. 345. *Itys* is the probable reading.

How this heart was the thorn
Which pierced that breast forlorn.—GILDER.

For he sings not now of wounding thorn,
He sings as the lark in the golden morn.—BAYARD TAYLOR.

A rose tree, and a nightingale
That bruised his bosom on the thorn.—ALDRICH.

The mountain-pink whose heart, you'd think,
The thorn-pierced sparrow's blood did drink.—CAWEIN.

We know thy breast was bleeding all life long,
O thou, the Nightingale of English Song!—MIFFLIN.
(*Ode to the Memory of Keats.*)

The metamorphosis of Philomela, Progne and Tereus:

Corpora Cecropidum pennis pendere putares:
Pendebant pennis. Quarum petit altera[1] silvas,
Altera[2] tecta subit, neque adhuc de pectore caedis
Excessere notae, signataque sanguine pluma est.
Ille dolore suo poenaeque cupidine velox
Vertitur in volucrem, cui stant in vertice cristae,
Prominet immodicum pro longa custide rostrum:
Nomen epops volucri, facies armata videtur.
—Ov., *Met.* VI, 666.

A reference to the myth:

Colchida respersam puerorum sanguine culpant,
Atque sua caesum matre queruntur Ityn.
Utraque saeva parens; sed tristibus utraque causis
Iactura socii sanguinis ulta virum.
Dicite, quis Tereus, quis vos irritet Iason
Figere sollicita corpora vestra manu?
—Ov., *Am.* II, 14, 33.

The crime from another point of view:

Arte mea Tereus, quamvis Philomela placeret,
Per facinus fieri non meruisset avis.
—Ov., *Rem. Am.* 61.

---

[1]Nightingale, Philomela.

[2]Swallow, Progne. Thus usually in the Roman poets, due perhaps to a volk-etymology of Philomela. In the Greek poets the names are reversed. Dante, curiously enough, follows the Greek tradition. Cf. for Nightingale, *Purg.* XVII, 19; for Swallow, *Purg.* IX, 13.

Philomela canoris
Evocat in silvis, et tu, soror hospita, tectis
Aciperis, solis Tereus ferus exulat agris.
—Aet. 587.

Cf. Ov., *Met.* VI, 668; Sen., *Ag.* 670; *Culex,* 250; Petr. 131; Silvestris aedon, atque urbana Progne.

The myth again with greater detail:

Aspice ut insignis vacua atria lustrat hirundo,
Vere novo maestis late loca questibus implet;
Victum infelicem maerens Philomela sub umbra
Adsiduo resonat cantu miserabile carmen.
Causa mali tanti coniunx, thalamique cruenti
Virginis os: notumque, furens quid femina possit.
Hic crudelis amor: crudelis tu quoque, mater;
Infelix puer, atque odium crudele tyranni.
Progeniem parvam curaeque iraeque coquebant,
Thrëicio regi cum iam securus amorum
Coniugis infandae inter deserta ferarum
Fas omne abrumpit, pariterque loquentis ob ore
Decidit exanimis vox ipsa [et] frigida lingua:
Haut impune quidem dementia cepit amantem.
Pectore in adverso saevi monumenta doloris
Fertque refertque soror, crimenque [et] facta tyranni
Sanguis ait. Solidae postquam data copia fandi,
(Vulnera siccabat circum praecordia) 'Sanguis,
Accipe' (ait) 'vocem,' ac saevo sic pectore fatur:
'Heu miserande puer, nunc te fata impia tangunt!'
Regalis inter mensas genitoris et ora
Polluit ore dapes, quidquid solamen humandi est.
Dum genitor nati morsu depascitur artus,
Et soror et coniunx petierunt aethera pinnis.
(*Progne et Philomela.*) —*Anth. Lat.* 13.

Cf. Sanguine muta probat facinus Philomela sorori,
Vimque vice linguae sanguine muta probat.
—*Anth. Lat.* 64.

Me sterilem Niobe, linguam Philomela rogant me.
—*Anth. Lat.* 199, 90.

There the lorn Philomel dissolves in tears.—R. T. Paine.

Iole in her distress prays that she may be changed into a bird and express her grief after the manner of Philomela:

Vel in Edonas tollite silvas
Qualis natum Daulias ales
Solet Ismaria flere sub umbra:
. . . . .
Fugit vultus Philomela suos
Natumque sonat flebilis Atthis.
Cur mea nondum capiunt volucres
Bracchia plumas? Felix, felix,
Cum silva domus nostra feretur
Patrioque sedens ales in agro
Referam querulo murmure casus
Volucremque Iolen fama loquetur.
—SEN., *Herc. Oet.* 191, 199.

Daulias ales is, I believe, the nightingale. Riese's derivation from δαυλός, 'the singer of the thicket,' seems very probable. Cf. Palmer, Ovid, Heroides, p. 432, and Note IV, RUSCINIA. Obviously the translation, "like a swallow, Procne" (Harris, *The Trag. of Sen.*, p. 363) is made without consideration of the habits of the bird as reflected in *silvas* and *Ismaria umbra.* In the later lines Philomela, in contrast to *Daulias ales* above, may possibly be taken as a swallow, following the Greek tradition. Cf. Mart. V, 67. In either case we have a curious parallelism and repetition in *natum.* In connection with the above cf. the following:

Qualia sub densis ramoram concinit umbris
Daulias, absumpti fata gemens Ityli.
—CAT. LXV, 13.

Talis in umbrosis, mitis nunc denique, silvis
Deflet Threicium Daulias ales Ityn.
—CONSOL. AD LIV. 105.

And back from Daulis came the nightingale.
—BAYARD TAYLOR.

Oh, all ye liquid-throated nightingales
Singing among the dusky leaves of the trees,
Pour forth your lamentable elegies
Along the twilight of Sicilian dales!—MIFFLIN.
(*The Lament for Bion.*)

Dido's lot is like that of Philomela:

Ramis male garrula pendens
Iam philomela tacet damno male victa pudoris,
Amplexuque fovens querulos sub culmine nidos,
Pensat amore nefas, miserasque alitura querellas
Nocte gemit, quod luce dolet.—*Anth. Lat.* 83, 53.

Philomela and her song. This passage is almost unique in the Latin poets in its denial of sorrow in the nightingale's song. There is even the modern suggestion of joy, which is so rare in the ancient poets with all birds because of the metamorphosis associations. For a discussion of this whole subject cf. infra and vid. Note IV, RUSCINIA:

Assonat Terei puella subter umbram populi;
Ut putes motus amoris ore dici musico,
Et neges queri sororem de marito barbaro.
Illa cantat: nos tacemus. Quando ver venit meum?
Quando faciam uti chelidon, ut tacere desinam.
—*Perv. Ven.* 87.

Your songs and pleasant tunes they are the same,
And so's the notes which nightingales do frame.
—ANNE BRADSTREET.

The joyous birds on every blossom'd spray,
Sung hymeneans to the important day,
While Philomela swell'd the spousal song
And Paradise with gratulations rung.
—WILLIAM LIVINGSTON.

'Tis the merry nightingale.—COLERIDGE.

Ah! sweeter than Philomel's song
Was the love-breathing strain of his lute.—LOW.

An ass munched thistles, while a nightingale
From passion's fountain flooded all the vale.—LOWELL.

Sweetly from yon hollow vaults of shade
The nightingales breathe out their souls in song.
—LONGFELLOW.

That's merrier than the nightingale.—LONGFELLOW.

The passion of the nightingale.—TIMROD.

When soft and deep in Sweden's skies
    Moons burn like golden fire,
And the nightingale thrills all the wood
    With exquisite desire.—HIGGINSON.

While musing thus, with contemplation fed,
And thousand fancies buzzing in my brain,
The sweet-tongu'd Philomel percht o'er my head,
And chanted forth a most melodious strain;
Which rapt me so with wonder and delight
I judg'd my hearing better than my sight,
And wisht me wings with her a while to take my flight.

"O merry bird," said I, "that fears no snares,
That neither toyles nor hoards up in thy barn,
Feels no sad thoughts, nor cruciating cares
To gain more good or shun what might thee harm;
Thy cloaths ne're wear, thy meat is every where,
Thy bed a bough, thy drink the water clear;
Reminds not what is past, nor what's to come dost fear.
The dawning morn with songs thou dost prevent,
Sets hundred notes unto thy feathered crew,
So each one tunes his pretty instrument
And, warbling out the old, begins anew;
And thus they pass their youth in summer season,
Then follow thee into a better region,
Where winter's never felt by that sweet airy legion."
(*Contemplations*, 1678.)—ANNE BRADSTREET.

Professor Melville B. Anderson, now residing in Italy, thus interprets the nightingale's song, which, to him, voices both sadness and joy:

When ashes of the day at last
Into the urn of night are cast,
And heavy odors clog the gale,
The leaf-enshrouded nightingale
Pours from the fountain of his throat
In many a rippling liquid note
Those cadences so rich and deep
That thrill the intervals in sleep,
Awakening dim rememberings
Of "old, unhappy, far-off things."
Hark! he again the theme repeats;
Who can tell how he sings but Keats—
"Now more" (his heart was in that sigh)
"Than ever seems it rich to die."
But, as I say the line, my soul
Whispers, "No truth if not the whole!"
By night old legends throw a spell
Upon the lay of Philomel.
Had you but from my oriel heard
At dawn to-day the happy bird
Make ring again the groves and hills
With warblings, runs, bravuras, trills
From yon tall poplar by the bridge,
You would have felt with Coleridge
That introspective bards obtrude
Upon the lay an alien mood,
And more by token listen wrong.
The nightingale: his lilting song
Is all of morning and delight,
Instead of crooning crimes of night;
In sooth, the minor strains are none
Except, for modulation, "one
Low piping sound more sweet than all,"—
So thought the poet musical.

(*La Capponcina*. An Epistle to Friends.
Settignano, Italy, April 1912.)

Hark! the nightingale is chanting
As if her mate but knew;
Yet the dream within me
Which the bird-voice wakens,
Takes from her unconscious
Prompting, form and hue.—BAYARD TAYLOR.

The moonbeams over Arno's vale in silver flood were
pouring,
When first I heard the nightingale a long-lost love deploring.
—HENRY VAN DYKE.

Tablet and coronal
From the Cephissan grove have vanished long,
Yet in the sacred dale
Still bides the nightingale,
Easing his ancient heart-break still with song.—STEDMAN.

Cf. also Emma Lazarus, *Critic and Poet.*

We stood grief-struck, till one clear note,
Of soulful song the miracle,
Upon our hearts its pathos smote—
The voice of Philomel!—MIFFLIN.
(*The Slopes of Helicon.*)

Octavia prays that she may be metamorphosed into a nightingale and thus lament her lot. Cf. the prayer of Iole, supra:

Quis mea digne deflere potest
Mala? Quae lacrimis nostris questus
Reddat aedon? Cuius pennas
Utinam miserae mihi fata darent!
Fugerem luctus sublata meos
Penna volucri procul et coetus
Hominum tristes caedemque feram.
Sola in vacuo nemore et tenui
Ramo pendens querulo possem
Gutture maestum fundere murmur.
—OCT. 914.

Then lull'd, by nightingales, to balmy rest.
—WILLIAM LIVINGSTON.

All the night
She lay awake, and heard the nightingales
Remind her of her sorrow and their own.—SUTHERLAND.

Somewhere a mourning-dove
Is plaining to the silence and the night—
A human heart-break in her grieving call.—HIGGINSON.

Octavia bids her grief exceed that of the daughters of Pandion:

Vince et volucres Pandionias:
Gravior namque his fortuna tua est.
—OCT. 8

Ceres bemoans the loss of Proserpina as Philomela does the loss of Itys:

Quacumque ingreditur, miseris loca cuncta querelis,
Implet, ut amissum cum gemit ales Ityn.
—Ov., *Fast.* IV, 481.

The nightingale as one of the harbingers of spring:

Nidum ponit, Ityn flebiliter gemens,
Infelix avis et Cecropiae domus
Aeternum opprobrium, quod male barbaras
Regum est ulta libidines.—Hor., *Od.* IV, 12, 5.

Best taken as referring to the nightingale. Horace, I believe, has in mind the Greek references to the nightingale as an announcer of spring (cf. Hom., *Od.* XIX, 518; Sappho, *Fr.* 19; Soph., *El.* 147), and as the mother of Itys (cf. inter al. Aes., *Ag.* 1116; Eur., *Frag.* 773; Ar., *Av.* 212), which is universally the Roman tradition, with the exception of Mart. V, 67 and possibly Sen., *Herc. Oet.* 199. Cf. Gemoss, op. cit., p. 25, who argues for the swallow. Cf. Verg., *Ecl.* VI, 79; Ov., *Am.* II, 6, 7; III, 12, 32; *Trist.* II, 3, 89; *Culex* 251; Mart. X, 51.

And, deep within their bloom, my heart
Sings like some nightingale apart
In orange grove, while winds of May
Up the still valley waft his lay!—Proctor.

Whence comes the magic? Listen, sweetheart, listen!
The mocking-bird is singing: Spring is begun.
—Henry Van Dyke.

The nightingale,[1] the blackbird and the thrush,
Now tune their layes on sprayes of every bush.
(*The Four Seasons of the Year. Spring.* 1650.)
—Anne Bradstreet.

The nightingale bereft of her young, bewails through the night her loss:

Qualis populea maerens Philomela sub umbra
Amissos queritur fetus, quos durus arator
Observans nido inplumes detraxit; at illa
Flet noctem, ramoque sedens miserabile carmen
Integrat, et maestis late loca questibus implet.
—Verg., *Geor.* IV, 511.

Cf. *Anth. Lat.* 17, 304.

[1]In the earlier colonial American poetry, the nightingale is one of the most common of the birds to appear. This was due both to the strength of the European associations and the false identification of certain American song birds.

So in some poplar's shade, with soothing song,
Sad Philomela mourns her captive young;
When some rude swain hath found the unfeather'd prey,
Her nest despoil'd, and borne the prize away;
Thro the long night she breathes her plaintive strain,
The slow, deep moan resounds, and echoes o'er the plain.
—JOHN TRUMBULL.

Leave to the nightingale her shady wood.—WORDSWORTH.

And Philomel shall teach the woods to mourn.—R. T. PAINE.

Sing me a song, my nightingale,
Hidden among the twilight flowers.—ALICE CARY.

I must be up later than the nightingale.—LONGFELLOW.

The mocking-bird, the American mimic, singing all the forenoon,
Singing through the moon-lit night.—WHITMAN.

Pour out thy heart in strains of woe
O bird: that in the willows' shade
Singst till the stars do pale and fade.—YOUNG (Stedman).

Or that lost soul men call the nightingale,
In bosky coverts hidden.—BAYARD TAYLOR.

And then a bird began to sing,
A bulbul hidden in a bough.—ALDRICH.

The while he slept at midnight, in his ears
The nightingale, whose sorrow is the world's,
Has pour'd the hopeless passion of her song.—SUTHERLAND.

As out of the gloom of the cypress grove
The mocking-bird sings at night.—DUNBAR.

Is heard the lonely serenade
Of some heart-broken nightingale.—MATTHEWS.

O nightingale! sweet nightingale!
In leafy covert dost thou mourn?—COX.

One mocking-bird, moon-saddened
Sobs on.—CAWEIN.

When Dian's lune hangs dewy in the sky,
And the wild nightingale with anguished might
Bewails in some dense bramble's spicy dusk
Its old heart-sorrow to the wild rose wan.—CAWEIN.
(*Nature-Notes.*)

Various references to the night song of the nightingale:

Sum noctis socia, sum cantus dulcis amica:
    Nomen ab ambiguo, sic filomela gero.
Insomnem filomela trahit dum carmine noctem,
    Nos dormire facit, se vigilare docet.
Dic, filomela, velis cur noctem vincere cantu?
    'Ne noceat ovis vis inimica meis.'
Dic age, num cantu poteris depellere pestem?
    'Aut possim aut nequeam, me vigilare iuvat.'
—*Anth. Lat.* 658.

Kind Philomela! whose sweet voice
    Beguiles the darksome hour;
Let your soft, warbling, tuneful throat
    The thrilling musick pour.
The daily toils of patriot kings require
Music at night, to check the patriot fire.
—PIETAS ET GRATULATIO.

And Philomela's plaintive strains complete the roundelay.
(*Evening.*) —SUSANNA ROWSON.

Then pours the plaintive Nightingale her notes,
And all night long her melting music floats.—BIRTHA.

Across my waking dreams, the tremulous, drowsy notes
    Of the enthralling nocturn of the mocking-bird.
—HIGGINSON.

Precor meritis qui nostra parent tibi dona
Annua, et manes placida tibi nocte quiescant
Et super in nido Marathonis cantet aëdon.
—BÜCHELER, *Carm. Epig.*, p. 220.

Surge, refer matri ne me noctesque diesque
Defleat ut maerens Attica mater Ityn.
—BÜCHELER, *Carm. Epig.*, p. 508.

Cf. But now the robin sings above thy tomb.
—SANBORN (Stedman).

A raven on the moldering tomb.—SARAH HELEN WHITMAN.

While, from the dagger-tree, the bubbling song
Of mocking-birds makes music all night long.
(*The Lonely Grave.*) —SPOFFORD (Sladen).

From the grave of a lonely maiden
    A white cross upward sprung,
And aloft on the carvèd marble,
    A bird in the sunset sung.—PROCTOR.

When greenest are the twinkling leaves
    Anear his silent couch of rest,
The Ji-a-yaik[1] is heard and weaves
Of velvet moss her little nest.—HOSMER.
  (*Grave of the Sachem.*)

Sappho and the night song of the nightingale, which is however wrongly portrayed as singing in the autumn:

Quin etiam rami positis lugere videntur
    Frondibus, et nullae dulce queruntur aves:
Sola virum non ulta, pie maestissima mater
    Concinit Ismarium Daulias ales Ityn
Ales Ityn, Sappho desertos cantat amores
    Hactenus ut media cetera nocte silent.
—Ov., *Her.* XV, 151.

I dreamed of Sappho on a summer night.
Her nightingales were singing in the trees.—CARMAN-HOVEY.

Cf. Keep the page till winter, when no thrush is heard.—SILL.

Cf. also Tabb, *Keats—Sappho.*

There is a whisper pale,
As if a rose awoke,
And, having heard in sleep the nightingale,
Still dreaming of it spoke.—CAWEIN.

The morning song of the nightingale:

Pendet summo stridula ramo
Pennasque novo tradere soli
Gestit querulos inter nidos
Thraecia paelex, turbaque circa
Confusa sonat murmure mixto
Testata diem.—SEN., *Herc. Fur.* 146.

Cf. Et mira lucem voce ciere novam,
Quam nec aëdoniae voces nec tibia possit
    Musica Cirrhaeis adsimulare modis,
Sed neque olor moriens imitari posse putatur
    Nec Cylleneae fila canora lyrae.
—LACT., *De Phoen.* 47.

Here Philomel high percht upon a thorn
Sings cheerful hymns to the approaching morn.
—ROGER WOLCOTT.

[1] Ji-a-yaik is the Seneca word for Robin.—*Author's note.*

The sweet lay of the mocking-bird
Rings in the morning air.—BRYANT.

The thrush that carols at dawn of day.—LONGFELLOW.

No more the robin pipes his lay
To greet the flushed advance of day.—ABBEY (Stedman).

Vid. Barker, *Is the nightingale the Herald of Day, as well as the Messenger of Spring? Class. Journ.*, vol. 27, p. 91; 29, p. 2, 255; 30, p. 180 and p. 341.

A hundred thousand birds salute the day,
One solitary bird salutes the night.
—CHRISTINA G. ROSETTI.

Cynthia's sorrow is greater than the nightingale's:

Quid quereris nostram sic cecidisse fidem?
Non tam nocturna volucris funesta querela
Attica Cecropiis obstrepit in foliis.
—PROP. II, 20, 4.

Thompson's identification (op. cit., p. 46), γλαῦξ, *noctua*, is not convincing. Cf. int. al. Mart. I, 53, 9 infra; X, 51, 4; Hor., *Od.* IV, 12. 5.

A spring poem. The sadness of Philomela:

Sentio, fugit hiems: Zephyrisque animantibus orbem
Iam tepet Eurus aquis. Sentio, fugit hiems.
Parturit omnis ager, persentit terra calores.
Germinibusque novis parturit omnis ager.
Laeta virecta tument, foliis sese induit arbor,
Vallibus apricis laeta virecta tument.
Iam Philomela gemit modulis, Ityn impia mater
Oblatum mensis iam Philomela gemit.
—*Anth. Lat.* 235, 1.

Martial and Fidentius suggest a comparison of nightingale and magpie:

Sic ubi multisona fervet sacer Atthide lucus,
Improba Cecropias offendit pica querelas.
—MART. I, 53, 9.

Cf. Tu facis, in lucis ut cantet tristis aedon.
—*Anth. Lat.* 199, 54.

Hunc lucum Filomela tenet: circumvolat alis
Et dulcis queritur fetus suspensa ramo.
—*Anth. Lat.* 808, 38.

Arabia's Nightingale was he,
His incense-breathing Rose was she.—Low.

Thrilled by the poet-nightingales,
I turn, dear native land, to thee.—READ.

The nightingale would never waken more;
But in the northland by a stormy shore
A poet-child was born.—MACE.
(*A Buddist Vision.*)

As well might tuneful Philomel complain,
That mute and grov'ling is the loathsome toad.—Low.
(*To a Lark.*)

Nightingales as table birds:

Quinti progenies Arri, par nobile fratrum,
Nequitia et nugis pravorum et amore gemellum
Luscinias soliti impenso prandere coēmptas.
—HOR., *Sat.* II, 3, 243.

Cf. Plut., *Apophth. Lacon. divers.* 13: Τίλας τις ἀηδόνα καὶ βραχεῖαν πάνυ σάρκα εὑρὼν εἶπε, φώνα τύ τίς ἐσσι καὶ οὐδὲν ἄλλο.

The Fable of the Peacock and Nightingale; Juno's reply to the former:

Pavo ad Iunonem venit, indigne ferens,
Cantus luscinii quod sibi non tribuerit.
Illum esse cunctis auribus admirabilem;
Se derideri, simul ac vocem miserit.
Tunc consolandi gratia dixit Dea:
Sed forma vincis, vincis magnitudine:
Nitor zmaragdi collo praefulget tuo,
Pictisque plumis gemmeam caudam explicas.
Quo mi, inquit, mutam speciem, si vincor sono?
Fatorum arbitrio partes sunt vobis datae:
Tibi forma, vires aquilae, luscinio melos,
Augurium corvo, laeva cornici omnia,
Omnes quae propriis sunt contentae dotibus.
—PHAED. III, 18.

The masculine form is unique, but is scientifically correct, as only the male bird sings. Occasionally a modern poet uses the masculine, but usually, in accord with the metamorphosis association, the feminine prevails.

The Fable of the Nightingale and the perfidious Hawk:

Accipiter ad lusciniae nidum dum sedet
Auritum speculans, illic pullos invenit.
Mater periculo mota prolis advolat
Supplexque, pullis ut parcat suis, rogat.
Accipiter: Quod vis, inquit, faciam, si bona
Cantaris voce carmen modulatum mihi.
At illa, quamvis excideret animus, tamen
Metu coacta est et cantavit denique
Dolore plena. Praedam qui captaverat
Accipiter illi: non tu cantasti bene,
Et unum e pullis apprehendit unguibus,
Coepitque devorare. Ex diverso venit
Auceps et calamo dam levato perfidum
Viscum contingit atque in terram deiicit.
—*Aes. Fab.* XVIII.

The caged nightingale struggles to regain her freedom, even as Ovid does:

Cum bene sit clausae cavea Pandione natae,
Nititur in silvas illa redire suas.—Ov., *Ex Pont.* I, 3, 39.

The same, but with opposite results:

Munera namque dedi, noster quae non dedit Idas,
Vocalem longos quae ducit, aedona, cantus;
Quae licet interdum, contexto vimine clausa
Cum parvae patere fores, ceu libera ferri
Novit et agrestes inter volitare volucres,
Scit rursus remeare domum tectumque subire,
Viminis et caveam totis praeponere silvis.
—NEMES. II, 60.

Cf. Jewett, *A Caged Bird.*

A proverbial reference to the nightingale's power of song:

Pol quoque metuo lusciniolae ne defuerit cantio.
—PLAUT., *Bacch.* 39.

An appreciation of the nightingale's song:

Dulcis amica veni, noctis solatia praestans;
Inter aves etenim nulla tui similis
Tu, filomela, potes vocum discrimina mille,
Mille vales varios rite referre modos.
Nam quamvis aliae volucres modulamina temptent,
Nulla potest modulos aequiperare tuos.
Insuper est avium, spatiis garrire diurnis.
Tu cantare simul nocte diesque soles.
—*Anth. Lat.* 762, 1.

For the *locus classicus* of the nightingale's song vid. Plin. X, 29, 43.

They are not the soft sounds of the flute or of the hautboy that I hear, but the sweeter notes of Nature's own music. The mellowness of the song, the varied modulations and gradations, the extent of its compass, the great brilliancy of execution, are unrivalled. There is probably no bird in the world that possesses all the musical qualifications of this king of song, who has derived all from nature's self. Yes, reader, all!—AUDUBON, *Common Mocking-Bird.*

That our mocking-bird, in his native haunts in the South, surpasses any bird in the world in compass, variety and execution, is highly probable.—JOHN BURROUGHS, *English and American Song-Birds. Cent.* I, 357.

And thou America's sole boast!
    Pour out the joy sincere;
Give each soft passion of the grove
    To charm the royal ear.
These distant realms, by British valour won,
Feel the warm rays of Britain's genial Sun.
—PIETAS ET GRATULATIO.

Another appreciation of the nightingale's song:

Vox, filomela, tua cantus edicere cogit,
    Inde tui laudem rustica lingua canit.
Vox, filomela, tua citharas in carmine vincit
    Et superat miris musica flabra modis.
Vox, filomela, tua curarum semina pellit,
    Recreat et blandis anxia corda sonis.
Florea rura colis, herboso cepite gaudes
    Frondibus arboreis pignera parva foves.
Cantibus ecce tuis recrepant arbusta canoris,
    Consonat ipsa suis frondea silva comis.
Indice me cycnus et garrula cedat hirundo,
    Cedat et inlustri psittacus ore tibi.
Nulla tuos umquam cantus imitabitur ales,
    Murmure namque tuo dulcia mella fluunt.
Dic ergo tremulos lingua vibrante susurros
    Et suavi liquidum gutture pange melos.
Porrige dulcisonas adtentis auribus escas;
    Nolo tacere velis, nolo tacere velis!
Gloria summa tibi, laus et benedictio, Christe,
    Qui praestas famulis haec bona grata tuis.
—*Anth. Lat.* 658.

The robin sounds a beggar's note
Where one the nightingale has heard,
But he for whom no silver throat
Its liquid music ever stirred,
Deems robin still the sweetest bird.—DUNBAR.

The chirrup of the robin, and the whistle of the quail
As he piped across the meadows, sweet as any nightingale.
—RILEY.

But once—but once—to hear the nightingale.—HIGGINSON.

MEMNONIDES. Μέμνονος ὄρνιθες. Birds of Memnon.

The Ruff. *Machetes pugnax.* Thompson, op. cit., p. 116.

The Ruff has been taken occasionally on our eastern coast. There are no parallels in the American poets.

The curious myth of the Birds of Memnon is undoubtedly based upon the observation of the springtime fighting or 'hilling' of rival Ruffs. This identification was first made by Cuvier (Plin. X, 26, 37. Ed. Grandidier). But an older myth not connected with this particular bird, may well have been in existence. Cf. Holland, op. cit., pp. 1-5 for a discussion of this point with various Greek and Roman versions. He concludes that the myth is oriental in origin. In Ovid's version he sees Egyptian influences and a confusion with the myth of the Phoenix. Certain it is, that the account of Ovid presents inharmonious details. For modern descriptions cf. Newton, op. cit. s. v. and Montagu, *Suppl. Orn. Dict.* s. v.

How the birds of Memnon arose from the tomb of that hero and how they fought and perished:

At primos similis volucri, mox vera volucris
Insonuit pennis; pariter sonuere sorores
Innumerae, quibus est eadem natalis origo.
Terque rogum lustrant, et consonus exit in auras
Ter clangor: quarto seducunt castra volatu.
Tum duo[1] diversa populi de parte feroces
Bella gerunt, rostrisque, et aduncis[2] unquibus iras
Exercent, alasque, adversaque pectora lassant,
Inferiaeque cadunt cineri cognata sepulto
Corpora, seque viro forti meminere creatas.
Praepetibus subitis nomen facit auctor; ab illo
Memnonides dictae, cum Sol duodena peregit
Signa, parentali perituræ Marte rebellant.
—Ov., *Met.* XIII, 606.

[1]The actual fighting of the Ruffs seems to be confined to rivals pitted one against the other and is naturally rarely fatal.

[2]Either conventional or points to another species, in the mind of the writer.

Quo properas, Aurora? Mane: sic Memnonis umbrae
Annua sollemnia caede parentet avis.
—Ov., *Am.* I, 13, 3.

Oh, not the swallows on the ridges high,
Nor plaintive note of piteous Philomels,
Nor dolphins rolling in the ocean swells
About the sea-banks, nor, in the summer sky,
The halcyon shrilling forth her mournful cry,
Nor that strange bird of Memnon in the dells
Of dawn, e'er sang such touching, sad farewells
As were poured forth, when, Bion, thou didst die!
(*The Lament for Bion.*) —MIFFLIN.

MERGUS. Κολυμβίς, αἴθυια et al.

Species indeterminate. Diver, cormorant, gull, grebe, merganser, et al.

American literary parallels: The above, with possibly also the loon.

Allen (Stedman): *Sea-birds.*

Brainard (Griswold): *The Sea-Bird's Song.*

Bret Harte: *To a Sea-Bird.*

Lampman: *The Loons.*

Proctor: *The Stormy Petrel.*

Gould: *The Sleeping Albatross.*

Erskine: *The Sea-Gull.*

A rock, that is a haunt dear to the *mergi*:

Est procul in pelago saxum spumantia contra
Litora, quod tumidis summersum tunditur olim
Fluctibus, hiberni condunt ubi sidera Cori:
Tranquillo silet, immotaque attollitur unda
Campus et apricis statio gratissima mergis.
—VERG., *Aen.* V, 124.

Cf. Ov., *Met.* XIII, 625, s. v. FULICA. Luc. V, 555. Aut siccum quod mergus amat.

The *mergi* frequent the hull of a shattered bark:

Ast vocat officium, trabe rupta, Bruttia saxa
Prendit amicus inops; remque omnem surdaque vota
Condidit Ionio; iacet ipse in litore, et una
Ingentes de puppe dei iamque obvia mergis
Costa ratis lacerae.—PERS. VI, 27.

Cf. But if, at last, upon some winding shore
A prey to hungry cormorants you lie.
—HOR., *Ep.* X, 21. (Trans. by Freneau.)

The *mergi* fortell the coming of storms:

Iam sibi tum curvis male temperat unda carinis,
Cum medio celeres revolant ex aequore mergi
Clamoremque ferunt ad litora.
—VERG., *Geor.* I, 360.

Vergil has here applied the name *mergus* to the ἐρωδιός (heron) of Aratus. Cf. Plin. 18, 87.

Blent with the sea-mew's clangor.—BAYARD TAYLOR.

The love of the *mergus* for the sea is like that of Gracinus for Ovid:

Nam prius incipiant turres vitare columbae,
Antra ferae, pecudes gramina, mergus aquas,
Quam male se praestet veteri Graecinus amico.
—OV., *Ex Pont.* I, 6, 51.

Cf. Mergus et aequora scandit.—*Anth. Lat.* 772, 38.

He came to the green ocean's brim
And saw the wheeling sea-birds skim.—EMERSON.

But lightly as the sea-bird swings
She floats the depths above.—HOLMES.

The feeding calls of *mergi* and other birds:

Postremo, genus alitum variaeque volucres,
Accipitres atque ossifragae mergique marinis
Fluctibus in salso victum vitamque petentes,
Longe alias alio iaciunt in tempore voces,
Et quom de victu certant praedaque repugnant.
—LUCR. V, 1076.

For the story of the metamorphosis of Aesacus into a *mergus* vid. Ov. *Met.* XI, 749 ff.

The actual metamorphosis of Aesacus into a *mergus,* with some description of the bird and its habits:

Dixit et e scopulo, quem rauca subederat unda,
Decidit in pontum. Tethys miserata cadentem
Molliter excepit nantemque per aequora pennis
Texit, et optatae non est data copia mortis
Indignatur amans, invitum vivere cogi

Obstarique animae, misera de sede volenti
Exire, utque novas umeris adsumpserat alas,
Subvolat atque iterum corpus super aequora mittit,
Pluma levat casus: furit Aesacus inque profundum
Pronus abit letique viam sine fine retemptat.
Fecit amer maciem: longa inter nodia crurum,
Longa manet cervix, caput est a corpore longe;
Aequora amat nomen tenet, quia mergitur illo.
—Ov., *Met.* XI, 783.

Suddenly drops the gull and breaks the glassy tide.
—LOWELL.

Up from the stream with sluggish flaps,
Struggles the gull and floats away.—LOWELL.

MERULA. Κόσσυφος. Blackbird.
Turdus merula.
American literary parallels: Grackle, redwing, blackbird, robin.
Tennyson: *The Blackbird.*
Ben King: *De Blackbird fetched de Spring.*
Ben King: *The Blackbird and the Thrush.*
A playful reference to the alarm-song of the blackbird:

Sed facitodum merula per vorsus quod cantat [tu] colas:
"Cum cibo cum quiqui" facito ut veniant, quasi eant Sutrium.
—PLAUT., *Cas.* 523.

The text adopted is that of Lindsay. For a discussion of the passage vid. *Cl. Rev.* 1891, p. 323; Id., 1892, p. 124 and p. 227. Lindsay thus translates: "But see that you follow what the blackbird sings in its stave, see that they come 'food or no food,' as if they were marching to Sutrium." Verbal interpretations of the songs of birds by children and country folk are fairly common. Lindsay quotes 'a little bit of bread and no cheese,' as applied to the song of the yellow-hammer by English children.

And the blackbird sang, 'She is sorry, sorry, sorry,
Let her in! Let her in!'—KINGSLEY.

Loquacious black-birds in the sunny brake
Thick settling.—M'KINNON.

The red-wing flutes his o-ka-lee.—EMERSON.

Just come the blackbirds chatt'rin' in tall trees.—LOWELL.

Within my limits, lone and still
The blackbird pipes in artless trill.—WARTON.

The blackbirds jangle in the tops
Of hoary, antlered sycamores.—HOWELLS.

Blackbirds are singing
Clear hylas ringing.—CHANNING (Stedman).

The flock of blackbirds chattering in council overhead.
—CROSBY (Stedman).

Then, like a congress of blackbirds, held
In ancient tree-tops in October eves.—BAYARD TAYLOR.

No blackbird bates his jargoning
For passing Cavalry.—EMILY DICKINSON.

The frolic of the blackbirds.—WHITTIER.

Even the blackbirds in yon leafless tree
Wheezing and squeaking in discordant glee.—LAMPMAN.

In English gardens, green and bright and full of fruity treasure,
I heard the blackbird with delight repeat his merry measure.
—HENRY VAN DYKE.

The sudden blackbirds bluster on the boughs.—MATTHEWS.

A 'blackbirder' with eyes aloft falls into a pit and calls for aid:

Hic, dum sublimis versus ructatur et errat,
Si veluti merulis intentus decidit auceps
In puteum foveamve, licet, 'Succurrite,' longum
Clamet, 'Io cives!' non sit qui tollere curet.
—HOR., *A. P.* 457.

Many years ago, one election day, when he and other boys or young men were out gunning to see how many birds they could kill, Jonathan Hildreth, who lived near by, saw one of these birds (Scarlet Tanager) on the top of a tree before him in the woods, but did not see a ditch that crossed his course between him and it. As he raised his gun, he exclaimed, 'Fire never redder!' and, taking a step or two forward, with his eyes fixed on the bird, fell headlong into the ditch; and so the name became a byword among his fellows.—THOREAU, op. cit., p. 328.

Blackbirds form part of a banquet:

Deinde secuti
Mazonomo pueri magno discerpta ferentes
Membra gruis sparsi sale multo non sine farre,
Pinguibus et ficis pastum iecur anseris albae,
Et leporum avolsos, ut multo suavius, armos,
Quam si cum lumbis quis edit; tum pectore adusto
Vidimus et merulas poni et sine clune palumbes,
Suaves res, si non causas narraret earum et
Naturas dominus. —HOR., *Sat.* II, 8, 85.

The blackbird's song:

Et merulus modulans tam pulchris zinzitat odis,
Nocte ruente tamen cantica nulla cantit.
—*Anth. Lat.* 762, 13.

These words of appreciation are remarkably modern in tone. Cf. Tennyson, *The Blackbird*. The blackbird like the lark did not get its full meed of honor among the ancients. As with the lark, there was lacking a great metamorphosis myth to fix and hold the bird in popular fancy.

Cf. the onomatopoetic verb *zinzitare* with Plaut., *Cas.* 524, Cum cibo cum quiqui. They may reflect the same notes, though more likely the Plautine words are taken from the bird's winter notes. Cf. Plin. X, 28, hieme balbutit.

The blackbird from a neighboring thorn
With music brims the cup of morn.—TIMROD.

Like the merle's note when its ecstatic heart
Is packed with summer-time.—ALDRICH.

And the blackbird left the piping of
His amorous airy glee.—ALICE CARY.

Or blackbirds' note, the harbinger of love.—FRENEAU.

To my ear the blackbird is the most satisfying of English birds.—CHAPMAN, *An American's Impression of English Birds*. *Scrib.* 39, 715.

MILVUS. Ἰκτῖνος, Kite.

Falco milvus, also *M. ictinus* and *M. ater,* both being migrants in Italy.

American parallels: Swallow-tailed kite, falcon.

Stoddard (Stedman): *The Falcon.*

A kite threatened with a law suit for theft:

Pulmentum pridem eripuit ei milvos;
Homo ad praetorem plorabundus devenit;
Infit ibi postulare plorans, eiulans,
Ut sibi liceret milvom vadarier.
—PLAUT., *Aul.* 316.

A picture of a kite hovering greedily in circling flight over the entrails of a sacrifice:

Ut volucris visis rapidissima milvus extis,
Dum timet et densi circumstant sacra ministri,
Flectitur in gyrum, nec longius audet abire,
Spemque suam motis avidus circumvolat alis.
Sic super Actaeas agilis Cyllenius arces
Inclinat cursus et easdem circinat auras.
—OV., *Met.* II, 716.

Cf. Vivit edax vultur ducensque per aera gyros
Milvus et pluviae graculus auctor aquae.
—OV., *Am.* II, 6, 33.

Another English name for the kite is *glead* or *gled*—cognate with glide.

The clocking hen her chirping chickins leads
With wings and beak defends them from the gleads.
(*Four Seasons. Spring.*)—ANNE BRADSTREET.

Has any Whitret's direfu' jaws,
Or greedy Gled's fell squeezing claws,
Made thy wee lord a feast?—ALEXANDER WILSON.

Save when the falcon, poised on wheeling wings.
—BAYARD TAYLOR.

Yonder bird,
Which floats, as if at rest,
In those blue tracts above the thunder.—TIMROD.

Don't the buzzards *ooze* around up thare jest like they've
allus done?—RILEY.

Er a hawk—away up there,
'Pearantly *froze* in the air.—RILEY.

And the shadder o' the buzzard as he goes *'a-lazein'* by.
—RILEY.

Distances were proverbially measured by the flight of the kite:

Dic, passer, cui tot montes, tot praedia servas
Appula, tot milvos intra tua pascua lassos?
—JUV. IX, 54.

Nostin' Vettidi praedia? Cuius?
Dives arat Curibus quantum non milvus errat.
—PER. IV, 25.

South as far
As ever eagle cleaved his way.—MILLER.

I know a falcon swift and peerless.—LOWELL.

The kite mounts to the very stars:

Hinc prope summa rapax milvus ad astra volat.
—MART. IX, 54.

Cf. Petr. 37, Qua milvi volant.

He followed his high heart
To swim on sunshine.—LOWELL.

A procurer likened to a kite and as such feared:

Tene sis me arte, mea voluptas; male ego metuo milvos.
Mala illa bestiast, ne forte me auferat pullum tuom.
—PLAUT., *Poen.* 1292.

The heartless falcon, poised for flight.—LATHROP (Sladen).

The greed of cooks and kites is on a par:

An tu invenire postulas quemquam coquom
Nisi milvinis aut aquilinis ungulis?
—PLAUT., *Pseud.* 851.

Cf. Petr. 49. Mulier, quae mulier! milvinum genus.

The kite's hunger was proverbial:

Madida quae mi adposita in mensam milvinam suggerant.
—PLAUT., *Men.* 212.

Cf. 'Hungry as a wolf.' 'Wolfsbären.' 'Βουλιμία.'

The swoop of the kite sometimes fails:

Vidi petere milvom, etiam quom nihil auferret tamen.
—PLAUT., *Rud.* 1124.

The flight of the kite as a weather sign:

Iugere volitans milvus
Aquam e nubibus tortam indicat
Fore ut tegellum pastor sibi sumat.
—VARR., *Men. Rel.* 464.

For the mating of kite and dove, as symbolic of the impossible, cf. Hor., *Ep.* XVI, 32; *Anth. Lat.* 729, 4.

Cf. 'Tis hard for one so good and young
To suffer thus! The poor white dove
Was murdered by a falcon's love.—READ.

And the swift hawk had ne'er the warbler torn.
—ALEXANDER WILSON.

Whilst dove and vulture, in promiscuous fright,
With staggering wing confusedly outpoured.
—WILLS (Kettell).

The eagle, with his soaring crest,
Disdained the robin's lowly nest.—STREET.

The falcon shrunk
From the meek dove.—HOLMES.

For the myth of how the kite became a constellation vid. Ov., *Fast.* III, 793.

For the Fable of the Kite, who having been made King of the Doves, later devoured them, cf. Phaed. I, *Fab.* 31. S. v. COLUMBA.

For the Fable of the marriage of the Eagle and Kite cf. Aes. Fab. 30. S. v. AQUILA.

The Fable of the sick Kite, whose vows were of no avail, because of his temple thefts and desecrations:

Multos cum menses aegrotasset milvus
Nec iam videret esse vitae spem suae,
Matrem rogabat, sancta circuiret loca.
Et pro salute vota faceret maxima.
Faciam, inquit, fili; sed opem ne non impetrem,
Vehementer vereor; nam qui delubra omnia
Vastasti et cuncta polluisti altaria
Sacrificiis nullis parcens, nunc quid vis, rogem?
—*Aes. Fab.*, App. II, Fab. I.

The cry of the kite:

> Accipitres pipant milvus hiansque lupit.
> —*Anth. Lat.* 762, 24.

> Dum milvus iugilat, trinnit tunc improbus anser.
> —*Anth. Lat.* 733, 11.

Cf. Wackernagel, op. cit. s. v. MILVUS.

MONEDULA. Κολοιός. Jackdaw.
Corvus monedula L. Vid. s. v. v. CORNICULUS, GRACULUS.
American parallels: Blue-jay, magpie.

> There the noisy blue-jay comes.—WHITTIER.

> The crested blue-jay flitting swift.—WHITTIER.

The jackdaw as a pet bird for boys:

> Nam ubi illo adveni, quasi patriciis pueris aut monerulae
> Aut anites aut coturnices dantur, quicum lusitent,
> Itidem haec mihi advenienti upupa qui me delectem datast.
> —PLAUT., *Capt.* 1002.

Monerula as a term of endearment:

> Dic igitur med aneticulam, columbam vel catellum,
> Hirundinem, monerulam, passerculum putillum.
> —PLAUT., *Asin.* 693.

Arne, who betrayed her country for gold, is changed into a jackdaw, which also has a passion for gold:

> Marmoreamque Paron, quamque impia prodidit Arne
> Mutata est in avem, quae nunc quoque diligit aurum,
> Nigra pedes, nigris velata monedula pennis.
> —Ov., *Met.* VII, 465.

As is the case usually with Ovid, the appearance and habits of the jackdaw are accurately described. Cf. Plin. X, 10, 41. Monedulae, cui soli avi furacitas auri argentique praecipue mira est. Cf. also Cic., *Flacc.* 31.

Cf. Grant Allen, *Aesthetic Feeling in Birds. Pop. Sci. Mo.* 17, 650.

> And in the hollow thereof was found the nest of the magpie
> Into whose clay-built walls the necklace of pearls was woven.
> —LONGFELLOW.

MEROPS. Μέροψ. The Bee-eater.

Merops apiaster L.

Broderip: *Bee-eaters, etc. Fraser,* 57, 342.

American literary parallels: King-bird, 'bee-bird.'

Alexander Wilson: *The King-bird.*

Crèvecœur: *Letters from an American Farmer. Letter II.*

The hostility of the *Merops* and of *Progne* to bees:

> Absint et picti squalentia terga lacerti
> Pinguibus a stabulis meropesque aliaeque volucres,
> Et manibus Progne pectus signata cruentis;
> Omnia nam late vastant ipsasque volantes
> Ore ferunt dulcem nidi immitibus escam.
> —VERG., *Geor.* IV, 13.

Cf. Serv. ad loc. Meropes aves vocantur apiastrae, quia apes comedunt.

> Did wasps or king-birds bring dismay?—FRENEAU.
> (*Honey Bee.*)

> The kingbird, hovers, darting on his prey;
> And takes the ventured argosy of sweets,
> Then boasts his conquest on the adjacent branch,
> Where, like a pirate hauled against the wind,
> He waits another sail.—READ.

> Here o'er the woods the tyrant Kingbird sails,
> Spreads his long wings, and every foe assails;
> Snaps the returning bee with all her sweets,
> Pursues the Crow, the diving Hawk defeats,
> Darts on the Eagle downwards from afar,
> And 'midst the clouds, prolongs the whirling war.
> —ALEXANDER WILSON.

> And the sunny chaplet spread
> O'er the sleeping fly-bird's head,
> Till, with dreams of honey blest,
> Haunted, in his downy nest,
> By the garden's fairest spells,
> Dewy buds and fragrant bells,
> Fancy all his soul embowers
> In the fly-bird's heaven of flowers.—THOMAS MOORE.
> (*Poems relating to America.*)

The poet here probably has in mind the humming-bird.

The note of the bee-eater is like that of wren and swallow:

Regulus atque merops et rubro pectore progne
Consimili modulo zinzizulare sciunt.
—*Anth. Lat.* 762, 43.

The bees have sucked the clover,
And the honey-birds call and hover
Over the hollow tree.—ROSE TERRY COOKE.

Strait he alights, and from the pear-tree spies
The circling stream of humming insects rise;
Selects his prey; darts on the busy brood,
And shrilly twitters o'er his savory food.
—ALEXANDER WILSON.

The bee-bird of the woodland,
That finds the honeyed hollows
Of ancient oaks, for others—
Even as these, am I.—BAYARD TAYLOR.

NOCTUA. Γλαῦξ. The little Owl.

Athene noctua.

American parallels: The screech owl, saw-whet owl, et al.

Low: *To the Owl.*

Hosmer: *The Owl.*

Cawein: *The Screech Owl.*

I'd say as much, wert thou Minerva's owl.—TIMROD.

The call of the *noctua* resembles *'Tu Tu'*:

Ma. Tu, tu istic inquam. Pe. Vin adferri noctuam,
Quae 'tu tu' usque dicat tibi? Nam nos iam defessi sumus.
—PLAUT., *Men.* 653.

My Owl sounds hoo-hoo-hoo-hoo.—THOREAU, op cit., p. 184.

Cf. *Anth. Lat.* 762, 40, Noctua lucifuga cucubit in tenebris.

Cf. Wackernagel, op. cit., 49.

The owl calls from the house tops at night, as a weather prophet:

At nebulae magis ima petunt campoque recumbunt,
Solis et occasum servans de culmine summo
Nequiquam seros exercet noctua cantus.
—VERG., *Geor.* I, 401.

Cf. Serv. ad. loc. Noctua significat pluviam, si cecinerat post solis occasum.

The heron on the sand-bar,
And the rain-owl made reply.—BALLARD.

Note—The *rain-owl* here is probably the cuckoo.

Cf. Echoes the owl aloof—
The last of all,—upon the roof.—READ.

The call as an ill omen:

Sive in finitimo gemuit stans noctua tigno,
Seu voluit tangi parca lucerna mero,
Illa dies hornis caedem denuntiat agnis,
Succinctique calent ad nova lucra popae.
—PROP. V, 3, 59.

Nor bird of night her hateful note resounds.—FRENEAU.

And as at Rome a like committee
Who found an owl within their city
With solemn rites and grave processions
At every shrine perform'd lustrations,
And, lest infection might take place
From such grim fowls with feather'd face,
All Rome attends him through the street.—TRUMBULL.
(*M'Fingal.* 1782.)

Entranced by Arion's voice, the crow and owl ceased their enmity. Vid. Ben King, *The Owl and the Crow.*

Et sine lite loquax cum Palladis alite cornix
Sedit, et accipitri iuncta columba fuit.
—Ov., *Fast.* II, 89.

For the hostility of other birds to the owl cf. Ov., *Met.* XI, 67; Plin. X, 19. For another reference to the owl in relation to Minerva cf. Ov., Met. II, 563. For the metamorphosis of Nyctimine into an owl by Minerva cf. Ov., *Met.* II, 589. Serv. ad. Verg., *Geor.* I, 403.

For Pallas, Goddess chaste, discreet and wise,
Gave thee that sober air and visage sad.—LOW.

Black from the forge of Belzebub,
And grim with metaphysic scowl,
With quill just pluck'd from wing of owl.
—DR. LEMUEL HOPKINS.

Awards her moping sage in common with the owl.
—HILL (Griswold).

His image flamed out on the terrible shield
That Pallas up-bore when arrayed for the field;
An Emblem that Wisdom, when others are blind,
Clear-sighted, a path through the darkness will find.
—HOSMER.

The wisest of the wild fowl,
Bird of Jove's blue-eyed maid—the owl.—HALLECK.

I ask my peers,
The erudite and learned in the law,
Why the recusant owl is singled out
As Wisdom's bird?—SIGOURNEY.

The Nightingale should be her bird
And not the Owl, big-eyed and solemn.—ALDRICH.

Dear goose, thou'rt greatly wrong'd. I move the owl
Be straightway swept from the usurper's seat,
And thou forthwith be voted for, to fill
Minerva's arms.—SIGOURNEY.

Once one of them (owls) perched over one of the windows and sat motionless, looking exactly like an owl of Pallas Athene.—ROOSEVELT.

Martial is an eagle, a plagiarist an owl:

Quid congregare cum leonibus vulpes,
Aquilisque similes facere noctuas quaeres?
—MART. X, 100, 3.

In the morning and by day the owl's eyesight is dim:

Et Hadrianus dulcius culex cantet,
Videasque quantum noctuae vident mane.
—MART. III, 93, 9.

Dim, like the day-struck owl, ye grope in light.
(*The Conspiracy of Kings.*) —BARLOW.

He faced the east, where the sunshine streamed
On the singing, sparkling sea,
And he blinked with his yellow eyes, that seemed
All sightless and blank to be.
(*The Great White Owl.*) —CELIA THAXTER.

Roll thy wild eyeballs like the day-struck owl.
(*The Anarchiad.*) —HUMPHREYS, BARLOW, HOPKINS, TRUMBULL.

The owl hoots at noon that the eagle is blind.—HOLMES.

Only a blind owl floating by.—MATTHEWS.

And the blinking owl from the dead oak peeps.—STRONG.

A reference to *owlish* eyes:

Tun etiam cum noctuinis oculis 'odium' me vocas?
—PLAUT., *Cur.* 191.

The owlet's eyes our lanterns be.—DRAKE.

The staring owl her note has sung.—FRENEAU.

The aforesaid owl,
With his dull, staring eyes, what hath he done
To benefit mankind?—SIGOURNEY.

And rolls around his wondering eyes,
Like a wise owl, in great surprise.—MAXWELL (Kettell).

Ez an owl by daylight amongst a flock of teazin chirpers.
Sees clear'n mud the wickedness o' eatin little birds.
—LOWELL.

But cf.

Thus pigeons, doves and other fowls,
Are often sacrificed by owls,
Barely because this bird of prey
Is blest with better eyes than they.—HITCHCOCK.

A house, which even owls would ignore:

Aedes emit Aper, sed quas nec noctua vellet
Esse suas: adeo nigra vetusque casa est.
—MART. XI, 34.

And when I tread the consecrated aisle,
And hear thee pour thy melancholy scream,
I'll ponder on my destiny the while;
The world of spirits shall be all my theme.—LOW.
(*To an Owl.*)

I know not if the night-owl calls
From Feudal battlements of stone
Inhabited by him alone.—DAVID STARR JORDAN.

The owlet roosts above its door.—CAWEIN.
(*The Haunted House.*)

The Fable of the Owl and the Cicada:

Cicada acerbum noctuae convicium
Faciebat, solitae victum in tenebris quaerere,
Cavoque ramo capere somnum interdiu.
Rogata est, ut taceret. Multo validius
Clamare coepit. Rursus admota prece,
Accensa magis est. Noctua, ut vidit sibi
Nullum esse auxilium, et verba contemni sua,
Hac est aggressa garrulam fallacia:
Dormire quia me non sinunt cantus tui,
Sonare cithara quos putes Apollinis,
Potare est animus nectar, quod Pallas mihi
Nuper donavit: si non fastidis, veni:
Una bibamus. Illa, quae ardebat siti,
Simul cognovit vocem laudari suam,
Cupide advolavit. Noctua, egressa e cavo,
Crepitantem consecuta est, et leto dedit.
Sic, viva quod negarat, tribuit mortua.
—PHAED. III, 16, 2.

Hark! 'twas the screech-owl's melancholy scream.—LOW. (*Winter.*)

Bird of Minerva! denizen of night!—LOW.

ONOCROTALUS. Ὀνοκρόταλος, πελεκάν. Pelican.
Pelecanus onocrotalus. P. crispus.
Thompson, op. cit., p. 122, 134, s. v. Πελεκάν.
Vid. Chapman, *An Intimate Study of the Pelican. Cent.* 71, 198.
American parallel: Pelican. *P. erythrorhynchus.*

The drowsy pelican wings home his way.—FRENEAU.

Full brother to the hungry pelican.—FRENEAU.

They swim like the swans and like pelicans call.—MILLER.

The flapping pelican feeds about.—STEDMAN.

And like as grim-beaked pelicans level file,
Across the sunset toward their nightly isle.—LANIER.

Gray Pelican, poised where yon broad shallows shine,
Know'st thou, that finny foison all is mine
In the bag below thy beak—yet thine, not less?
. . . I sail with thee,
Thy Pelican's self is mine.—LANIER.

A spot it was the bronzen fishermen
Had fancied not, and left inviolate
To screaming gull and wheeling pelican.—SUTHERLAND.

The gullet of the pelican is referred to in a simile:

Lydia tam laxa est, equitis quam culus aeni,
. . . . .
Quam veteres braccae Britonis pauperis et quam
Turpe Ravennatis guttur onocrotali.
—MART. XI, 21.

Cf. Martialis Ravennatem onocrotalum cognominat, a civitate Italiae circa quam conspicitur (in paludibus scilicet), quamquam Bellonius Galliae et Italiae incognitum esse scribit, nisi quod interdum in lacu Mantuae videatur.—GESNER, op. cit., p. 606.

Uteri, qui huius avis faucibus haeret, tanta est capacitas, ut ipsi viderimus, ingentis staturae hominem ocreatum pedem usque ad genu in fauces immittentem eximentemque sine laesione.—PEROTTUS, GESNER, op. cit., p. 607.

The later myth of how 'the pelican turneth her beak against her breast and therewith pierces it till the blood gusheth out, wherewith she nourisheth her young' is easily explained by the coloring and feeding habits of the bird. It was used by the early Christians, like the hibernation fallacy, as an emblem of 'piety,' and as such passed over into heraldic symbolism. I have not found a trace of it in the Latin and American poets covered in this study. Vid. Thompson, op. cit., p. 134; Broderip, *Fraser* 58, 537; *Acad.* 25, 97; *Sci. Am. S.* 55, 22952; and cf.:

The painful pelican
Self-sacrificial.—BAILEY.

OSSIFRAGA. Vid. s. v. HALIAEETOS.

PALUMBES. Φάσσα. Ring-dove.

Columba palumbus, Wood-pigeon, ring-dove. *Columba aenas*, Stock-dove.

Thompson, op. cit., pp. 177-179, identifies the above as the ring-dove. Fowler, *A Year with the Birds*, pp. 218-223, thinks the stock-dove was most commonly meant by *palumbes*. The two species were no doubt confused by the Romans. Vid. s. v. v. COLUMBA, TURTUR.

American parallels: Mourning dove, passenger-pigeon.

How the *palumbes* appears on the Roman table:

Tum pectore adusto
Vidimus et merulas poni et sine clune palumbes,
Suaves res, si non causas narraret earum et
Naturas dominus. —HOR., *Sat.* II, 8, 90.

Quidquid ponitur hinc et inde verris,
Mammas suminis, imbricemque porci
Communemque duobus attagenam,
Mullum dimidium lupumque totum
Muraenaeque latus femurque pulli
Stillantemque alica sua palumbum.
—MART. II, 37, 1.

Inquina torquati tardant hebetantque palumbi:
Non edat hanc volucrem qui cupit esse salax.
—MART. XIII, 67.

The *palumbes* as a typical pastoral gift:

Parta meae Veneri sunt munera: namque notavi
Ipse locum, aeriae quo congessere palumbes.
—VERG., *Ecl.* III, 68.

His tamen, his isdem manibus tibi saepe palumbes,
Saepe etiam leporem, decepta matre, paventem
Misimus in gremium: per me tibi lilia prima
Contigerunt, primaeque rosae: vixdum bene florem
Degustabat apis, tu cingebare coronis.
—CALP. III, 76.

Praeterea tenerum leporem geminasque palumbes
Nuper, quae potui, silvarum praemia misi.
—NEMES. II, 67.

For her the chestnut drops its prickly hulls
And the wood-pigeon yields its sav'ry meat.—T. C. JAMES.
(*The Country Meeting.*)

Cf. Ov., *Met.* XIII, 833. Neither the ring-dove nor the stock-dove now breeds in Italy. This fact is due to changes in climate and the disappearance of forests, swamps and marshes. America furnishes a parallel in the case of the now all but extinct passenger-pigeon. Vid. Nissen, *Italische Landeskunde,* p. 373; Deecke, *Ital.*, p. 185; Fowler, *A Year with the Birds,* loc. cit. supra; Glover, op. cit., p. 112.

Innumerae volitare solent hic saepe columbae;
Unde frequens multis obvia praeda datur.
(*Descriptio Pennsylvaniae,* anno 1729.) —THOMAS MAKIN.

Translation:

> Here, in the fall, large flocks of pigeons fly,
> So numerous that they darken all the sky.—PROUD.
> (*History of Pennsylvania*, p. 366.)

> Darkening the sun in their flight
> With naught in their craws but an acorn.—LONGFELLOW.

> There are deer on the mountains, and wood-pigeons fly
> From the crack of our muskets, like clouds on the sky.
> (*Song of the Vermonters*, 1779.)—FESSENDEN (?).

A suggestion of how the *palumbes* were taken by the bird catchers:

> Pi. Viscus meru' vostrast blanditia. Ba. Quid iam? Pi. Quia enim intellego,
> Duae unum expetitis palumbem, peri, harundo alas verberat.
> —PLAUT., *Bacch.* 51.

> Nos tibi palumbem ad aream usque adduximus:
> Nunc te illum meliust capere, si captum esse vis.
> —PLAUT., *Poen.* 676.

A possible reference to the spring migration:

> Iam mare Tyrrhenum longe penitusque palumbes
> Relliquit. —CIC., BAEHRENS, *P. L. M.*, p. 306.

Cf. Plin. X, 41. In agrum Volaterranum palumbium vis e mari quotannis advolat.

A reference to the exchange of nesting habits of the *palumbes* and halcyon as an 'affirmatio τοῦ ἀδυνάτου.'

> Ante sub Aegaeo optabunt pia tecta palumbes
> Et versa alcyone componet in arbore nidos.
> —LICENT., *Carm. ad Aug.* 92.

Palumbus as a title of endearment, on a Christian grave:

> Respice quam parbus cubat hic sine felle palumbus
> Dum luce est ista frunitas.—BÜCHELER, *Carm. Epig.* 1839.

Vid. s. v. COLUMBA.

The story of how the *palumbes* saved Horace when a child:

> Me fabulosae Vulture in Apulo
> Altricis extra limen Apuliae
> Ludo fatigatumque somno
> Fronde nova puerum palumbes
> Texere, mirum quod foret omnibus,

Quicumque celsae nidum Acherontiae
Saltusque Bantinos et arvum
Pingue tenent humilis Forenti,
Ut tuto ab atris corpore viperis
Dormirem et ursis, ut premerer sacra
Lauroque collataque myrto,
Non sine dis animosus infans.
—Hor., *Od.* III, 4, 9.

I see an infant, tired with play,
Sleep sweetly in Apulia's wild,
And doves bring myrtle leaves and bay
To cover the courageous child.—Sargent (Stedman).

Cf. Piatt, *The Watch of the Swan.*

Voracious ravens yield him up their prey,
Glad angels to his succor wing away.
(*Elijah's Translation.*) —Benjamin Colman (Kettell).

Tradition tells a tale of thee
Forever dear to memory:
When the lost children, side by side,
In the dark wood lay down and died,
Arm locked in arm, a heavenly pair,
For earth too sweet, for life too fair,
Dropping bright leaves, their forms to cover,
Above them thou didst gently hover.
(*Robin Red-Breast.*) —Hosmer.

How flocks of robins brought
In the old time, leaves, and sang, the while they covered
The innocent babes forsaken.—Hirst (Duyckinck).

And my bird-buried darlings, hidden under
Lost leaves—why, it is your dead selves I mean!
(*My Babes in the Wood.*) —Sarah M. B. Piatt.

Robin the Redbreast
Boasted on bush and tree it was he, it was he and no other
That had covered with leaves the Babes in the wood.
—Longfellow.

The note of the *palumbes*:

Nec tamen interea raucae, tua cura, palumbes,
Nec gemere aeria cessabit turtur ab ulmo.
—Verg., *Ecl.* I, 57.

Pausitat arborea clamans de fronde palumbes.
—*Anth. Lat.* 762, 21.

Gemit hinc palumbes, inde cereus turtur.
—MART. III, 58, 19.

Cf. Plin. XVIII, 267. A sign that summer is passing. Palumbium utique exaudi gemitus. Transisse solstitium caveto putes, nisi cum incubantem videris palumbem.

Cf. Wackernagel, op. cit., p. 59; Winteler, op. cit., p. 17.

The stock-dove plaining through its gloom profound.
(*Gertrude of Wyoming.*) —THOMAS CAMPBELL.

Quiet by nothing harsher broken
Than wood-doves' meditative coo.—LOWELL.

In the covert of the pine trees
Cooed the pigeon, the Omime.—LONGFELLOW.

Groves where Cowper's stock-dove cooes.—BROWN.
(*First Sight of England.*)

PARRA. Οἰνάνθη(?). An unidentified bird.

Perhaps one of the owls. "Grünspecht oder Schleiereule." Gemoss.

The various owls are possible American parallels.

Cf. Larcom, *The Sunset-bird of Dominica.*

The *parra,* when seen on the right, is a good omen:

Unde sumam? Quem intervortam? Quo hanc celocem
conferam?
Inpetritum, inauguratumst; quovis admittunt aves.
Picus et cornix ab laeva; corvus, parra ab dextera
Consuadent. —PLAUT., *Asin.* 257.

The call of the *parra* associated with other inauspicious omens:

Impios parrae recinentis omen
Ducat, et praegnans canis, aut ab agro
Rava decurrens lupa Lanuvino
Fetaque vulpes. —HOR., *Od.* III, 27, 1.

There rose an owl's cry, from the woods below,
Like a lost spirit.—SILL.

The hollow, quivering, loud-repeated howl,
Full overhead, betrays the haggard owl;
Who, well for her, in muffling darkness past,
Else this heart-sinking scream had been her last.
(*The Foresters.*) —ALEXANDER WILSON.

PARRUS. Αἰγίθαλος (?). Titmouse (traditional identification).

American literary parallels—which seem best to suit the references below: Song-sparrow, ground-sparrow. The Chickadee is a literary parallel for the traditional identification.

Vid. Trowbridge, *Midwinter*.

Marian Douglas (Griswold): *My Winter Friend* (*The Chickadee*).

Frances H. Green: *The Chickadee's Song*.

Hathaway: *Chickadee*.

Bryant: *The Song-sparrow*.

Jones Very: *Our Native Sparrow; English Sparrows*.

Dinsmoor (Duyckinck): *The Sparrow*.

> A bird that stays in wintry days,
> A friend indeed is he;
> And better than all other birds
> I love the chickadee.—MARIAN DOUGLAS (Griswold).
> (*My Winter Friend*.)

The *parrus* sings all night long, but pleases no one with its song:

> Parrus enim quamquam per noctem tinnipet omnem,
> Sed sua vox nulli iure placere potest.
> —*Anth. Lat.* 762, 9.

The reference here may be to one of the the smaller owls.

Cf. The *whetsaw's tinkle*, and the owl's loud shout.—STREET.

The *parrus* is a field-bird:

> Haec inter merulae dulci modulamine cantus
> Zinzilat et laetis parrus nunc tinnipat arvis.
> —*Anth. Lat.* 733, 8.

> He your steadfast brother was,
> Lowly field-bird of the grass.—CARMAN-HOVEY.

PASSER. Στρουθός. Sparrow.

Various species were connoted by *passer*.

American parallels: Song-sparrow, et al.

Burroughs: *The Golden Crowned Sparrow of Alaska*.

Cawein: *The Bush-Sparrow*.

Dunbar: *The Sparrow*.

Henry Van Dyke: *The Song-Sparrow*.

Forsyth: *The English Sparrow*.

Gould: *The Sparrow.*

Hirst (Stedman): *The Fringilla melodia.*

Lampman: *The Song-sparrow.*

Larcom: *A Song-Sparrow in March; The Field Sparrow; The Sing-away Bird* (the white-throated sparrow).

Lathrop: *The Song-Sparrow.*

Thomas: *The Vesper Sparrow.*

Valentine: *Sparrows.*

West: *The White-throated Sparrow.*

Carman-Hovey: *Ornithology.*

Vid. s. v. PARRUS.

> Like Apollonius of old,
> Who knew the tales of sparrows told.—WHITTIER.

Lesbia's sparrow:

> Passer, deliciae meae puellae,
> Quicum ludere, quem in sinu tenere,
> Qui primum digitum dare atpetenti
> Et acris solet incitare morsus.
> —CAT. II, I.

> The free-born sparrows of the air,
> That flit about her windows fair,
> Enjoy her smile and have her care.—WALLACE.

> Lugete, o Veneres Cupidinesque
> Et quantum est hominum venustiorum.
> Passer mortuus est meae puellae,
> Passer, deliciae meae puellae,
> Quem plus illa oculis suis amabat:
> Nam mellitus erat suamque novat
> Ipsam tam bene quam puella matrem.
> Nec sese a gremio illius movebat,
> Sed circumsiliens modo huc modo illuc
> Ad solam dominam usque pipilabat.
> —CAT. III, I.

Vid. Matthew Arnold, *Poor Mathias.*

Best taken as the common sparrow, but to the Roman reader other associations would inevitably occur. Cf. Gesner, op. cit., p. 622.

Passer ille Catullianus allegorice, ut arbitror, obsceniorem quempiam celat intellectum, quem salva verecundia nequimus enuntiare. Cf. Festus, s. v. *Strutheum.*

For echoes of these two inimitable bird poems vid. Juv. VI, 8; Mart. I, 7; I, 109; IV, 14; VII, 14; XIV, 77, et al.

Poe's *Raven* holds an analogous position in American literature.

Cf. Sarah Helen Whitman, *The Raven* (passim).

> There comes Poe, with his *Raven.*—LOWELL.

> The terrible might do, mother,—some wild, unearthly story;
> I might ride, for a Pegasus, a nightmare into glory.
> But then that "Raven" there, mother, above that 'chamber-door,'
> I asked *him* if 'twould be a hit,—quoth the raven,
> "Never more!"—'GRACE GREENWOOD.'

For *passerculus* as a term of endearment vid. s. v. COTURNIX. Plaut., *Asin.* 666, s. v. ANAS. Plaut., *Asin.* 693. Cf. also Varro, *Maripor.* For *pullus passer* in the same connotation vid. s. v. COLUMBA.

The association of the sparrow with Venus does not occur in the Latin poets. Vid. Sappho, *Fr.* 1, 9.

> To thy chariot yoked, fair fleet sparrows drew thee,
> Flapping fast their wings; round the dark earth circling
> From the lofty heaven down through middle ether
> Quickly descending.—ELIZABETH AKERS.
> (*Ode to Aphrodite. Sappho.*)

Passer as a term of reproach:

> Dic, passer, cui tot montes, tot praedia servas.
> —JUV. IX, 54.

Cf. Plin. X, 107. *Priap.* 26, 6.

For the Fable of the Sparrow and the Hare, vid. s. v. AQUILA. For the mother bird and the eight young devoured by the serpent at Aulis, vid. Ov., *Met.* XII, 15; Sil. Ital., *Il. Lat.* 147.

> Perhaps, while here thou sweetly sung,
> Some serpent stole thy new-fledg'd young;
> Or boys, perhaps, in cruel play
> Have borne thy tender care away.—BAYARD.
> (*Address to the Robin Red-Breast. The Columbian Muse, 1794,* p. 179.)

The sparrow as a harbinger of spring:

> Nunc sturnos inopes fringillarumque querelas
> Audit, et arguto passere vernat ager.
> —MART. IX, 55, 7.

While the song-sparrow warbling from her perch
Tells you that spring is near.—BRYANT.

The Easter sparrow repeats her song,
A merry warbler, she chides the blossoms,
The idle blossoms that sleep so long.—BRYANT.

Here when the Spring begins to call
The sparrow sings his madrigal;
Through sleet and hail, in shine or rain,
I hear him o'er and o'er again:
"Resilio! Silio! Silio! Sil!"—ROSE TERRY COOKE.

The gray song-sparrows, full of spring, have sung
Their clear thin silvery tunes in leafless trees.—LAMPMAN.

The autumn song:

And sparrows fill the autumn air
With merry muting.—MITCHELL (Stedman).

Other references to the sparrow's song. Vid. Wackernagel, op. cit., p. 58.

Hinc titiare cupit diversa per avia passer.
—*Anth. Lat.* 733, 4.

Pessimus et passer sons titiare solet.
—*Anth. Lat.* 762, 30.

Every little sparrow twitters.—SILL.

The sparrow with its simple notes.—WHITMAN.

The song-sparrow's exquisite warble
Is born in the heart of the rose.—LARCON.

Here cat- and blue-bird and wood-sparrow wrote
Their presence on the silence with a tune.—CAWEIN.

PASSER MARINUS. Στρουθοκάμηλος. Ostrich.
Struthio camelus.
The ostrich in the circus:

Vola curriculo. Pa. Istuc marinus passer per circum solet.
—PLAUT., *Pers.* 198.

The *ales equus* of Cat. LXVI, 54, is probably an ostrich.

Cf. Giant-paced *mooa;* ostrich, feathery steed.—BAILEY.

The boast of the kite in the Fable of the Eagle and the Kite:

Aquila cum tristis assideret milvo
In arbore. Vultu quid te tam maesto, hic ait,
Conspicio? Quaero, dixit illa, coniugem
Parem nec invenire possum. Me accipe,
Te multo qui sum fortior. Quid? An potes
Ex rapto victum quaerere? Unguibus meis
Struthiocamelum rapui prensum saepuis.
—*Aes. Fab.* XXX.

No entail
The first-born lifting into bloated pomp,
Tainting with lust, and sloth, and pride, and rage,
The world around him: all the race beside,
Like brood of ostrich, left for chance to rear,
And every foot to trample.—TIMOTHY DWIGHT.
(*Greenfield Hill.*)

Didst thou the ostrich clothe with plumes so neat,
Who leaves her eggs exposed to heedless feet?
Hatch'd by the genial influence of the sun,
Alone, the unfledged brood are left to run.
In flight she scorns the rider and his steed;
Through eddies of the sand unspurn'd, her speed
Impetuously she skims; than winds more fleet,
She triumphs in th' alertness of her feet.—DEVENS (Kettell).

As desert birds are by the sun
Warmed into life within their nests.—CLARKE.

For Love, when he would safely keep
His head in secret hiding deep
Is but an ostrich in the sand.—READ.

PAVO. Ταώς. Peacock. *Pavo cristatus.*
The peacock's beauty is typical of its kind;

Aurea pavonum ridenti imbuta lepore
Saecla, novo rerum superata colore iacerent
Et contemptus odor smyrnae mellisque sapores,
Et cycnea mele Phoebeaque daedala chordis
Carmina consimili ratione oppressa silerent.
—LUCR. II, 502.

Colors due to the effect of sunshine:

Caudaque pavonis, larga cum luce repleta est,
Consimili mutat ratione obversa colores.
—Lucr. II, 806.

Full on the morn the peacock op'd his beams.
(*Creation.*) —Timothy Dwight.

Sylvia shone out, no peacock finer.—Trumbull.

Brilliant traits of mind,
And genius, clear and countless as the dies
Upon the peacock's plumage.—Halleck.

She brings the magic of an Indian night
Where smolder peacock-breasts of phosphor-green,
Ruffled by jungle zephyrs ne'er so light.—Riggs.

Men laud the peacock's beauty:

Laudatas homini volucris Iunonia pennas
Explicat, et forma muta superbit avis.
—Ov., *Med. Fac.* 33.

But cf. Et praeter pennas nihil in pavone placebat.
—Ov., *Fast.* VI, 177.

Cui comparatus indecens erat pavo,
Inamabilis sciurus, et frequens phoenix.
—Mart. V, 37, 12.

Didicit iam dives avarus
Tantum admirari, tantum laudare disertos,
Ut pueri Iunonis avem.—Juv. VII, 30.

The parrot is more beautiful than the peacock:

Occidit aeriae celeberrimae gloria gentis
Psittacus, ille plagae viridis regnator Eoae;
Quem non gemmata volucris Iunonia cauda
Vinceret adspectu, gelidi non Phasidis ales.
—Stat. Silv. II, 4, 24.

Cf. Mart. III, 58, 13. Gemmeique pavones.
The phoenix has some of the colors of the peacock:

Effigies inter pavonis mixta figuram
Cernitur et pictam Phasidis inter avem.
—Lact., *De Phoen.* 143.

The peacock's pride and haughtiness:

Laudatas ostendat avis Iunonia pennas:
Si tacitus spectes, illa recondit opes.
—Ov., *A. A.* I, 625.

Cf. Plin. X, 22; Col. IX, 11. Pavo etiam ad libidem extimulatur, semet ipsum, veluti mirantem, caudae gemmantibus pennis protegit, idque cum facit, rotare dicitur.

Cic., *Fin.* III, 5, 18. Cauda pavoni ad ornatum data est.

Laudato pavone superbior; acrior igni;
Asperior tribulis; feta truculentior ursa.
—Ov., *Met.* XIII, 801.

Explicat ipsa suas ales Iunonia pennas.
—Ov., *Am.* II, 6, 55.

Miraris quoties gemmantes explicat alas,
Et potes hunc saevo tradere, dure, coquo?
—Mart. XIII, 70.

Quin tu igitur, summa nequidquam pelle decorus
Ante diem blando caudam iactare popello
Desinis, Anticyras, melior sorbere meracas.
—Pers. IV, 14.

Saepe etiam perdix iacet et Iunonius ales,
Gemmatam pinnis solitus producere caudam.
—*Anth. Lat.* 199, 69.

The peacock view, still exquisitely fair,
When clouds forsake, and when invest the air:
His gems now brightened by a noontide ray;
He proudly waves his feathers to the day.
A strut, majestically slow, assumes,
And glories in the beauty of his plumes.—Devens (Kettell).

On the hitching-block, boys, grandly satisfied,
See the old peacock, boys, on the sunny side.—Riley.

The peacock as a table bird:

Vix tamen eripiam, posito pavone velis quin
Hoc potius quam gallina tergere palatum,
Corruptus vanis rerum; quia veneat auro
Rara avis, et picta pandat spectacula cauda;
Tanquam ad rem attineat quidquam. Num vesceris ista,
Quam laudas, pluma? Cocto num adest honor idem?
Carne tamen quamvis distat nihil hac magis illa,
Imparibus formis deceptum te patet. Esto.
—Hor., *Sat.* II, 2, 23.

Quanta est gula, quae sibi totos
Ponit apros, animal propter convivia natum!
Poena tamen praesens, cum tu deponis amictus
Turgidus, et crudum pavonem in balnea portas:
Hinc subitae mortes atque intestata senectus.
—Juv. I, 140.

For other references to the peacock in this connection int. al. vid. Hor., *Sat.* I, 2, 115; Pub. Syr. 304; Plin. X, 20; Var., R. R. III, 6; Col. VIII, 11.

A fan made of peacock feathers:

Et modo pavonis caudae flabella superbae,
Et manibus dura frigus habere pila.
—Prop. III, 15, 11.

Cf. Ov., *Met.* XV, 385. Iunonis volucrem, quae cauda sidera portat.

The ruffling bird of Juno.—Hale (Stedman).

At her side
The women stood and fann'd her, with their fans
Of scented peacock feathers, bound with gold
Where come the plumes together, set in rods
Of ebony and silver, bright with gems.—Sutherland.

A peacock spread his thousand dies to screen
The yellow sunlight from the head of one
Who sat upon the throne.—Moody.

A *muscaria pavonina*:

Lambere quae turpes prohibet tua prandia muscas,
Alitis eximiae cauda superba fuit.
—Mart. XIV, 67.

How the eyes of Argus, slain by Hermes, were transferred to the tail of her favorite bird by Juno:

Arge, iaces; quodque in tot lumina lumen habebas,
Exstinctum est; centumque oculos nox occupat una.
Excipit hos, volucrisque suae Saturnia pennis
Collocat, et gemmis caudam stellantibus implet.
—Ov., *Met.* I, 719.

Di maris annuerant. Habili Saturnia curru
Ingreditur liquidum pavonibus aera pictis:
Tam nuper pictis caeso pavonibus Argo.
—Ov., *Met.* II, 531.

Nomina dat spondae pictis pulcherrima pennis
Nunc Iunonis avis; sed prius Argus erat.
—MART. XIV, 85.

Innumerous peacocks midst the o'erhanging glooms,
Perch'd in proud state, display their gold-eyed plumes.
—ALSOP.

When a peacock, plumage trembling,—gaudy occelli resembling,
Myriad evil eyes dissembling,—rose again from out the ground.—KITTREDGE.

For the association of peacock with Juno vid. passim.

Matronam magni vehit ardens pavo Tonantis.
—*Anth. Lat.* 939, 1.

Scare not the sacred peacock where he spreads
His fan upon the wall.—MOODY.

Singing still
Their hymns in praise of Juno, bearing boughs
And peacock's plumes.—SUTHERLAND.

Proudly advancing, drawn by peacocks fair,
With gorgeous plumery, dancing in the air.
On that bright chariot, in imperial state,
The queen of Oberon, fair Titania, sate:
On downy cushion, rich with gold and green,
Aloft she sat, like Jove's celestial queen,
When, through the skies, she drives her glowing car,
And gazing gods adore her from afar.
(*Crystalina, a Fairy Tale.*)—BY AN AMERICAN (Kettell).

For the Fable of the Graculus Superbus et Pavo vid. s. v. GRACULUS.

The Fable of the Peacock's complaint to Juno:

Pavo ad Iunonem venit, indigne ferens,
Cantus luscinii quod sibi non tribuerit;
Illum esse cunctis auribus admirabilem:
Se derideri, simul ac vocem miserit.
Tunc consolandi gratia dixit dea.
"Sed forma vincis, vincis magnitudine;
Nitor zmaragdi collo praefulget tuo,
Pictisque plumis gemmeam caudam explicas."
"Quo mi," inquit, "mutam speciem, si vincor sono?"
Fatorum arbitrio partes sunt vobis datae;
Tibi forma, vires aquilae, luscinio melos,
Augurium corvo, laeva cornici omnia,
Omnes quae propius sunt contentae dotis.—PHAED. III, 18.

Is it a spike of azure flowers,
    Deep in the meadows seen,
Or is it the peacock's neck, that towers
    Out of the spangled green?—BAYARD TAYLOR.

Ennius was once a peacock:

Cor iubet hoc Enni, postquam destertuit esse
Maeonides, Quintus pavone ex Pythagoreo.
—PERS. VI, 10.

Cf. Enn., Baehrens, *P. L. M.*, p. 60. Memini me fieri pavom.

Or exiled to some humbler sphere,
    In yonder wood-dove dost thou dwell,
And murmuring in the stranger's ear,
    Thy tender melancholy[1] tell?—GALLANDET (Kettell).
  (*Lines to a Western Mummy.*)

Each golden note of music greets
The listening leaves, divinely stirred,
As if the vanished soul of Keats
Had faced its new birth in a bird.—HAYNE.

The peacock in the garden of Eden:

The eye-plumed bird, King Taous, who, so starred,
God's garden entered, but crawled out, a snake.—BAILEY.

High over head, his body hid,
A peacock reared its crest amid
The Persian apple's crimson bloom,
Whence floats a sweetly faint perfume;
His sinuous neck, of brilliant blue,
Each moment changing in its hue,
As quick he turns from side to side
His haughty head in conscious pride,
A serpent seems, who, hid in flowers,
Is seeking 'neath its leafy bowers
This Eden's Eve, that he may win
Her virgin soul to shame and sin.
  (*Clytie and Zenobia.*) —CLARKE.

The note of the peacock:

Cucurrire solet gallus, gallina cacillat,
    Pulpulat et pavo, trissat hirundo vaga.
—*Anth. Lat.* 762, 26.

---

[1]These lines briefly set forth the whole doctrine of metamorphosis,—as portrayed (by the ancient poets) in its effect upon bird-life. Vid. passim and Note IV, RUSCINIA.

Cf. Varr., *L. L.* 5, 75. Pavo etiam, ut pleraeque volucres a sua voce, dictus est.

Cf. Wackernagel, op. cit., p. 56.

From the hill-side, no longer discordant or harsh,
Comes the cry of the peacock, the jubilant cackle.
—TROWBRIDGE.

PERDIX. Πέρδιξ. Partridge.

Perdix graeca. P. saxatilis. P. cinerea.

American literary parallels: Quail, 'bobwhite,' ruffed grouse, et al.

A partridge (the nephew of Daedalus, and treacherously slain by him, but now metamorphosed into the bird of the same name) gleefully prattles as he beholds Daedalus burying his son Icarus:

Hunc miseri tumulo ponentem corpora nati
Garrula ramosa prospexit ab ilice perdix
Et plausit pennis testataque gaudia cantu est,
Unica tunc volucris nec visa prioribus annis,
Factaque nuper avis, longum tibi, Daedale, crimen.
—Ov., *Met.* VIII, 236.

Ovid, because of the dramatic situation and metamorphosis, is here thinking more of the lad Perdix than of the bird. Cf. infra. for habits of the bird.

The partridge in the brake.—WHITTIER.

A partridge whistled the whole day through.—MILLER.

The slaying by Daedalus of Perdix, who is metamorphosed by Pallas into the bird of the same name. A good account of the partridge's habits:

Daedalus invidit sacraque ex arce Minervae
Praecipitem misit, lapsum mentibus. At illum
Quae favet ingeniis, excepit Pallas avemque
Reddidit et medio velavit in aëre pennis.
Sed vigor ingenii quondam velocis in alas
Inque pedes abiit; nomen, quod et ante, remansit.
Non tamen haec alte volucris sua corpora tollit,
Nec facit in ramis altoque cacumine nidos:
Propter humum volitat ponitque in saepibus ova
Antiquique memor metuit sublimia casus.
—Ov., *Met.* VIII, 250.

For the accuracy of these details of observation cf. Newton, op. cit., s. v.; Hudson, op. cit., p. 267.

And partridges here keep in memory,
How to their loss they soared once too high.
(*Connecticut River.*) —ROGER WOLCOTT.

With drumming wings the mottled pheasant flew.
—HIGGINSON

Where the partridge is pluming his brown, mottled wing.
And beating his morning drum.—BROWN.

Where near her brood the hunter strayed
With trailing limp the partridge stirred.—STREET.

The Fable of the Partridge and the Fox:

Resedit alta quondam perdix arbore;
Advenit vulpes; deinde sic coepit loqui:
O quanta vultus species est, perdix, tui!
Ut ostrum crura fulgent et coralium.
At si dormires, quanto pulchrior fores!
Ut stulta perdix clausit oculos, illico
Rapit credentem vulpes. Illa fletibus
Haec mixta gravibus verba supplex edidit:
Tuarum, vulpes, per virtutes artium,
Ut ante, quaeso, nomen proferas meum:
Sic devorabis. Vulpes, ubi voluit loqui,
Aperuit os; at perdix evasit necem.
Decepta vulpes: Quid opus erat loqui mihi?
Respondit perdix: Et dormire quid mihi
Erat necisse, somnus cui non venerat.
—*Aes. Fab.* XII.

For the partridge in a Roman farm-yard scene vid. s. v. AFRA AVIS.
The partridge on the Roman table:

Ponitur Ansoniis avis haec rarissima mensis:
Hanc in lautorum mandere saepe soles.
—MART. XIII, 65.

Rustica sim an perdix, quid refert, si sapor idem est?
Carior est perdix. Sic sapit illa magis.
—MART. XIII, 76.

Nobis quae copia, dicam.
Silva feras tribuit, pisces mare et aura volucres,
Dat vinum Bromius, Pallas mihi praestat olivam,
Datque sues Calydona et saepe ego condio dammas,
Saepe etiam perdix iacet et Iunonius ales,
Gemmatam pinnis solitus producere caudam.
—*Anth. Lat.* 199, 65.

Perna, lepus, turtur, perdix, Iunonius ales,
Agnus, porcellus iunguntur, candidus anser.
Aethera quod pontusque, altrix quod terra creavit,
Cernimus esciferum paulatim sumere ventrem.
—*Anth. Lat.* 230.

'*Toujours perdrix,*' snipe, woodcock, trout or rabbit
Offends the simplest palate, it appears.—WILLIS.

The partridge is one of the birds, 'quis nobile fandi ius Natura dedit.' Asked to bewail the death of the parrot:

Plangat Phoebeius ales
Auditasque memor penitus dimittere voces
Sturnus et Aonio versae certamine picae.
Quique refert iungens iterata vocabula perdix,
Et quae Bistonio queritur soror orba cubili:
Ferte simul gemitus cognataque ducite flammis
Funera et hoc cunctae miserandum addiscite carmen.
—STAT., *Silv.* II, 4, 18.

Iterata refers, I believe, to the repeated call note reflected in κακκαβάζειν and cacare. Cf. *Anth. Lat.* 762, 19: Cacabat hinc perdix. *Anth. Lat.* 733, 12: Interea perdix cacabat nidumque revisit.

Like a rusty key
Turned in a lock.—TENNYSON.

PHASIDIS ALES. Φασιανὸς ὄρνις. Pheasant.

Phasianus colchicus.

American parallels: Partridge, pheasant, quail, et al.

Pheasants in a farm-yard scene, vid. s. v. AFRA AVIS.

For the very common association of pheasants and guinea-fowls vid. Mart. XIII, 45; III, 77, 4; Juv. XI, 139; Stat., *Silv.* II, 4, 27.

For the breeding of pheasants vid. Col. VIII, 8; Athen. 14, p. 654.

For prices vid. Plin. XXI, 43. Edict. Dioclet. C. I. L., vol. III.

Pheasants were first imported by the Argonauts:

Argiva primum sum transportata[1] carina,
Ante mihi notum nil, nisi Phasis,[2] erat.
—MART. XIII, 72.

[1]A very doubtful bit of lore, as the pheasant may have been indigenous in Greece and Italy. Cf. Newton, op. cit., p. 713; Hehn, op. cit., p. 297.

[2]Cf. Juv. XI, 139. Scythicae volucres.

Certain Roman *bon vivant* distinctions:

> Ah miseri! quos nosse iuvat, quid Phasidis ales
> Distet ab hiberna Rhodopes grue: quis magis anser
> Exta ferat: cur Tuscus aper generosior Umbro.
> —STAT., *Silv.* IV, 6, 8.

> And, nested in the spicy paste, repose
> The timid quail, that lately from their haunts
> In trepidation scar'd, sulphureous hail
> Pursuing, in their eager flight brought down.—M'KINNON.

> Pheasants stuffed with spice.—BAYARD TAYLOR.

> May canvass-backs and terrapins still be within your means!
> May *pheasants* not destroy your taste for homely jowl and greens!
> —GEN. ALBERT PIKE.

Cf. Hor., *Sat.* II, 23.

A princely gift to the people at the amphitheatre:

> Inter quae subito cadunt volatu
> Immensae volucrum per astra nubes,
> Quas Nilus sacer, horridusque Phasis,
> Quas udo Numidae legunt sub Austro.
> Desunt qui rapiant; sinusque pleni
> Gaudent, dum nova lucra comparantur.
> Tollunt innumeras ad astra voces.
> Saturnalia Principis sonantes.—STAT., *Silv.* I, 6, 75.

The parrot surpasses the pheasant in beauty:

> Quem non gemmata volucris Iunonia cauda
> Vinceret adspectu, gelidi non Phasidis ales,
> Nec quas humenti Numidae rapuere sub Austro.
> —STAT., *Silv.* II, 4, 26.

The phoenix has some of the markings of the pheasant:

> Effigies inter pavonis mixta figuram
> Cernitur et pictam Phasidis inter avem.
> —LACT., *De Phoen.* 143.

> De Capone Phasianacio.
>
> Candida Phoebeo praefulgunt ora rubore,
> Crista riget radiis, ignea barba micat.
> Alae colla comae pectus femur inguina cauda
> Paestanis lucent floridiora rosis.
> Flammea sic rutilum distinguit pinna colorem,
> Ut vibrare putes plumea membra faces.
> —*Anth Lat.* 132.

PHOENICOPTERUS. Φοινικόπτερος. Flamingo.

Phoenicopterus antiquorum L.

Scollard: *Flamingos.*

Mentioned in Greek literature only by Arist. [Av. 271], apparently unknown to Aristotle.

American parallel: *P. ruber.* Scarlet flamingo. (Florida and Southern States.)

Then, where of Indian hills the daylight takes
His leave, now might you the flamingo see
Disporting like a meteor on the lakes.
(*Gertrude of Wyoming.*)—THOMAS CAMPBELL.

Campbell's ornithology is here throughout pitched in too southern a key for northern Pennsylvania.

Cf. And every sound of life was full of glee,
From merry *mock-bird's* song, or hum of men.
The *crocodile,* the *condor* of the rock,
Shall be the pastime of thy sylvan wars.

Cf. as a corrective Halleck, *Wyoming.*

Vid. also from Thomas Moore (*Poems relating to America*), these lines, descriptive of the wilderness near Buffalo:

Where the pale witch feeds her snakes,
And the *cayman* loves to creep,
Torpid, to his wintry sleep.

The flamingo (seemingly domesticated) in a Roman farm-yard.

Vagatur omnis turba sordidae chortis,
Argutus anser gemmeique pavones
Nomenque debet quae rubentibus pinnis.
—MART. III, 58, 12.

Vid. Alexander Wilson, op. cit., s. v. Red Flamingo.

Before him like a blood-red flag
The bright flamingo flew.—LONGFELLOW.

Then—o'er the far savannah's utmost bourn—
Flare the wide wings of the flamingo morn!—MIFFLIN.

Nature sent Iris of the rosy plume.—STEDMAN.

Till Dawn, as some fair angel, wide out flings
The rose-meshed pinions of her silent wings
Along the dreaming east.—SYMMES.

The feathers of the flamingo used as a throat irritant to cause vomiting:

> Stat exoletus suggeritque ructanti
> Pinnas rubentes cuspidesque lentisci.
> —MART. III, 82, 8.

The flamingo is named from its bright color, but its tongue is its greatest fame:

> Dat mihi pinna rubens nomen, sed lingua gulosis
> Nostra sapit. Quid si garrula lingua foret?
> —MART. XIII, 71.

Cf. Plin. X, 68. Phoenicopteri linguam praecipui saporis esse, Apicius docuit. Vid. also Thompson, op. cit., s. v.

> Some pelican's eggs, a la Cairo,
> And fried *phenicopters* on toast.—BEN KING.

The flesh of these birds is esteemed pretty good meat; and the young thought by some equal to that of the partridge; but the greatest dainty is the tongue, which was esteemed by the ancients an exquisite morsel.
—ALEXANDER WILSON, op. cit., s. v. Red Flamingo.

Cf. How the old steeples hand the scarlet,
Till the ball is full,—
Have I the lip of the flamingo
That I dare to tell.—EMILY DICKINSON.

Carvers might practise on huge wooden flamingos at the carving school of Professor Trypherus. Juv. XI, 137.

In Stat., *Silv.* I, VI, 77 (vid. supra s. v. PHASIDIS ALES), Vollmer with considerable probability argues for flamingos as the birds of the 'sacred Nile.'

> And the shy flamingo rises like a wingèd oriflamme.
> (*Cuba.*) —TROWBRIDGE.

> And a great flamingo, winged in flight,
> A giant rose in the gloaming light.
> (*At the Desert's Marge.*) —SCOLLARD.

> Broken, I rust beside this Northern roar
> 'Mid rocks of desolation and of doom—
> I who once dropped through waters filled with bloom
> Of lotus-lilies where flamingoes soar
> In coves of El Dorado.—MIFFLIN.
> (*An old Anchor on the Coast.*)

Radiant, remote and sense-evading,
They are like a dream o'er which we joyed,
Flashing on the vision and then fading
In the golden-blue Egyptian void.
(*Flamingos.*) —SCOLLARD.

PHOENIX. Φοῖνιξ. The Phoenix.

A mythical bird.

The Fable of the Phoenix. Death. The young. The nest:

Una est, quae reparet seque ipsa reseminet, ales:
Assyrii phoenica vocant. Non fruge neque herbis,
Sed turis lacrimis et suco vivit amomi.
Haec ubi quinque suae complevit saecula vitae,
Ilicet in ramis tremulaeque cacumine palmae
Unguibus et puro nidum sibi construit ore.
Quo simul ac casias et nardi lenis aristas
Quassaque cum fulva substravit cinnama murra,
Se super imponit finitque in odoribus aevum.
Inde ferunt, totidem qui vivere debeat annos,
Corpore de patrio parvum phoenica renasci.
Cum dedit huic aetas vires, onerique ferendo est,
Ponderibus nidi ramos levat arboris altae
Fertque pius cunasque suas patriumque sepulchrum
Perque leves auras Hyperionis urbe potitus
Ante fores sacras Hyperionis aede reponit.
—Ov., *Met.* XV, 391.

In Am. II, 6, 51, Ovid portrays the phoenix as living in the Elysian fields of the birds.

For the age of the phoenix vid.:

Alipedem cervum ter vincit corvus, et illum
Multiplicat novies Phoenix, reparabilis ales.
—*Anth. Lat.* 647, 6.

In the *De Ave Phoenice* of Lactantius(?), one of the most curious and delightful bird poems in literature, is given a full account of the phoenix. Cf. also Claud., *Idyll.* I. *Phoenix.*

The beautiful grove of the sun, where the phoenix dwells:

Hoc nemus, hos lucos avis incolit unica Phoenix,
Unica, sed vivit morte refecta sua.
—LACT., *De Phoen.* 31.

The phoenix there welcomes the rising sun with a morning song unsurpassed by that of nightingales and dying swans:

Tollitur ac summo consedit in arboris altae
Vertice, quae totum despicit una nemus,
Et conversa novos Phoebi nascentis in ortus
Expectat radios et iubar exoriens.
Atque ubi Sol pepulit fulgentis limina portae
Et primi emicuit luminis aura levis,
Incipit illa sacri modulamina fundere cantus
Et mira lucem voce ciere novam,
Quam nec aëdoniae voces nec tibia possit
Musica Cirrhaeis adsimulare modis,
Sed neque olor moriens imitari posse putatur
Nec Cylleneae fila canora lyrae.

—LACT., *De Phoen.* 39.

I mourn not like the swan
That ready is to die,
But with the Phoenix I rejoice,
When she in fire doth fry.

—JOHN WINTHROP (Duyckinck).

I struck the sweetest notes on Memnon's lyre,
And quiver'd on the Phoenix' funeral pyre.

—GILMAN (Kettell).

Like a Phoenix in the nest
Burned the red sun in the West.

—LONGFELLOW.

Like a Phoenix from its shroud
Came the red sun back again.

—LONGFELLOW.

After a thousand years the phoenix leaves the grove and repairs to a hidden forest, where in a palm tree it builds its nest and sepulchre composed of the rarest fragrant shrubs and plants. On this the bird is consumed by fire, but from the ashes there arises a new phoenix of wondrous beauty.

Thus in endless cycles passes the life of the phoenix:

Mors illi Venus est, sola est in morte voluptas
Ut possit nasci, appetit ante mori.
Ipsa sibi proles, suus est pater et suus heres,
Nutrix ipsa sui, semper alumna sibi.
Ipsa quidem, sed non eadem est, eademque nec ipsa est,
Aeternam vitam mortis adepta bono.

—LACT., *De Phoen.* 165.

Sparrows when they choose to pair,
Meet their matches anywhere;
But the Phoenix, sadly great,
Cannot find an equal mate.—MAXWELL (Kettell).

That, like the Phoenix, die but to renew.
—CLASON (Griswold).

Like the sole Phoenix in his perfumed nest.
—SARAH HELEN WHITMAN.

The birds greet the phoenix, as it comes to the banks of the Nile for death and resurrection:

Sic ubi fecunda reparavit morte iuventam
Et patrios idem cineres collectaque portat
Unguibus ossa piis Nilique ad litora tendens
Unicus extremo Phoenix procedit ab Euro,
Conveniunt aquilae cunctaeque ex orbe volucres,
Ut solis mirentur avem: procul ignea lucet
Ales, odorati redolent cui cinnama busti.
—CLAUD., *De Cons. Stilich.* II, 414.

Cf. Mart. IX, 11, 4; Plin. XII, 85; Aus., *Idyll.* XI, 15.

The nest of the phoenix is renewed by fire:

Qualiter Assyrios renovant incendia nidos,
Una decem quotiens saecula vixit avis,
Talitur exuta est veterem nova Roma senectam
Et sumpsit vultus praesidis ipsa sui.
—MART. V, 7, 1.

The phoenix builds its nest in the spring time:

Nomen cum violis rosisque natum,
Quo pars optima nominatur anni,
Hyblam quod sapit Atticosque flores,
Quod nidos olet alitis superbae.
—MART. IX, 12, 1.

The treasures of the nest:

Accipe Callaicis quidquid fodit Astur in arvis,
Aurea quidquid habet divitis unda Tagi,
Quidquid Erythraea niger invenit Indus in alga,
Quidquid et in nidis unica servat avis.
—MART. X, 16, 3.

The phoenix rises from the flames:

Senio nec fessus inerti
Scandet odoratos phoenix felicior ignes.
—STAT., *Silv.* II, 4, 36.

And stately London, (our Great Britain's glory)
My raging flame did make a mournful story,
But maugre all, that I or foes could do,
That Phoenix from her bed, is risen new.
(*The Four Elements. Fire*).—ANNE BRADSTREET.

Reviving Norfolk from her ashes springs,
A golden phoenix on refulgent wings.—BARLOW.
(*Columbiad.*)

If every age, in new unconscious prime,
Rose, like a phoenix, from the fires of time,
To wing its way unguided and alone.—THOMAS MOORE.
(*Poems relating to America.*)

Out of her ashes let a Phoenix rise
That may outshine the first and be more wise.
(*New England's Crisis.*) —BENJAMIN TOMPSON.

This phoenix built her nest of spice,
Like to the Birds of Paradise;
Which, when a fever set on fire,
Her soul took wing and soared higher;
But left choice ashes here behind,
Christ will for resurrection find.—NOYES.
(*A consolatory poem—to Cotton Mather, at the death of his wife.* 1703.)

Thou art but ashes—dust; no Phoenix thou,
That, after crumbling on the funeral pyre,
Rises triumphant by its own bright fire.—STODDARD.

As Phoenix, 'mid consuming flame,
Takes on new life and upward springs.—WALLACE.
(*Love.*)

A wicked wag, who meant to deride,
Called honest John, "Old *Phoenix* Macbride,"
Because he rose from his ashes.—SAXE.

The resurrection of the phoenix was a hopeful parallel to the early Christians:

Sicut avis Phoenix meditatur a morte renasci,
Dat nobis exemplum, post funera surgere posse;
Hoc Deus omnipotens vel maxime credere suadet,
Quod veniet tempus defunctorum vivere rursum,
Sint licet nunc pulvis, iaceant licet ossa nudata.
—COMMOD., *Carm. Apol.* 139.

Sed tamen ad Manes foenix me serbat in aura
Qui mecum properat se reparare sibi.
—BÜCHELER, *Carm. Epig.* 1318.

Post flammas cineresque suos nova surgere foenix
Scit. —BÜCHELER, *Carm. Epig.* 1802.

Vita mihi mors est; morior si coepero nasci.
Sed prius est fatum leti, quam lucis origo
Sic solus Manes ipsos mihi dico parentes.
(*Phoenix.*) —*Anth. Lat.* 286, XXXI.

Th' ostrich with her plumes, th' eagle with her eyn
The phoenix too (if any be) are mine.—ANNE BRADSTREET.
(*The Four Elements. Air.*)

No fabled Phoenix from his bier revives;
His ashes perish, but his Country lives!—R. T. PAINE.

The resurrection of the phoenix associated with the rays of the sun:

Namque docet Phoenix, ustis reparata favillis
Omnia Phoebeo vivescere corpora tactu.
Haec vitam de morte petit, post fata vigorem,
Nascitur ut pereat, perit ut nascatur ab igni,
Una cadit totiens surgitque ac deficit una;
Rupe sedet, capitur radiis, et lumine Phoebi
Suscipit inmissum recidiva morte calorem.
—*Anth. Lat.* 389, 31.

A second Pope, like that Arabian bird
Of which no age can boast but one, may yet
Awake the muse of Schuylkill's stream.—FRENEAU.

And man once more, self-ruin'd Phoenix, rise
On wings of Eden, to his native skies.
(*Greenfield Hills.*) —TIMOTHY DWIGHT.

Here, Science, thy last stage of being lies,
No other Phoenix from thy dust shall rise—CLIFFTON.

PICA. Κίσσα. Magpie, jay.

P. rustica. Thompson, op. cit., p. 84, takes κίσσα as the jay, *Garrulus glandarius. Pica,* as among the Italians of today, seems to have been applied to both magpie and jay. Plin. X, 29, describes the magpie as a recent addition to the birds about Rome.

American parallels: Blue jay, crow, and in the West the magpie. Vid. Alexander Wilson, op. cit., s. v. Magpie.

Emily Dickinson: *The Blue Jay.*

Ben King: *I'm a Blue Jay.*

The nine daughters of Pierus, metamorphosed into magpies, salute Minerva and the nine muses:

Musa loquebatur, pennae sonuere per auras,
Voxque salutantum ramis veniebat ab altis.
Suspicit et linguae quaerit tam certa loquentes
Unde sonent, hominemque putat Iove nata locutum.
Ales erat, numeroque novem, sua fata querentes,
Institerant ramis imitantes omnia picae.
—Ov., *Met.* V, 294.

Changed (not degraded) as a Magpie talk'd.
(*Hamiltoniad.*) —JOHN WILLIAMS.

A plowman, saluted by a magpie, answers:

Inde salutatus picae respondet arator.
—MART. IX, 54, 9.

Cf. Pica salutatrix si tibi, Lause, placet.
—MART. VII, 87, 6.

Jay-bird tol' me,
Tol' me in the morning.
—CARMAN-HOVEY.

When domesticated he is easily taught to imitate the human voice, and to articulate words pretty distinctly.—ALEXANDER WILSON, op. cit., s. v. Magpie.

The actual metamorphosis of the daughters of Pierus into magpies:

Rident Emathides spernuntque minacia verba,
Conataeque loqui et magno clamore protervas
Intentare manus, pennas exire per ungues
Aspexere suos, operiri bracchia plumis;
Alteraque alterius rigido concrescere rostro
Ora videt, volucresque novas accedere silvis;
Dumque volunt plangi, per bracchia mota levatae
Aëre pendebant, nemorum convicia, picae.
Nunc quoque in alitibus facundia prisca remansit
Raucaque garrulitas studiumque immane loquendi.
—Ov., *Met.* V, 669.

Cf. Stat., *Silv.* II, 4, 19. Sturnus et Aonio versae certamine picae.

But chatt'ring magpies, perching on each spray,
Devoured the blooms or pick'd the fruit away.
—CHATTERTON.

Heard them chattering like the magpies.—LONGFELLOW.

The 'raven poets and poetess pies.' Persius alludes to the literary ladies of his time:

> Quis expedivit psittaco suum chaere
> Picasque docuit verba nostra conari?
> Magister artis ingenique largitor
> Venter, negatas artifex sequi voces.
> Quod si dolosi spes refulserit nummi,
> Corvos poetas et poetridas picas
> Cantare credas Pegaseium nectar.
>
> —PERS., *Prol.* 8.

Cf. Mart. I, 53, 10.

A magpie comments on the clearness of his speech:

> Pica loquax certa dominum te voce saluto:
> Si me non videas, esse negabis avem.
>
> —MART. XIV, 76.

> Jaybird chattin' wif a bee,
> Trying to teach him grammah.—DUNBAR.

Martial complains when a magpie instead of a dove is served to him:

> Sunt tibi boleti, fungos ego sumo suillos:
> Res tibi cum rhombo est, at mihi cum sparulo.
> Aureus immodicis turtur te clunibus implet.
> Ponitur in cavea mortua pica mihi.
>
> —MART. III, 60, 5.

> De Pica, quae humanas voces imitabatur.
>
> Pica hominum voces cuncta ante animalia monstrat
> Et docto externum perstrepit ore melos.
> Nec nunc oblita est, quidnam prius esset in orbe:
> Aut haec Picus erat aut homo rursus inest.
>
> —*Anth. Lat.* 370.

> And the noisy magpies about the gables,
> Chattered and gossiped of this and that.—STRONG.

The note and imitative powers of the magpie:

> Pica loquax varias concinnat gutture voces,
> Scurrili strepitu omne quod audit ait.
>
> —*Anth. Lat.* 762, 32.

> Kept by a woman as chipper as a jay.—BRET HARTE.

> De Catto qui comedens picam mortuus est.
>
> Mordaces morsu solitus consumere mures
> Invisum et domibus perdere dente genus
> Cattus in obscuro cepit pro sorice picam
> Multiloquumque vorax sorbuit ore caput.

Poena tamen praesens praedonem plectit edacem,
Nam claudunt rabidam cornea labra gulam.
Faucibus obsessis vitalis semita cessit
Et satur escali vulnere raptor obit.
Non habet exemplum volucris vindicta peremptae.
Hostem pica suum mortua discruciat.
—*Anth. Lat.* 181.

A later myth:

The magpies fly in pairs (an evil omen
It were to see but one).—MRS. PIATT.
(*Early Spring in Ireland.*)

PICUS. Δρυοκολάπτης, κελεός. The green woodpecker. *P. viridis.* Πιπώ. The greater and lesser spotted woodpeckers. *P. major* and *minor*. Cf. Aristotle, *H. A.* VIII, 3, 593 and IX, 9, 614. Among the Romans the name *Picus* was applied to all the various species of woodpeckers. The occasional identification of the particular species a Roman poet had in mind is dependent upon descriptive epithets and the weighing of probabilities. The woodpecker is more prominent in the lore of the Romans than in that of the Greeks because of the *Picus* myth and the association with Mars.

Vid. Broderip, *Woodpeckers*. *Fraser* 57, 46.

McManus: *The Flicker on the Fence.*

American parallels: Red-headed woodpecker, yellow-hammer (flicker), (high-hole), et al.

Hic avis est quaedam rubro formosa colore,
Gutture quae plumis est maculata nigris.
(*Descriptio Pennsylvaniae,* Anno 1729.)—THOMAS MAKIN.

Translation:

The various woodpeckers here charm the sight;
Of mingled red, of beauteous black and white!
(*History of Pennsylvania,* p. 366.)—PROUD.

The *picus* (here) on the left is a good omen, although ominous when he works upon an elm:

Impetritum, inauguratumst; quovis admittunt aves;
Picus et cornix ab laeva, corvus, parra ab dextera
Consuadent; certum herclest vostram consequi sententiam.
Sed quid hoc quod picus ulmum tundit? non temerariumst.
Certe hercle ego quantum ex augurio eius pici intellego,
Aut mihi in mundo sunt virgae aut atriensi Saureae.
—PLAUT., *Asin.* 259.

And woodpeckers explore the sides
Of rugged elms.—COWPER.

The vaulting high-ho flings abroad his glee
In fluty laughter from the towering elm.—LAMPMAN.

Naught heard but the tap of the woodpecker's bill.—STREET.

And *Picus minor* plies his trade,
Hunting for dens by insects made;
Knocking off flakes of dropping wood
To pound with his hammer their loathsome brood.—HOSMER.

The robins are the pipers,
The flickers beat the drum.—CRANDALL.
(*The Bird Army.*)

The woodpecker drums on the birch.—TROWBRIDGE.

The woodpecker, with curious bill,
Had made the wilderness reëcho, shrill.—MARKS.

Peckawood erpon de tree
Tappin' lak a hammah.—DUNBAR.

Where the hammering 'red-heads' hopped awry.—RILEY.

And that sassy little critter jes a-pecking all the day.
—RILEY.

And from the frondous pine did ring
The hammer of the golden-wing.—MAURICE THOMPSON.

Above him in the sycamore
The flicker beats a dull tattoo.—MAURICE THOMPSON.

Hear the woodpecker, rap-a-tap!
See him with his cardinal's cap.—MAURICE THOMPSON.

His bill an auger is,
His head, a cap and frill.
He laboreth at every tree,
A worm his utmost goal.
(*The Woodpecker.*) —EMILY DICKINSON.

The crested wood-cocks hammer on high.
(*The Foresters.*) —ALEXANDER WILSON.

Every leaf was at rest, and I heard not a sound
But the woodpecker tapping the hollow beech-tree.
(*Poems relating to America.*) —THOMAS MOORE.

The *picus* (here) on the left is with the *cornix* a bad omen:

Sis licet felix ubicumque mavis,
Et memor nostri, Galatea, vivas,
Teque nec laevus vetet ire picus
Nec vaga cornix.—HOR., *Od.* III, 27, 13.

The Greeks faced the north, the Romans the south, when taking note of birds in augury, hence 'right' and 'left' are frequently confused when the Romans followed the Greek tradition. Cf. Plin. X, 18, 20.

'Tis yon wood-pecker's warning note.
He is their seer and sentinel.—SILL.

For the myth of *Picus,* who, on refusing the advances of Circe, by virtue of his love for Canens, was metamorphosed into a woodpecker, vid. Ov., *Met.* XIV, 320.

The actual metamorphosis of Picus:

Ille fugit, sed se solito velocius ipse
Currere miratus: pennas in corpore vidit,
Seque novam subito Latiis accedere silvis
Indignatus avem[1] duro fera robora rostro
Figit et iratus longis dat vulnera ramis;[2]
Purpureum chlamydis pennae traxere colorem;
Fibula quod fuerat vestemque momorderat aurum,
Pluma fit, et fulvo cervix praecingitur auro,
Nec quicquam antiqui Pico, nisi nomina, restat.
—Ov., *Met.* XIV, 388.

[1]Ovid probably had in mind the greater spotted woodpecker, *P. major*.

[2]A bit of true observation, as so often in Ovid. Cf. Newton, op. cit., p. 1047: "Both of these birds (*P. major* and *P. minor*) have an extraordinary habit of causing, by quickly repeated blows of their beak on a branch, or even on a small bough, a vibrating noise, louder than that of a watchman's rattle, and enough to excite the attention of the most incurious."

Hudson, op. cit., p. 182: "The most curious sound he makes is instrumental: it is the love-call of the bird, produced by striking the beak on a branch so rapidly as to produce a long jarring or rattling note." Vid. supra.

The woodpecker loud hammered.—EMERSON.

The only hammer that I hear
Is wielded by the woodpecker.—LOWELL.

A woodpecker pounded a pine top shell.—MILLER.

Two other descriptions of the metamorphosed Picus:

Ipse Quirinali lituo parvaque sedebat
Succinctus trabea, laevaque ancile gerebat
Picus, equum domitor, quem capta cupidine coniunx
Aurea percussam virga versumque venenis
Fecit avem Circe, sparsit coloribus alas.
—VERG., *Aen.* VII, 187.

Hoc Picus, quondam nomen memorabile ab alto
Saturno, statuit genitor, quem carmine Circe
Exutum formae volitare per aethera iussit
Et sparsit croceum plumis fugientis honorem.
—SIL. ITAL. VIII, 439.

Both Vergil and Silius seem to have *P. major* in mind. Cf Serv. ad loc.

Rhea Silvia in a vision beholds a woodpecker and a she-wolf fighting in defence of two palm trees (Romulus and Remus).

Terreor admonitu, corque timore micat,
Martia, picus, avis gemino pro stipite pugnant
Et lupa. Tuta per hos utraque palma fuit.
—Ov., *Fast.* III, 36.

Romulus and Remus, when exposed, were fed by a woodpecker:

Lacte quis infantes nescit crevisse ferino,
Et picum expositis saepe tulisse cibos?
—Ov., *Fast.* III, 53.

The name *pici* applied to the fabulous griffins:

Picis divitiis, qui aureos montes colunt,
Ego solus supero.
—PLAUT., *Aul.* 701.

Cf. Non. 2, 641. Picos, veteres esse voluerunt, quos Graeci γρύπας appellant.

I love their orchards where the gay woodpecker
Flits, flashing o'er you, like a wingéd jewel.
(*Old Homes.*) —CAWEIN.

PORPHYRION. Πορφυρίων. Purple gallinule(?).

Porphyrio hyacinthus. Vid. s. v. GALLINULA.

American parallel: Purple gallinule, a rare straggler in the Northern States.

A play upon the name:

> Nomen habet magni volucris tam parva gigantis?
> Et nomen prasini Porphyrionis habet.
> —MART. XIII, 78.

> The marsh-hen cried and the tide was ailing
> Under the skies of Augustine.—CAWEIN.

PSITTACUS. Ψιττάκη. Parrot.

P. cubicularis. Vid. Thompson, op. cit., p. 199.

American literary parallels: Parrot, parroquet, cockatoo.

William Lake: *Fable of the Parrot.*

Ovid's lament over the dead parrot is one of the most graceful and tender bird poems ever written. It must be read in the ancient spirit, with its mingling of nature and human characteristics. The *Psittacus* of Statius is vastly less attractive. Greek literature shows no parallel. In English one is apt to recall Cowper's *Elegy to the Bullfinch;* Keat's *Ode to the Nightingale,* and Wordsworth's *Ode to the Cuckoo.* The American poets have always turned to our native birds. In addition to the specific titles given under each Roman species, wherever there seemed to be certain points of resemblance, the following unattached titles will show the wide range covered by our own poets. The list is of course only representative.

Stoddard: *The Albatross.*
Holmes: *My Aviary.*
Dana: *The little Beach-bird.*
Aldrich: *The Bluebird.*
Akers: *The Bobolink.*
Hill: *The Bobolink.*
Stedman: *The Songster* (Canary).
Gallagher: *The Cardinal Bird.*
Venable: *My Catbird.*
Anon.: *To the Catbird.*
Goodrich: *Birth-night of the Humming-birds.*
Clarke, Tabb, Murray: *The Humming-bird.*
Street: *The Loon.*

Burroughs: *To the Lapland Longspur.*
Roberts: *The Night-hawk.*
Flagg: *The O'Lincoln Bird.*
Fawcett: *To an Oriole.*
Howells: *The Song of the Oriole.*
Bolles: *The Oven-bird.*
Trowbridge: *The Pewee.*
Hathaway: *Phebe.*
Lathrop: *The Phoebe-bird.*
Stratton: *The Robin's Madrigal.*
Chadwick: *The Golden-robin's Nest.*
Doane: *Robin Red-breast.*
Thaxter: *The Sandpiper.*
Mason, Benton: *The Scarlet Tanager.*
Hathaway: *Snow-bird.*
Lampman: *Snowbirds.*
Roberts: *A Secret Song* (Snow-bird).
Payne: *The Southern Snow-bird.*
Lampman: *The Warbling Vireo.*
Bryant: *To a Waterfowl.*
The first poetic list of American birds:

Of Birds, there is a knavish robbing crew,
Which constantly the smaller tribes pursue;
The hawk and eagle swoop the azure blue,
With sharp eyes prying.
The chicken saker-hawk, with talons fell;
The sparrow-hawk; the vigilant castrel
Watching his enemy, till he may reel
And faint in flying.
The duck, the goose, the turkey, the proud swan,
The diver and the heron and the crane,
The snipe, the curlew, merlin and moorhen,
The foremost vieing;
The dove and pheasant, thievish blackbird, quail;
The widgeon, which an epicure may hail;
The teal and bob-o'-lincoln, all avail
For man's enjoyment.
But names are wanting wholly to explain
The numerous species of the feathered train;
And surely the recital were a vain
Misspent employment.—JACOB STEENDAM.
(*'Tlof van Niuv-Nederland, 1661.*
Translated by Henry C. Murphy, 1861.)

Ovid's lament at the death of a parrot, which he had given Corinna. The poet summons all good birds to the parrot's obsequies:

Psittacus, Eois imitatrix ales ab Indis,
Occidit: exsequias ite frequenter, aves;
Ite, piae volucres, et plangite pectora pinnis
Et rigido teneras ungue notate genas;
Horrida pro maestis lanietur pluma capillis.
Pro longa resonent carmina vestra tuba!
—Ov., *Am.* II, 6, 1.

Note throughout Ovid's poem the human attributes assigned to the birds.

Hark to my Indian beauty—
My cockatoo, creamy white,
With roses under his feathers
That flash across the light.—STORY (Stedman).

Before all others is summoned the affectionate turtle-dove, whose friendship for the parrot was comparable to that of Pylades for Orestes:

Omnes, quae liquido libratis in aere cursus,
Tu tamen ante alios, turtur amice, dole!
Plena fuit vobis omni concordia vita,
Et stetit ad finem longa tenaxque fides.
Quod fuit Argolico iuvenis Phoceus Orestae,
Hoc tibi, dum licuit, psittice, turtur erat.
—Ov., *Am.* II, 6, 11.

Cf. Ov., *Her.* XV, 38. Et niger a viridi turtur amatur ave.
Viridi ave is here, of course, the parrot.

On her hand a parrot green.—HOLMES.

Of pea-green paraquets 'twixt neighbor trees.—LANIER.

The beauty of the parrot and his powers of mimicry and speecn:

Quid tamen ista fides, quid rari forma coloris,
Quid vox mutandis ingeniosa sonis?
Quid iuvat, ut datus es, nostrae placuisse puellae?
Infelix, avium gloria, nempe iaces!
Tu poteras fragiles pinnis hebetare zmaragdos
Tincta gerens rubro Punica rostra croco.
Non fuit in terris vocum simulantior ales.
Reddebas blaeso tam bene verba sono!
—Ov., *Am.* II, 6, 17.

Occidit illa loquax, humanae vocis imago,
Psittacus, extremo munus ab orbe datum!
—Ov., *Amor.* II, 37.

In plumes of gold and array'd in red.—MILLER.

Hung all red-crowned and robed in green,
With belts of gold and blue between.—MILLER.

To me a painted paroquet
Hath been a most familiar bird.—POE.

Brighter plumes may greet the sun
By the banks of Amazon.—HILL.

That bright-wing'd paroquet.—SIGOURNEY.

Over the curtained door Simorga sits,
The Bird of Ancient Days, whose wondrous green
Was caught from glimmering shades in tropic bower
Where first his eyes were opened to the day:
A bird mysterious, who climbs and speaks
And laughs and stretches out a hand like one
Of human kind.—MRS. J. G. SMITH.

Strange birds like the cockatoos, lories,
    Spread wings, like great blossoms, illumed.—CAWEIN.

The parrot needed but little for sustenance. He talked so much that he had little time for feasting.

Plenus eras minimo nec prae sermonis amore
    In multos poteras ora vacare cibos;
Nux erat esca tibi causaeque papavera somni,
    Pellebatque sitim simplicis umor aquae.
        —Ov., *Am.* 6, 29.

The last words of the dying parrot:

Nec tamen ignavo stupuerunt verba palato:
    Clamavit moriens lingua, 'Corinna, vale!'
        —Ov., *Am.* II, 6, 47.

A description of the Elysian grove, where the souls of the birds that are blessed consort:

Colle sub Elysio nigra nemus ilice frondet,
    Undaque perpetuo gramine terra viret:
Siqua fides dubiis, volucrum locus ille piarum
    Dicitur, obscenae quo prohibentur aves;
Illic innocui late pascuntur olores
    Et vivat phoenix, unica semper avis:
Explicat ipsa suas ales Iunonia pinnas,
    Oscula dat cupido blanda columba mari.
Psittacus has inter nemorali sede receptus
    Convertit volucres in sua verba pias.
        —Ov., *Am.* II, 6, 49.

Where spirit-birds may fold their wings
Within Elysian portal,
And gleaners of divinest things
May gather sweets immortal.—BRIDGE.

The parrot's grave and burial inscription:

Ossa tegit tumulus, tumulus pro corpore magnus,
Quo lapis exiguus par sibi carmen habet:
"Colligor ex ipso dominae placuisse sepulcro,
Ora fuere mihi plus ave docta loqui."
—Ov., *Am.* II, 6, 59.

Another funeral poem, in honor of a parrot which belonged to Melior, a friend of Statius. How the parrot spent his last day and night:

Psittace, dux volucrum, domini facunda voluptas,
Humanae sollers imitator, psittace, linguae,
Quis tua tam subito praeclusit murmura fato?
Hesternas, miserande, dapes moriturus inisti
Nobiscum et gratae carpentem munera mensae
Errantemque toris mediae plus tempore noctis
Vidimus. Adfatus etiam meditataque verba
Reddideras. At nunc aeterna silentia Lethes
Ille canorus habes. Cedat Phaethontia vulgi
Fabula: non soli celebrant sua funera cygni.
—STAT., *Silv.* II, 4, 1.

Birds with the gift of speech are summoned to the funeral:

Huc doctae stipentur aves, quis nobile fandi
Ius Natura dedit: plangat Phoebeius ales[1]
Auditasque memor penitus dimittere voces
Sturnus et Aonio versae certamine picae
Quique refert iungens iterata vocabula perdix[2]
Et quae Bistonio queritur soror orba cubili:
Ferte simul gemitus cognataque ducite flammis
Funera et hoc cunctae miserandum addiscite carmen.
—STAT., *Silv.* II, 4, 16.

Cf. Plin. X, 117, 120, 121, 124; Apul., *Flor.* II; Manil. V, 379.

A description of the parrot. His powers of speech. His last rites and the words uttered by the birds at his funeral:

---

[1]The raven.

[2]The reading *cornix* is attractive (cf. Plin. X, 124 et al.), but *quique* is then of course impossible.

Occidit aeriae celeberrima gloria gentis
Psittacus, ille plagae viridis regnator Eoae,
Quem non gemmata volucris[1] Iunonia cauda
Vinceret aspectu, gelidi non Phasidis ales[2]
Nec quas[3] humenti Numidae rapuere sub austro,
Ille salutator regum nomenque locutus
Caesareum et queruli quondam vice functus amici,
Nunc conviva levis monstrataque reddere verba
Tam facilis, quo tu, Melior dilecte, recluso
Numquam solus eras. At non inglorius umbris
Mittitur: Assyrio cineres adolentur amomo
Et tenues Arabum respirant gramine plumae
Sicaniisque crocis, senio nec fessus inerti
Scandet odoratos Phoenix felicior ignes.

—STAT., *Silv.* II, 4, 24.

Or leave me here as now,
Bill, parrot-like and old with cracked voice, harping, screeching.

—WHITMAN.

That screaming parrot makes my blood run cold.—MOODY.

Other references to the parrot and his powers of speech:

Quis expedivit psittaco suum *chaere*,
Picasque docuit verba nostra conari?
Magister artis ingenique largitor
Venter, negatas artifex sequi voces.

—PERS., *Prol.* 8.

Greek was the language of small talk, love talk, parrot talk.

—GILDERSLEEVE.

Voce ut loquatur psittacus coturnicis
Et concupiscat esse Canus ascaules?

—MART. X, 3, 6.

Psittacus a vobis aliorum nomina discam:
Hoc didici per me dicere, *Caesar*. *Have*.

—MART. XIV, 73.

Iudice me cycnus et garrula cedat hirundo,
Cedat et inlustri psittacus ore tibi.

—*Anth. Lat.* 658, 19.

Psittacus humanas depromit voce loquelas
Atque suo domino *chaere* sonat vel *ave*.

—*Anth. Lat.* 762, 31.

---

[1]The peacock. [2]The pheasant. [3]The guinea-fowl.

Cf. Macaw; and gold-green parrot, human-tongued,
For craft and wit prediction famed of yore.—BAILEY.

Behind us at our evening meal
The gray bird ate his fill,
Swung downward by a single claw,
And wiped his hooked bill.—WHITTIER.

QUERQUEDULA. Κερκουρίς and κερκιθαλλίς have been assumed as possible originals for the *cerceris* in Varr., *L. L.* V, 79.

Cf. Keller, *Lateinische Volksetymologie*, p. 52.

Κερχήδης, as a gloss, also occurs.

Vid. Thompson, op. cit. s. v. v. Νῆττα, βοςκάς, and γλαύκιον.

The *querquedula* is probably the Teal (*Anas crecca*) or the Garganey (*Anas querquedula*). Cf. Gesner, op. cit., p. 103. "Easdem omnino Ferrariae in Italia rustici qui in foro vendebant, nomen interroganti mihi *scavolos* et *cerceuolos* (quasi *querquedulas*) appellarunt. Mediolani audio *garganello* dici, quod nomen aliqui etiam aliis anatibus aut mergis improprie tribuant. Eliota Anglus *querquedulas* interpretatur *teale*."

American parallel: Teal.

He told how teal and loon he shot.—WHITTIER.

Above the marshy islands flew
The green teal and the swift curlew.—MAURICE THOMPSON.

A possible reference to the fall migration of the *querquedulae*:

Et ratione
Aut frigidos nimbos cito ac caduciter ruentis
Pertimuerunt aquatilis querquedulae natantes.
—VARR., *Men.* 576.

The teal and mallard wanton o'er the flood.—ALSOP.

O Nature! gentle is thy might:—
Thy action is repose;—the Eagle's flight
Is tranquil as the teal that sails so light
The hill-defended tarn.—BROWN.

REGULUS. Τροχίλος and probably ὀρχίλος, βασιλεύς. Wren.
Troglodytes europaeus or *Regulus cristatus*.
American parallels: Wren, kinglet, king-bird.
Alexander Wilson: *The Disconsolate Wren.*
Henry Van Dyke: *The Ruby-Crowned Kinglet.*

It is noteworthy that the wren, although one of the most observable and sociable of the smaller birds and about which much later lore has collected, seems to have touched the ancient poets scarcely at all. This is due, as in several other cases, largely to the fact that no great metamorphosis myth with the wren gained popular acceptance.

Cf. int. al. Newton, op. cit., p. 1050. The myth of the wren as 'King of all the birds' is post-classical.

The fire-crowned king of the wrens,
From out the pines.—TENNYSON.

I'll be king of the queen of the wrens
And all in a nest together.—TENNYSON.

Where's your kingdom, little king?
Where the land you call your own,
Where your palace and your throne?
Fluttering lightly on the wing
Through the blossom-world of May,
Whither lies your royal way,
Little king?—HENRY VAN DYKE.

The wren's song is like that of the bee-eater and swallow:

Regulus atque merops et rubro pectore progne
Consimili modulo zinzizulare sciunt.
—*Anth. Lat.* 762, 43.

Sibilous shivering voice.
(*Wood-wren.*) —GILBERT WHITE of Selborne.

For other references vid. Plin. VIII, 37; Plin., *Ep.* I, 5, 14.

Then came the wren with carols gay,
The customed roof and porch to greet.
(*Frontenac, Canadian Spring.*)—STREET.

There are notes of joy from the hang-bird and wren.
—BRYANT.

When first the wren
Was heard to chatter.—BRYANT.

There's the hum of the bee and the chirp of the wren.
—BRYANT.

The wren
Comes twittering from his brushy den.
—MAURICE THOMPSON.

And from his pigmy house the wren looked out.
—BAYARD TAYLOR.

Wrens sing all the winter through: frost excepted.
—GILBERT WHITE of Selborne.

RUSTICA. Σκολόπαξ and ἀσκαλώπας. Woodcock.
Scolopax rusticula.
American parallels: Woodcock, snipe.
A table bird. Compared with the partridge:

Rustica sim an perdix, quid refert, si sapor idem est?
Carior est perdix. Sic sapit illa magis.
—MART. XIII, 76.

The seasons send
Their wildest wanderers: the secret snipe,
That on the borders of the slimy field
Sucks up its draining juice.—M'KINNON.

The woodcock in his moist retreat,
Heard not the falling of their feet.—HOSMER.

Bubbling within some basin green
So fringed with fern, the woodcock's bill
Scarce penetrates the leafy screen.—STREET.

SCOLOPAX. Σκολόπαξ and ἀσκαλώπας. Woodcock.
Scolopax rusticula.
American parallels: Woodcock, snipe.

A striking description of the appearance and feeding habits of the bird:

Cum nemus omne suo viridi spoliatur honore,
Fultus equi niveis silvas pete protinus altas
Exuviis: praeda est facilis et amoena scolopax.
Corpore non Paphiis avibus maiore videbis
Illa sub aggeribus primis, qua proluit humor,
Pascitur, exiguos sectans obsonia vermes.
At non illa oculis, quibus est obtusior, etsi
Sint nimium grandes, sed acutis naribus instat;
Impresso in terram rostri mucrone sequaces
Vermiculos trahit et vili dat praemia vitae.
—NEMES. (?), *Anth. Lat.* 884.

For discussion of authorship vid. *Rhen. Mus.* 52, p. 457.

Tread softly now, Carlo! The woodcock is here;
He rises—his long bill thrust out like a spear.—STREET.

When but a brown snipe flutters by
With rustling wing and piping cry.—MAURICE THOMPSON.

The woodcock whirrs by bush and brake.
—BROWNELL.

The lonely snipe
O'er marshy fields, high in the dusky air
Invisible, but with faint, tremulous tones,
Hovering or playing o'er the listener's head.—WILCOX.

From yon grove the woodcock rises,
Mark her progress by her notes;
High in air her wings she poises,
Then like lightning down she shoots.
—BLEECKER (Kettell).

As thick as pine trees in the wood,
Or snipes on Jersey shore.
(*Eolopoesis.*) —BIGELOW (?).

The snipe darts from it like an arrow.—STREET.
And the tilting snipe stood fearless of the truants wayward cry
And the splashing of the swimmer, in the days gone by.
—RILEY.

Watch the snipes and killdees foolin' half the day.—RILEY.

Or give me the marsh, with the brown snipe aflush,
And my gun's sudden flashes and resonant din.
—MAURICE THOMPSON.

When but a brown snipe flutters by
With rustling wing and piping cry.—MAURICE THOMPSON.

SPINTURNICIUM. Σπινθαρίς An unknown bird. Possibly one of the smaller owls.

A comparison, which seems to suggest the habits of an owl:

> Pithecium haec est prae illa et spinturnicium
> Viden tu illam oculis venaturum facere atque aucupium
> auribus? —PLAUT., *Mil. Glor.* 989.

Cf. Fest. 330. Spinthurnix est avis genus turpis figurae, ea Graece dicitur, ut ait Santra, σπινθαρίς. Vid. also Plin. X, 13, 17; Baehrens, *P. L. M.*, p. 52.

> Whippoorwill and owlet-things,
> Whose far call before you brings
> Wonder-worlds of happenings.—CAWEIN.

STRIX. Στρίξ, et al. An Owl. Exact species indeterminate. Vid. Plin. XI, 95.

Cawein: *The Owlet.*

A bit of folklore combining references to harpies, witches and night owls, with some description of the latter, a derivation and an incantation:

> Sunt avidae volucres, non quae Phineia mensis
> Guttura fraudabant, sed genus inde trahunt:
> Grande caput, stantes oculi, rostra apta rapinis,
> Canities pinnis, unguibus hamus inest.
> Nocte volant puerosque petunt nutricis egentes
> Et vitiant cunis corpora rapta suis.
> . . . . . .
> Est illis strigibus nomen, sed nominis huius
> Causa, quod horrenda stridere nocte solent.
> Sive igitur nascuntur aves seu carmine fiunt
> Naeniaque in volucres Marsa figurat anus:
> . . . . . .
> 'Noctis aves, extis puerilibus,' inquit
> Parcite: 'pro parvo victima parva cadit.
> Cor pro corde, precor, pro fibris sumite fibras.
> Hanc animam vobis pro meliore damus.'
> —Ov., *Fast.* VI. 131 ff.

Cf. Ov., *Am.* I, 8, 13; Prop. IV, 5, 17.

The *strix* in magic and incantations:

> Iubet sepulcris caprificos erutas,
>   Iubet cupressos funebres,
> Et uncta turpis ova ranae sanguine,
>   Plumamque nocturnae strigis.
>
> —HOR., *Epod.* V, 17.

> Addit et exceptas luna pernocte pruinas
> Et strigis infamis ipsis cum carnibus, alas.
>
> —OV., *Met.* VII, 268.

> Illum turgentis ranae portenta rubetae
>   Et lecta exuctis anguibus ossa trahunt,
> Et strigis inventae per busta iacentia plumae,
>   Cinctaque funesto lanea vitta viro.
>
> —PROP. III, 6, 27.

> Maestique cor bubonis, et raucae strigis
> Exsecta vivae viscera. —SEN., *Med.* 733.

> A nest of vipers, mix'd with adders foul;
> The screeching night-bird, and the greater owl.
> (*The Anarchiad.*) —HUMPHREYS, BARLOW, HOPKINS, TRUMBULL.

> Serpents and caw-caws and bats,
>   Screech-owls and crickets and adders—
> These were the guides of that witch
>   Through the dank deeps of the forest.—FIELD.

> The screech-owl's voice makes wild the breeze.
> Mourn, mourn, thou feathered witch
>   Above the frozen ditch!—CAWEIN.
> (*Nature-Notes.*)

The accursed birds of Hades:

> Palus inertis foeda Cocyti iacet;
> Hic vultur, illic luctifer bubo gemit,
> Omenque triste resonat infaustaeque strigis:
> Horrent opaca fronde nigrantes comae,
> Taxo imminente, quam tenet segnis Sopor.
>
> —SEN., *Herc. Fur.* 686.

> Nor barking Satyrs breathe, nor dreary clouds
> Exhaled from Styx, their dismal drops distill
> Within these fairy, flowery fields, nor shrouds
> The screeching night raven, with his shady quill.
>
> —JOHN ROGERS.

> Where once was nought but desert, howling,
> And swamps, scarce fit to pasture owl in.—FESSENDEN.

Within, the screech-owl made her mournful home,
And birds obscene that hover round the tomb.
—Alsop.

With thrilling shrieks his dirge the Death-owl sings,
And birds ill-omen'd flap their dusky wings.—Alsop.

With thee to guide my steps I'll creep
In some old haunted nook to sleep,
Lull'd by the dreary night-bird's scream,
That flits along the wizard stream,
And there, till morning 'gins appear,
The tales of troubled spirits hear.—Cliffton.

It is a wild, a fearful spot,
And sinless birds they love it not.—Hosmer.

The owlet hoots;
A voice that shivers as with fear,
That cries in fear:
"Who is it, who is it, who?"
Who creeps with his glow-worm crew
Above the mire
With a corpse-light fire,
As only dead men do?
"Who, who, who!
Who is it, who is it, who?"
(*The Owlet.*) —Cawein.

A yewtree in Hades the abode of the accursed birds:

Dextra vasta comas nemorosaque bracchia fundit
Taxus, Cocyti rigua frondosior unda.
His dirae volucres pastusque cadavere vultur
Et multus bubo ac sparsis strix sanguine pennis
Harpyiaeque fovent nidos atque omnibus haerent
Condensae foliis; saevit stridoribus arbor.
—Sil. Ital. XIII, 595.

Another accursed tree with the same birds:

Illa dedit turpes raucis bubonibus umbras
Vulturis in ramis et strigis ova tulit.
—Ov., *Am.* I, 12, 19.

Deep thro' the turnings of a darksome vale,
Where blasted trunks hung from th' impending steep,
Where oft was heard the owl's wild dreary wail.
—Alexander Wilson.

Was it the owl, the koko-koko,
Hooting from the dismal forest?—LONGFELLOW.

The ill-omened note of the *strix*:

Hanc volitent animae circum sua fata querentes
Semper, et e tectis strix violenta canat.
—TIB. I, 5, 51.

Omenque triste resonat infaustae strigis.
—SEN., *Herc. Fur.* 688.

Resounding with the sad noises of the night owl.—WHITMAN.

Wail, wail, thou bird of ill omén,
Within thy freezing glen!
Screech, screech through all the frosty night
Where gleams the cold moonlight!
(*Nature-Notes.*) —CAWEIN.

Quod trepidus bubo, quod strix nocturna queruntur.
—LUC. VI, 686.

Monstra volant, dirae strident in nube volucres
Nocturnaeque gemunt striges et feralia bubo
Damna canens. —STAT., *Theb.* III, 510.

Strix nocturna sonans et vespertilio stridunt.
—*Anth. Lat.* 762, 39.

And bat and owl above his head
From out their gloomy caverns swing.—MILLER.

The bat and owl inhabit these.—LOWELL.

STURNUS. Ψάρ. Starling.

Sturnus vulgaris.

American parallels: The meadow-lark, red-winged blackbird, and the rusty and purple grackles furnish some points of contact as to habits and folk observation.

Cf. Holbrook, op. cit., p. 280 for comparison of Dànte, *Inf.* V, 31 and Verg., *Aen.* VI, 308 (cf. Plin. X, 24; Hudson, op. cit., p. 156).

The bird commonly called the Meadow Lark with us is more nearly related to the Starling of this country (England) than to any other bird. I was particularly surprised that a low note, resembling the noise made by a wheel not well greased, was precisely the same in both, that the style of their walk and gait was also precisely alike, and that in short flights the movement of the wings had the same tremulous action before they alighted.—AUDUBON, *Journal,* vol. I, p. 24.

The spring song of the paltry starling:

Nunc sturnos inopes fringillorumque querellas
Audit et arguto passere vernat ager.
—MART. IX, 55, 7.

A list of harmful birds:

Non sturnus mihi graculusve raptor
Aut cornix anus aut aquosus anser
Aut corvus nocuit siticulosus:
Sed quod carmina pessimi poetae
Ramis sustineo laboriosis. —*Priap.* LXI, 10.

The farmers' planted fields forlorn,
Will make a poor return of corn,
And thievish birds wax fat, I fear,
Since all the scarecrows volunteer.—READ.

This done, behold,
The hideous shape is throned upon the field!
A figure built awry, with outstretched arms,
And, like a drunken maudlin, in the wind
Flutters its rags, and frightens the pilfering crow.—READ.

Next the dawn
Falls gray and indistinct, upon a shape
Gaudily decked within the cornfield's midst,
Nodding its limbs to every breath of air.
The crow commander, from the hemlock's top,
Eyes the strange form askance; from greater height
Still looks, and as the object yet remains,
Leads off his legions to the neighboring field.—STREET.

Men think, grim wight, his rags affright
The wingèd thieves from root and ear;
But on his hat pert sparrows light—
Crows have been friends too long to fear!—CANTON.

The starling as one of the talking birds:

Huc doctae stipentur aves, quis nobile fandi
Ius Natura dedit: plangat Phoebeius ales
Auditasque memor penitus dimittere voces
Sturnus et Aonio versae certamine picae.
—STAT., *Silv.* II, 4, 16.

Cf. Plin. X, 59. Habebant Caesaris iuvenes sturnum, etiam luscinias, Graeco atque Latine sermone dociles. Vid. also Aul. Gell. XIII, 20.

The song of the starling:

Dum turdus trucilat, sturnus tunc pusitat ore,
Sed quod mane canunt, vespere non recolunt.
—*Anth. Lat.* 762, 17.

STYMPHALIDES. Στυμφαλίδες. Stymphalian birds.

Mystical birds. For description and astronomical interpretation vid. Thompson, op. cit. s. v.

The slaying of the Stymphalian birds by Hercules:

En cernite, urbes, cernite ex illo Hercule
Quid iam supersit. Herculem agnoscis, pater?
Hisne ego lacertis colla Nemeaei mali
Elisa pressi? Tensus hac arcus manu
Astris ab ipsis detulit Stymphalidas?
—SEN., *Herc. Oet.* 1233.

Cf. Mart. IX, 101, 7. Stymphalidas astris abstulit.

Has hydra sensit, his iacent Stymphalides
Et quidquid aliud eminus vici malum.
—SEN., *Herc. Oet.* 1650.

Solitasque pennis condere obductis diem
Petit ab ipsis nubibus Stymphalidas?
—SEN., *Her. Fur.* 243.

Vidit Hyppolyte ferox
Pectore e medio rapi
Spolium, et sagittis
Nube percussa Stymphalis alto
Decidit caelo.—SEN., *Ag.* 847.

Cf. Verg., *Aen.* XI, 580; Sen., *Herc. Oet.* 17; Claud., *De R. P.* II, *Praef.* 37; *Anth. Lat.* 641, 5.

No leaden thunder strikes the fowl in air,
Nor from my shaft the winged death do fear.
(*An invitation into the country, in imitation of Horace.*) —JANE TURELL (Kettell).

An eagle, sailing with sunward ken,
Receives from the heartless archer's bow
The envious arrow winged from below.—READ.

Your arrow stays the eagle's flight no more.—SIGOURNEY.

The untamed eagles whom a shaft had brought
From highest heaven to her sandal'd feet.—SUTHERLAND.

And told her how the deadly instrument
Had brought to earth the fleetest footed deer
And birds that seem'd a speck against the sky.
—SUTHERLAND.

But suddenly, from unseen hand
In thicket hid, an arrow sped,
The noblest and the fairest bird
Fell from the sunlight, dead.—MACE.

My rifle for thy feast shall bring,
The wild swan from the sky.—BRYANT.

She swam the lake or climbed the tree,
Or struck the flying bird in air.—WHITTIER.

The feathers of a Stymphalian bird used by Medea in an incantation:

Reliquit istas invio plumas specu
Harpyia, dum Zeten fugit.
His adice pinnas sauciae Stymphalidos
Lenaea passae spicula.—SEN., *Med.* 781.

Cf. Hyg. XXX. Aves Stymphalides in insula Martis quae emissis pennis suis iaculabantur sagittis interfecit.

Serv. ad Verg., *Aen.* VIII, 300. Stymphalides aves, quae alumnae Martis fuisse dicuntur, quae hoc periculum regionibus inrogabat, quod, cum essent plurimae volantes, tantum plumarum stercorumque de se emittebant, ut homines et animalia necarent, agros et semina omnia cooperirent.

Jocasta prays that she may be borne away by a Stymphalian bird:

Quis me procellae turbine insano vehens
Volucer per auras ventus aetherias aget?
Quae Sphynx vel atra nube subtexens diem
Stymphalis avidis praepetem pennis feret?
—SEN., *Phoen.* 420.

Cf. Sen., *Herc. Oet.* 1390. Hinc feris clangoribus, Aetheria me Stymphalis.

TERRANEOLA. Ground-bird. Possibly the lark, κορυδαλός. Exact identification of course impossible.

American parallels: Ground-bird, ground-sparrow.

Larcom: *The Field-Sparrow.*

A bit of folk bird nomenclature:

> Avis, quam dicunt terraneolam rustici,
> In terra nidum quia imponit scilicet.
> —PHAED., *Fab. Nov.* XXX.

> Where the ground-bird nests in the warm green shade.
> —STRONG.

> Nod o'er the ground-bird's nest.—BRYANT.

> And, by the little ground-bird's nest,
> He lays him down to sleep.—SARAH HELEN WHITMAN.

TETRAX. Τέτραξ. Identification doubtful.

The description in Athen. IX, (c. 58) 398, *c-f* seems to apply most closely to the Guinea-fowl. Cf. Thompson, op. cit. s. v. In the passage below the *tetrax* is taken (with a fair degree of probability) as the Capecaillie (*Tetrao urogallus*) by Longolius, op cit., but as a kind of Bustard by Gesner, op cit. s. v., who however emends *dorsum* in line twelve to *collum*. Ihm (*Rhein. Mus.* 52, p. 454 ff.) following Longolius, does not seem to me to have made good his contention that both the Tetrax and the Scolopax (vid. sup. s. v., *Anth. Lat.* 883, 884) are from Nemesianus. Both fragments seem curiously late in tone and view-point.

The trapping of the *tetrax* with some description of the bird and its habits:

> Et tetracem, Romae quem nunc vocitare *taracem*
> Coeperunt. Avium est multo stultissima.[1] Namque
> Cum pedicas necti sibi contemplaverit adstans,
> Immemor ipse sui tamen in dispendia currit.
> Tu vero adductos laquei cum senseris orbes,
> Appropera et praedam pennis crepitantibus aufer.
> Nam celer oppressi fallacia vincula colli
> Excutit et rauca subsannat voce magistri
> Consilium et laeta fruitur iam pace solutus.
> Hic prope Peltvinum radicibus Apennini
> Nidificat, patulisque se sol obicit agris,

[1]Cf. the name 'Fool-hen' given to one of our mountain grouse in the Western States, and the 'Fool-duck' applied to the little Ruddy Duck. Such a title or epithet is almost unparalleled in the ancient poets.

Persimilis cineri dorsum, maculosaque terga
Inficiunt pullae cacabantis imagine guttae[2]
Tarpeiae est custos arcis non corpore maior[3]
Nec qui te volucres docuit, Palamede, figuras.
Saepe ego nutantem sub iniquo pondere vidi
Mazonomi puerum, portat cum prandia, circo
Quae consul praetorve novus construxit ovanti.
—NEMES.(?), *Anth. Lat.* 883.

TURDUS. Κίχλη. Song-thrush, mavis. *Turdus musicus.* Missel-thrush, *T. viscivorus.* Fieldfare, *T. pilaris.*

American parallels: Brown-thrush, robin, wood-thrush, et al.

Vid. int. al.

Aldrich: *The Winter Robin.*
Benton: *The Hermit Thrush.*
Bridge: *The Thrush.*
Bridges: *The Robin.*
Caldwell: *Robin's Come.*
Cliffton: *To a Robin.*
Daly: *To a Thrush.*
Davis: *The Wood Thrush.*
Emily Dickinson: *To a Robin.*
Hardy: *The Darling Thrush.*
Hirst (Duyckinck): *The Robin.*
Larcom: *The Brown Thrush.*
Larcom: *Sir Robin.*
Keats: *The Thrush's Song.*
Pattee: *The Hermit Thrush.*
Gen. Albert Pike: *To a Robin.*
(Written in New Mexico in 1832, on hearing the song of the only red-breast he ever saw there.)
Roberts: *The Hermit Thrush.*
Stratton (Sladen): *The Robin's Madrigal.*
Taff: *Robin.*
Taylor: *The Veery-Thrush.*
Tennyson: *The Throstle.*
Valentine: *The Robin's Creed.*
Van Dyke: *The Veery.*
Waterman: *A Thrush's Song.*

[2]Vlitius, Ms. *notae.*

[3]These references to the goose and crane surely point to a bird larger than the 'guinea-fowl.'

Epithets: Advena, avidus, crassus, edax, gravis, macrus, peregrinus, pinguis, raucus, trutilans, vagus.

The song of the thrush (drosca):

Dulce per ora sonat, dicunt quam nomine droscam[1]
Sed fugiente die illa quieta silet.[2]
—*Anth. Lat.* 762, 11.

The brown rossignol's carol shrill.—STREET.
(*Frontenac, Canadian Spring.*)

Song-throstles, bold and fond
From Smyrna and from ancient Trebizond,
That sing in lofty tree-tops, at still noon,
A musical and melancholy tune.—GEN. ALBERT PIKE.

From choirs that lurk in hedge and birch
From black bird and from mavis.—LOWELL.

What was it the mournful wood-thrush said?—WHITTIER.

And where the shadows deepest fell
The wood-thrush rang his silver bell.—WHITTIER.

The winding water's sounding rush,
The long note of the hermit thrush.—WHITTIER.

And the robin through the long
Twilight sang his slumber song.—SILL.

'Twas spring, and loud the mavis piped outside.—ALDRICH.

The wood-thrush of the west, shall sing
Earth's last sweet even-song.—HOLMES.

And best of all, through twilight's calm
The hermit-thrush repeats his psalm.—HENRY VAN DYKE.

I hear the wood-thrush piping one mellow descant more.
—BRYANT.

I muse, while still the wood-thrush sings down the golden day.
—BRYANT.

And while the wood-thrush pipes his evening lay.—BRYANT.

Her thrushes sing in Rathburn bowers.—WHITTIER.

---

[1]Cf. O. H. Germ. Drosce, M. Germ. Drossel.

[2]Cf. Hudson, op. cit., p. 43: "The throstle is a very persistent singer; throughout the day he sings at intervals, and again, more continuously, in the evening, when he keeps up an intermittent flow of melody until dark."

And in a thick, melodious rain
The mavis pours her mellow strain.—TIMROD.

Already sings with sweet and lyric ease
The western thrush.—HIGGINSON.

A wood-thrush gurgled in a vine.—CAWEIN.

The wood-thrush from his leafy tower
Rings, Hymen, Hymen, all day long.—WRIGHT.

Save when the robin's melancholy song
Is heard amid the coppice.—SARAH HELEN WHITMAN.

In the woods of America I have never been in such silence; for in the most retired places I have had the gentle murmuring streamlet, or sound of the Woodpecker tapping, or the sweet melodious strains of that lovely recluse, my greatest favorite, the Wood-Thrush.—AUDUBON, *Journal*, vol. I, p. 339. London.

I estimated that the nightingale had a most wonderful compass and was the greatest of all bird *vocalists,* but with a less individual and exquisite genius than our Wood-Thrush.—MINOT, *English Birds compared with American. Am. Nat.* 14, 56.

In melody, and above all in that finer, higher melody, where the chords vibrate with the touch of eternal sorrow, it (nightingale) cannot rank with such singers as the wood-thrush and hermit-thrush.—ROOSEVELT. Cf. Note IV, RUSCINIA.

The thrush as a table delicacy. Details:

Tendemus hinc recta Beneventum, ubi sedulus hospes,
Paene macros arsit dum turdos versat in igni.
—HOR., *Sat*. I, 5, 71.

The *macros* by itself points rather to spring than to autumn:
Cf. *Anth. Lat*. 395. October pinguis dat tibi ruris aves.

In the fall, birds and fowls of all lands become very fat.
—BURROUGHS.

At simul assis
Miscueris elixa, simul conchylia turdis,
Dulcia se in bilem vertent stomachoque tumultum
Lenta feret pituita. —HOR., *Sat*. II, 2, 72.

Turdus
Sive aliud privum dabitur tibi, devolet illuc
Res ubi magna nitet domino sene.
—HOR., *Sat*. II, 5, 11.

'Non hercule miror,'
Aiebat, 'si qui comedunt bona, cum sit obeso,
Nil melius turdo, nil volva pulchrius ampla.'
—HOR., *Ep.* I, 15, 39.

Nec tenuem sollers turdarum nosse salivam.
—PERS. VI, 24.

Nec nullus nec te delectat, Baetice, turdus.
—MART. III, 77, 1.

Pylades, Marce, bibebat idem,
Nec melior panis turdusve dabatur Orestae.
—MART., VI, 11, 2.

Cum mittis turdumve mihi quadramve placentae,
Sive femur leporis, sive quid his simile est,
. . . . . .
Buccellas misisse tuas te, Pontia, dicis.
Has ego non mittam, Pontia, sed nec edam.
—MART. VI, 75, 1.

Nec erubescit peierare de turdo.
—MART. VII, 20, 6.

Si mihi Picena turdos palleret oliva.
—MART. IX, 54, 1.

Palleret is due to the food of the bird. Cf. Auson., *Epist.* 31. Qualis Picenae populator turdus olivae clunes opimat cereas. Calp. III, 47. Non sic destricta marcescit turdus oliva.

Inter aves turdus, si quid me iudice certum est,
Inter quadrupedes mattea prima lepus.
—MART. XIII, 92.

Netting thrushes; sending them as gifts and the like:

Nunc ab transenna hic turdus lumbricum petit;
Pendebit hodie pulchre, ita intendi tenus.
—PLAUT., *Bach.* 792.

Aut amite levi rara tendit retia
Turdis edacibus dolos. —HOR., *Epod.* II, 33.

Quin etiam turdoque licet missaque corona
Te memorem dominae testificere tuae.
—OV., *A. A.* II, 269.

Texta rosis fortasse tibi vel divite nardo
At mihi de turdis facta corona placet.
—MART. XIII, 50.

Uri Tongiluis malo dicitur hemitritaeo:
Novi hominis mores: esurit atque sitit.
Subdola tenduntur crassis modo retia turdis.
—MART. II, 40, 1.

Illic coronam pinguibus gravem turdis
Leporemque laesum Gallice canis dente.
—MART. III, 47, 10.

Sed tendit avidis rete subdolum turdis.
—MART. III, 58, 26.

Silva graves turdos exagitata dedit.
—MART. IV, 66, 6.

Quam quae rara vagos expectant retia turdos.
—MART. XI, 21, 5.

Whilst pecking corn, and void of care,
They fall un'wares in fowlers' snare.
Or whilst allur'd with bell and glass,
The net be spread, and caught, alas.—ANNE BRADSTREET.

The sportive urchins oft will skip away,
To chase the partridge from the neighb'ring bush;
And oft, with balls of well-attemper'd clay,
Will from its covert fright the trembling thrush.
(*The Country Meeting.*) —T. C. JAMES.

That's a brown thrush
In the underbrush,
Conceited, self-conscious, inclined to gush,
His is a voice that will not wear;
Faulty timber and volume weak,
He wings from his beak
A spiral squeak
That bores like a gimlet through the air!
And the cat-bird, too,
With its feline mew,
Is only fit for the springe and the snare!
(*To an English Nightingale.*)
—MAURICE THOMPSON.

TURTUR. Τρυγών. Turtle-dove.

Columba turtur.

American parallels: Mourning dove, turtle-dove.

Thomas: *The Mourning Dove.*

Keeler: *To a Mourning Dove.*

A play on the spelling of *turtur*:[1]

> Prima sonat quartae, respondet quinta secundae,
> Tertia cum sexta: nomen habet avis.
> —*Anth. Lat.* 738a.

Cf. Morris, *Whip-poor-will.* S. v. LUSCINIA.

> The whip-poor-will, her name her only song.—WILCOX.

The turtle-dove as a delicacy:

> Tu tibi istos habeas turtures, piscis, avis,
> Sine me aliato fungi fortunas meas.
> —PLAUT., *Most.* 44.

> Aureus immodicis turtur te clunibus implet,
> Ponitur in cavea mortua pica mihi.
> —MART. III, 60, 7.

> At ille retro flexus ad pedum turbam
> Inter catellas anserum exta lambentes
> Partitur apri glandulas palaestritis
> Et concubino turturum nates donat.
> —MART. III, 82, 18.

> Et devorato capite turturem truncum.
> —MART. VII, 20, 15.

> Dum pinguis mihi turtur erit, lactuca valebis;
> Et cocleas tibi habe. Perdere nolo famem.
> —MART. XIII, 53.

> Sed placet Ursidio lex Iulia, tollere dulcem
> Cogitat heredem, cariturus turture magno
> Mullorumque iubis et captatore macello.
> —JUV. VI, 38.

> Fulcit utrumque latus turdus cum turture pinguis
> Multaque perniferum corpore pandit opus.
> —*Anth. Lat.* 176, 5.

---

[1]Cf. Isid., *Orig.* 12, 17. Turtur de voce vocatur. Morris, op. cit. IV, p. 173. "The note resembles the syllable 'tur, tur,' more or less often repeated, and more or less quickly—doubtless the origin of the name."

Perna, lepus, turtur, perdix, Iunonius ales,
Agnus, porcellus iunguntur, candidus anser.
(*De mistu asso.*) —*Anth. Lat.* 230, 1.

How turtle-doves (by implication) were killed when captured, by piercing their brains with their own feathers:

In fundas visci indebant grandiculos globos,
Eo illos volantis iussi funditarier.
Quid multa verba? Quemquem visco offenderant,
Tam crebri ad terram reccidebant quam pira.
Ut quisque acciderat, eum necabam ilico
Per cerebrum pinna sua sibi quasi turturem.
—PLAUT., *Poen.* 481.

Fell as an eagle pierced with stabs from his own wing.
—STEDMAN.

How the turtle-dove was loved by the parrot:

Candida si non sum, placuit Cephaia Perseo
Andromede, patriae fusca colore suae:
Et variis albae iunguntur saepe columbae,
Et niger a viridi turtur amatur ave.
—OV., *Her.* XV, 35.

Vid. Ov., *Am.* II, 6, 12, s. v. PSITTACUS. Cf. Plin. X, 96. Gesner, op. cit., p. 305: "Est contra quod mihi et item multis exploratum saepe fuit." Morris, op. cit. IV, p. 173: "Turtle-doves may be kept in confinement, but in that state are quarrelsome with other birds."

Niger, like the *purpureis* in Hor., Od. IV, 1, 11, must not be taken literally.

How the turtle-dove cooes with mournful note:

Nec tamen interea raucae, tua cura, palumbes
Nec gemere aeria cessabit turtur ab ulmo.
—VERG., *Ecl.* I, 58.

Through dark and dismal groves
Where the sad turtle loves
To pass the night and kill the day.—FRENEAU.

May is passing:
'Mid the apple boughs a pigeon cooes.—LARCOM.

"Coo-loo! Coo-loo!"
Hear the doves in the tree-tops croon,
"Coo-lou! Coo-loo!"
Love comes soon.—CARMAN-HOVEY.

Sonantque turres plausibus columbarum,
Gemit hinc palumbus, inde cereus tutur.
—MART. III, 58, 18.

Et castus[1] turtur atque columba gemunt.
—*Anth. Lat.* 762, 20.

Will she or nill the chastest turtle must
Taste of the pangs of their unbridled lust.
(*New England's Crisis.*) —BENJAMIN TOMPSON.

The moan of doves in immemorial elms.—TENNYSON.

No closer sound than sob of distant dove.—SILL.

The turtle cooes his sweet refrain.—FIELD.

The drowsy moan of doves.—RILEY.

And that low, sweet voice, like a widow's moan.
—DOANE (Griswold).

Ye could not mourn with more melodious art
Than daily doth yon dim sequestered dove.—LANIER.

The lark's clear note, the dove's melodious moan.—MIFFLIN.

Or as the pensive dove doth all alone
(On withered bough) most uncouthly bemoan
The absence of her love, and loving mate,
Whose loss hath made her so unfortunate:
Ev'n thus do I, with many a deep sad groan
Bewail my turtle true, who now is gone,
His presence and his safe return, still wooes,
With thousand dolefull sighs and mournfull cooes.
(*Letters to her Husband.*)—ANNE BRADSTREET.

Or mourning dove which grieves and grieves,
And "Lost! Lost! Lost!" still seems to say.
—COOLIDGE.

The wood-dove's note of sad complaint.—WHITTIER.

Nor sadly wept the sympathising dove.—FRENEAU.

Since then the Poet ever hears
The mourning dove's undying plaint,
He knows not why with kindred pain
His inmost heart is faint.—MACE.
(*The Two Doves.*)

[1]Cf. She's . . . modest as the dove.—SHAKESPEARE.. Vid. Plaut., *Bacch.* 68, for obscene reference to turtle-dove.

ULULA. Αἰγώλιος. Sceech-owl or possibly the barn-owl. *Strix flammea.*
American parallels: Screech-owl, barn-owl, etc.
Tennyson: *The Owl.*
Timrod: *To a Captive Owl.*
A striking contrast. Proverbial:

> Certent et cycnis ululae, sit Tityrus Orpheus.
> —VERG., *Ecl.* VIII, 55.

> Yon heron! What? Shall herons grapple hawks?—LANIER.

The mournful note of the *ulula:*

> Ast ululant ululae lugubri voce canentes.
> —*Anth. Lat.* 762, 41.

Cf. Thoreau, op. cit., p. 173: "And when all is still at night, the owls take up the strain, like mournful women their ancient *ululu* (cf. s. v. v. STRIX, BUBO). Their most dismal scream is truly Ben-Jonsonian. Wise midnight hags! It is no honest and blunt *tu-whit-tu-who* of the poets, but, without jesting, a most solemn graveyard ditty."

UPUPA. Ἔποψ. Hoopoe.
Vid. s. v. EPOPS.

VULTUR, VULTURIUS. Γύψ. Vulture.
Griffon vulture, *V. fulvus.* Black vulture, *V. cinereus,* et al.

Vultur, as usual when there are many species, is generic. The habits of the vulture, eagle and hawk are sometimes confused in both the ancient and modern poets.

Perhaps no other bird (without metamorphosis associations) from Homer down has been so strongly enmeshed in the bonds of poetic tradition. The real bird is well nigh lost—even in the American poets. Cf. Robinson, *Foreign Birds and English Poets. Liv. Age,* 155, 241.

American parallels: Turkey-buzzard, condor.

> Dove beneath the vulture's beak.—EMERSON.

> And the condor beat with black wings the blue.—MILLER.

> And preying no more as tiger and vulture do.—HOLMES.

Far above the roof-tree failing,
See the hoary vulture sailing;
Marketh he the serpent trailing
Underneath the threshold-stone.
(*The Deserted House.*) —WARFIELD-LEE (Griswold).

The myth of Tityus and the vulture is the most common vulture motive in the Latin poets. Vid. Verg., *Aen.* VI, 595; *Cul.* 237; Prop. III, 11, 31; Stat., *Theb.* VI, 754; Sil. Ital. XIII, 597; Sen., *Thyest.* 8; *Hippol.* 1232; *Her. Fur.* 687; *Oct.* 621; Boeth., *Consol.* III, 12, 38, et al.

Cf. While Envy, like a rav'nous Vulture, tears
His canker'd heart to see your Brother's triumph.—GODFREY.
(*The Prince of Parthia.* 1759.)

For doubt and darkness, o'er thy head,
Forever waved their Condor wings.
—SARAH HELEN WHITMAN.

May no vulture beak
Transpierce thee for thine hospitality.—SIGOURNEY.

Prey to the vulture of a vast desire
That feeds upon my life.—HOLMES.

Chained to the icy peak,
Rent by the vulture's beak.—TICHNOR.

No chained Prometheus feasts the vulture there.—BARLOW.
(*Columbiad.*)

My reward hath been the rock and vulture.—LONGFELLOW.

But still, as when Prometheus bare
From heaven the fiery dart,
I saw the "vulture passions" tear
The proud Caucasian heart.—SARAH HELEN WHITMAN.

There Prometheus lay,
Chain'd to the cold rocks of Mount Caucasus—
The vulture at his vitals, and the links
Of the lame Lemnian festering in his flesh.—WILLIS.

Her memory is no Caucasus for thee,
And e'en her hovering hate would o'er thee fling
Too much of glory from its shadowy wing!
—GRACE GREENWOOD.

While thus with fiery eye, and outspread wings,
The ruthless vulture to his victim clings,
With whetted beak deep in the quivering heart.
Oh, thou embodied meaning, master wrought.
(*Tityus Chained in Tartarus.*)—STEBBINS (Griswold).

In one passage the horror of the vultures themselves is portrayed:

> Ipsae horrent, si quando pectore ab alto
> Emergunt volucres immensaque membra iacentis
> Spectant, dum miserae crescunt in pabula fibrae.
> —STAT., *Theb.* XI, 13.

The myth of Prometheus and his torture:

> Cingitur inde sinus, et, qua sibi fida magis vis
> Nulla, Prometheae florem de sanguine fibrae
> Caucasium, tonitru nutritaque gramina promit,
> Quae sacer ille nives inter tristesque pruinias.
> Durat editque cruor, cum viscere vultur adeso
> Tollitur e scopulis, et rostro irrorat aperto.
> —VAL. FLACC. VII, 355.

Vid. s. v. AQUILA. Thompson, op. cit. s. v. 'Αετός.

> The eagles of incessant thought still prey
> Upon me here; so, as Prometheus stood
> Chained in Caucasus, there in his blood
> The eternal Vulture gnawed.—MIFFLIN.

> The beak-torn Titan's hungering pain!—WHITTIER.

> God's bird of wrath! Swift is thy wrath, O God,
> Strong is thy jealousy!—MOODY.
> (*The Fire-Bringer.*)

> Prometheus thus, in fabled days of old
> Crown'd with success, grew arrogant and bold;
> Braved heaven's high lord, with blest immortals strove,
> And raised his arm against the throne of Jove;
> The god enraged, with mighty vengeance hurl'd
> The daring miscreant to the nether world;
> In durance stretch'd, and bound with massy chains,
> Condemn'd to torment and eternal pains;
> On his torn breast a greedy vulture fares,
> Sucks the warm blood, the tender liver tears;
> In vain devours, in vain the torrent flows,
> Still, still, the bloody feast immortal grows.
> —PEIRCE (Kettell).

Cf. supra for other definite references to the Prometheus myth and vid. passim Longfellow, *Prometheus;* Lowell, *Prometheus;* Moody, *The Fire-Bringer.*

For vultures as scavengers feeding upon the dead vid. Enn. Baehrens, *P. L. M.* 93; Luc. IV, 680; Ov. *Am.* II, 6, 33; *Trist.* I, 6, 11; *Ib.* 169; Juv. IV, 3; Mart. VI, 62, 4; Luc. VII, 835; Stat., *Theb.* III, 509; Val. Flacc. IV, 69; et al.

And buried corpses there
Be raised, to feast the vultures of the air.—FRENEAU.

Gray captains leading bands of veteran men
And fiery youths to be the vultures' feast.—BRYANT.

Thou passest o'er the battlefield
Where the dead lie stiff and stark
Where naught is heard save the vulture's scream.
—W. H. TIMROD.

For a time in our colonial poets, the hawk came into fashion (of course quite wrongly) as the typical scavenger bird of the battle-field:

Your bodies limb from limb this arm shall tear,
Nor sons nor wives nor sires nor infants spare,
But bid the hungry *hawks* your race devour
And call grim wolves to feast in floods of gore.
(*Conquest of Canaan.*) —TIMOTHY DWIGHT.

The beasts shall rend them, and the *hawks* devour.
(*Conquest of Canaan.*) —TIMOTHY DWIGHT.

Left in the field for foreign *hawks* to tear
Nor can our own vultures the banquet share.
(*Columbiad.*) —BARLOW.

The wide beak'd *hawk* that now beholds me die,
Soon with his cowering train my flesh shall tear.
(*Columbiad.*) —BARLOW.

The *hawks* who range the fields of air
Are fatten'd with our gore.—WILLIAM MUNFORD.
(*Patriots, who fell Nov. 4th, 1791.*)

But compare:

No hungry *vulture,* from the rock's tall brow,
Eyes the red field, and slaughtering host, below.
(*Conquest of Canaan.*) —TIMOTHY DWIGHT.

And the vulture ghoul, in the lofty pine,
Looks down with an eager eye and beak.—STRONG.

To be alone in this wide plain,
To hear the hungry vulture's wing,
And watch the fainting light of my existence wane.
(*Death in the Desert.*) —GEN. ALBERT PIKE.

For how vultures anticipate their days of plenty vid. Plaut., *Truc.* 335; *Capt.* 840.

The evil birds of carnage hung and watched,
As ravening heirs watch o'er the miser's couch.
—FAIRFIELD (Griswold).

O God, from vulture dreams my soul defend.—LANIER.

The vulture as a type of reproach and detestation:

Non hercle humanus ergo—
Nam volturio plus humani credo est.
—PLAUT., *Mil. Glor.* 1043.

Tum autem sunt alii qui te volturium vocant
Hostisne an civis comedis parvi pendere.
—PLAUT., *Trin.* 101.

Cf. Cic., *In Pis.* 16, 31; Cat. LXVI, 124; CVI, 4.

An imaginary fresco representing satirically a crow (Tranio), bedeviling two vultures (Theopropides, Simo).

Tr. Viden pictum ubi ludificat una cornix vultorios duos?
Th. Non edepol video. Tr. At ego video: nam inter volturios duos.
Cornix astat: ea volturios duos vicissim vellicat.
Quaeso huc ad me specta, cornicem ut conspicere possies.
Iam vides? Th. Profecto nullam equidem illic cornicem intuor.
Tr. At tu istoc ad vos optuere, quoniam cornicem nequis
Conspicari, si volturios forte possis contui.
Th. Omnino, ut te apsoluam, nullam pictam conspicio hic avem.
Tr. Age, iam mitto, ignosco: aetate non quis optuerier.
—PLAUT., *Most.* 832.

Prof. G. D. Kellog's clever interpretation as an architectural joke (*Trans. and Proc. Amer. Phil. Assoc.*, vol. XLI, p. xliii), postulates, I fear, more ornithology, architecture and Greek than either Plautus himself could have used or his audience follow.

For the Fable of the 'Canis, Thesaurus et Volturius' vid. Phaed. I, 27:

The mother-love of the vulture. This myth was later associated with the pelican. Vid. Thompson, op. cit., p. 48. S. v. ONOCROTALUS.

Cf. The vulture, all maternal, typing thus
Earth, mountain crowned, the glory of the sea,
And mother of us all.—BAILEY.

The vulture in proverbial sayings. An unlucky throw of dice:

Iacit vulturios quattuor.
—PLAUT., *Curc.* 2, 3, 78.

Of something impossible:

Vultur profert cornua.
—CLAUD., *In Eutrop.* I, 352.

Praepes funereo cum vulture ludat hirundo.
—*Anth. Lat.* 390, 27.

The cry of the vulture:

Dum clangunt aquilae, vultur pulpare probatur.
—*Anth. Lat.* 762, 27.

She could scream like a vulture or wink like an owl.
—FRENEAU.

NOTE I.

THE SPRING MIGRATION AND SPRING SONG.

To the poets of northern lands the return of the birds in the spring is a nature motive which has been very widely recorded. After the long period of songless autumn and winter, the eagerly awaited songs of the harbingers of spring, associated with the sunshine and joy of the season, naturally aroused the emotions of both folk and poetic consciousness.

The climatic conditions of America are preeminently conducive to such results; consequently it is not surprising to note how fully throughout their pages our own poets have voiced this feeling, for the most part referring to the birds that are equally familiar to every observer. The following citations chosen from scores will indicate the general range and temper of this particular impulse:

In vain the razor-bill'd auk sails far north to Labrador.
—WHITMAN.

And new-come birds each morning sing.—LOWELL.

Two feathered guests from Alabama, two together.
—WHITMAN.

And warmed the pinions of the early bird.—THOREAU.

A tropic bird blown through the north frost wind.—MILLER.

New birds still sing with every spring.—LOWELL.

'Tis the noon of the spring-time, yet never a bird
In the wind-shaken elm or maple is heard.—WHITTIER.

The birds are here, for all the season's late.—LOWELL.

Whence, oh, whither have they come?
From what rugged, wintry home,
That thus suddenly they bring
These glad messages of spring?
From the hollows of the rocks
Come these sable-coated flocks?
Or, in the forest deep
Have they shivered into sleep,
Where the fir tree or the pine
Their thick boughs intertwine?—LUNT.
(*Blackbirds.*)

O wild-birds flying from the south,
What saw and heard ye, gazing down?—WHITTIER.

May with her flowers and singing birds, had gone.—BRYANT.

A thousand black birds kept on wing
In walnut tops and it was Spring.—MILLER.

Sparrows far off, and nearer April's bird
Blue-coated flying before from tree to tree.—EMERSON.

The winter goes and the summer comes
And the merry blue birds twitter and trill.—ALICE CARY.

And blue birds in the misty spring
Of cloudless skies and summer sing.—BRYANT.

The blue bird chants, from the elm's long branches
A hymn to welcome the budding year.—BRYANT.

And from the stately elms I hear
The blue bird prophesying Spring.—LONGFELLOW.

A laugh which in the woodland rang,
Bemocking April's gladdest bird.—WHITTIER.

To northern lakes fly wind-borne ducks.—EMERSON.

Soars high with canticle of the blest
The jubilant bobolink.—MACE.

Gladness on wings, the bobolink has come.—LOWELL.

And lo! the bobolink—he soars and sings
With all the heart of summer in his wings.—LAMPMAN.

And in flocks the wild goose Wawa,
Flying to the fenlands northward.—LONGFELLOW.

Back into their lakes and marshes
Came the wild gooose and the heron.—LONGFELLOW.

Hill lads at dawn shall hearken the wild goose
Go honking northward over Tennessee.—MOODY.

I hear the whispering voice of Spring
The thrush's trill, the robin's cry.—HOLMES.

The robin the forerunner of spring.—LONGFELLOW.

The robins are come again
With tender, melodious note.—MACE.

While the song sparrow warbling from his perch
Tells you that spring is near.—BRYANT.

Already, close by our summer dwelling
The Easter sparrow repeats her song.—BRYANT.

Dusky sparrows in a crowd
Darting, darting northward free.—EMERSON.

At last I saw her watch the swan
Surge toward the north.—MILLER.

The coming of the first robin was a jubilee beyond crowning of monarch or birthday of pope.—MABEL LOOMIS TODD. (Preface, *Poems of Emily Dickinson.* Second Series.)

Yea, the stork in the heaven knoweth her appointed times; and the turtle and the crane and the swallow observe the time of their coming. —*Jer.* VIII, 7.

In Greece and Italy climatic conditions differ widely from our own. The winter is less long and severe. Many northern birds winter there but fewer stay during the summer after spending the winter across the sea. Yet the Greek poets note at least eight species in connection with the northern flight of birds in their spring migration. (Vid. Pischinger, *Der Vogelzug bei den Griechischen Dichtern.* Kap. I. *Der Frühjahrszug.*) The swallow holds the chief place of honor as the harbinger of spring. Vid. Hom., *Carm. Min.* XV, 11; *Carm. pop.* 41 (*Athen.* VIII, 360c); Ar., *Eq.* 419; Simon. 74; Ar., *Av.* 714; Cratin., *Frag.* 33; Sapp., *Frag.* 39; cf. also Thompson, op. cit., p. 188; Pischinger, op. cit., p. 8. The others are as follows: Nightingale, vid. Sappho, *Frag.* 39; Soph., *Elect.* 149. For the spring song of the nightingale, int. al. vid. Hom., *Od.* XIX, 518; Simon., *Frag.* 73; Ar., *Av.* 683; Anth. Pal. IX, 363. Cuckoo, vid. Hes., op. 486. Kite, Ar., *Av.* 713. Wild duck and crane, *Carm. Anac.* 44. Κηρύλος (a seabird, as yet unidentified), Alc. 12 (20). Black bird, Theoc., *Epig.* IV, 9. These citations collected by Thompson and Pischinger represent about all the Greek poets have left us, but we must remember that we have only very scanty remains from the lyric poets, to whom the poetry of spring and its attendant associations must have been especially dear. The references, in this connection, to the swan, jackdaw and birds of Memnon are rather too vague to be convincing.

In the Latin poets recognition of the spring migration, spring song and nesting is somewhat more widely attested, and the tone is ofttimes surprisingly modern. As with the Greeks, the swallow and nightingale hold the chief places. For the full record in the Latin poets vid. s. v. v. HIRUNDO, LUSCINIA, ACREDULA, CICONIA, CYCNUS, FRINGILLA, GRUS, PALUMBES, PASSER, STURNUS, TURDUS.

The verses (int. al.) which follow, referring to birds in general, show even more fully the wide sympathy which the Romans felt for the varied bird life of spring time.

Simile. The funeral of Cyzicus was as silent as Memphis and the Nile after the birds have gone north:

> Tandemque quiescunt
> Dissona pervigili planctu vada, qualiter arctos
> Ad patrias avibus medio iam vere revectis
> Memphis et aprici statio silet annua Nili.
> —VAL. FLACC. III, 358.

The emotions of a migrant bird:

> Fixerat ille gradus, totoque ex agmine solus
> Stabat, ut extremis desertus ab orbibus axis,
> Quem iam lassa dies Austrique ardentis arenae,
> Aut quem Rhiphaeas exstantem rursus ad arces
> Nix et caerulei Boreae ferus abstulit horror:
> Cum subito attoniti longissima Phasidis unda
> Caucasiaeque trabes omnisque Aeetia tellus
> Fulsit, et ardentes stabula effudere tenebras.
> —VAL. FLACC. VII, 557.

The joy of the birds on reaching their northern haunts:

> Qualia trans Pontum Phariis defensa serenis
> Rauca Paraetonio decedunt agmina Nilo,
> Cum fera ponit hiems: illae clangore fugaci
> Umbra fretis arvisque volant: sonat avius aether:
> Iam Boream imbresque pati, iam nare solutis
> Amnibus et nudo iuvat aestivare sub Haemo.
> —STAT., *Theb.* V, 11.

The spring song of birds is general:

> Avia tum resonant avibus virgulta canoris.
> —VERG., *Geor.* II, 328.

> Prataque pubescunt variorum flore colorum
> Indocilique loquax gutture vernat avis.
> —OV., *Trist.* III, 12, 7.

> Et tepidum volucres concentibus aëra mulcent.
> —OV., *Fast.* I, 155.

Vere prius volucres taceant, aestate cicadae,
Maenalius lepori det sua terga canis,
Femina quam iuveni blande temptata repugnet.
—Ov., *Ars Amat.* I, 271.

Hinc verno platanus folio viret
Et Phoebo laurus carum nemus;
Garrula per ramos avis obstrepit.
—Sen., *Oed.* 452.

Vere novo, cum iam tinnere volucres
Incipient.
—Calp., *Ecl.* V, 16.

Nunc cuncta veris: frondibus annuis
Crinitur arbor, nunc volucrum novi
Questus inexpertumque carmen
Quod tacita statuere bruma.
—Stat., *Silv.* IV, 5, 9.

Caesareae et Veneris mensis, quo floribus arva
Compta virent, avibus quo sonat omne nemus.
—*Anth. Lat.* 665, 7.

Has per umbras omnis ales plus canora quam putes
Cantibus vernis strepebat et susurris dulcibus.
—*Anth. Lat.* 809, 15.

The nesting of the birds in spring:

Nunc fecundus ager, pecoris nunc hora creandi,
Nunc avis in ramo tecta laremque parat.
—Ov., *Fast.* III, 241.

Quodcumque tellus vere nidifico creat.
—Sen., *Med.* 714.

Ver novum, ver iam canorum, vere natus orbis est,
Vere concordant amores, vere nubunt alites.
—*Perv. Ven.* 2.

NOTE II.

THE FALL MIGRATION AND THE FALL SONG.

Upon the Greeks and Romans the fall migration made deeper impressions and aroused a wider range of observation and fancy than was occasioned by the corresponding springtime flight. This was due in part to geographic and climatic conditions. In the spring the birds appeared in smaller numbers and their stay as migrants was for a shorter time. But in the fall they returned in flocks augmented by the young of the year. At this time, too, they were widely dispersed over the country and being in good condition were eagerly sought for the table. Thus to both Greeks and Romans the autumn flight of the birds was associated with good cheer and was pretty largely free from the sentimental associations of more northern lands, where the fall migration was grouped in thought and feeling with the waning of summer and the coming of winter with its cold and gloom.

Pischinger (op. cit.) and Thompson record at least eight species noted by the Greek poets as fall migrants. The Crane (γέρανος, *grus*) is preeminently first with the poets of both lands in this regard. The others (vid. s. v. v.) are the Stork (πελαργός, *ciconia*), Wild Goose (χήν, *anser*), Swan (κύκνος, *cygnus*), Starling (ψάρ, *sturnus*), Jackdaw (κολοιός, *monedula*), Thrush (κίχλη, *turdus*), Swallow (χελιδών, *hirundo*).

A summary of the most striking of the passages referring to these birds will make clear to the reader the trend and tone of the ancient observation of this phenomenon.

Crane. The Trojans are compared to flocks of migrating cranes which with loud cries flee southward from approaching winter to wage war upon the pygmies. Hom., *Il.* III, 2. The cry of the migrant crane is a signal to the farmer to begin his fall plowing. Hes., *Op.* 448; *Theog.* 1197. The same cry is a sign to the sailor to leave the sea for the winter. Ar., *Av.* 710. The finest passage in the ancient poets regarding the crane is in Eur., *Hel.* 1418, where the chorus accompany Menelaus and Helen, as they leave Egypt for home—with the wish that they, like migrant cranes, might fly to the banks of the Eurotas and announce the homecoming of the royal pair. Flocks of migrating cranes sink a ship at sea. *Anth. Pal.* VII, 543. The tale of Ibycus and the migrant cranes. *Anth. Pal.* VII, 745. Migrant cranes as foes to the fields in autumn. *Anth. Pal.* VII, 172. Cf. also Theoc. X, 30. The crane (and black bird) as innocent, carefree travelers. Ar., *Frag.* 10. The myth of the cranes and pygmies recurs again and again, vid. Hom., *Il.* III, 2, which is the earliest reference to it. Then, though failing to appear in the lyric and dramatic poets, it comes to light again in the later remains. Vid. *Anth. Pal.* XI, 265; XI, 369; Opp., *Hal.* I, 620.

Pischinger, after reviewing the literature on the subject and arguing chiefly from the fact that the later prose writers do not localize the pygmies in Africa, concludes that the myth originated in the realm of folk phantasy. It seems to me that Thompson is more likely correct when he attempts to rationalize the myth on a naturalistic basis. He cites a parallel in the Indian story of the warfare between the Garuda bird and the dwarfs, and suggests also that the myth may have arisen "in the pursuit of the ostrich by some southern dwarfish race." That reports of African pygmies had reached Europe at a very early date is quite probable.

How the Crane steadies its flight by a ballast of stones, Ar., *Av.* 1136; *Av.* 1428; Dionys. XL, 515. Pischinger's naturalistic rationalization is of interest (vid. op. cit.). The other birds recorded in this connection may be passed over very quickly. The Stork captured with Cranes in the fall, Babr. 13. The Wild Goose, Hom., *Il.* II, 460; XV, 692; *Anth. Pal.* VII, 546. The Swan, Hom., *Il.* II, 460; XV, 692; Eur., *Rhes.* 618; Ar., *Av.* 774. The Starling and Jackdaw, Hom., *Il.* XVII, 755 ff. The Thrush, *Aes. Fab.* 194. The Swallow, Anac., *Carm.* 25 (33). The last reference is of especial interest as clearly opposed to the hibernation lore of the north. Vid. Note III.

In the Latin poets again, as with the spring migration and the observation of spring song, the appreciation of this phenomenon also, seems to have grown and to be portrayed with a wider range of fancy.

The Crane (vid. s. v. GRUS). In Luc. V, 711, we have a picture of their flight from the north to Egypt. In Stat., *Theb.* XII, 515, a portrayal of the joy of the cranes on arriving at their winter haunts on the Nile. In Claud., *De Bell. Gild.* 474, an allusion to the warfare between pygmies and cranes and a reference to the letters formed by the cranes in flight. In Ov., *Met.* VI, 90, the myth of Gerana, who was metamorphosed into a crane and doomed to wage eternal warfare with her own people, the pygmies. In Juv. XIII, 167, a description of a battle between cranes and pygmies. In *Priap.* 46, 3; *Anth. Lat.* I, p. 158; II, p. 365; Namat. I, 285, et al., varying references to the myth. In

Verg., *Geor.* I, 373, the crane is hunted in the late fall and winter, in Hor., *Ep.* II, 30, the crane is called the *advenam gruem.*

The Swallow (vid. s. v. HIRUNDO).

In Ov., *Ex Pont.* IV, 14, Ovid dreads the land of the Getae as much as swallows do the coming of winter.

In Mart. V, 67, is told the story of the swallow that did not migrate in the fall, and how she was killed by the others when they returned in the spring. Vid. Note III.

In Ov., *Her.* XV, 151, the absence of bird-song in the fall is expressly noted. But the nightingale (wrongly, of course) is said to still bemoan the loss of Itys at this season. There is the same error in the fall song of the nightingale in Ov., *Her.* X, 7, but my collections show no record of the fall migration of Philomela. Once or twice the wild goose is associated with the crane as a foe to the fields of grain, and the migration of the fall seems to lie back of this observation.

The following passages (int. al.) relating to birds in general show more fully the Roman manner of utilizing this motive.

Three similes. The fall migrants are as numerous as the ghosts of the dead.

> Quam multa in foliis avium se milia condunt,
> Vesper ubi aut hibernus agit de montibus imber.
> —VERG., *Geor.* IV, 473.

> Quam multae glomerantur aves, ubi frigidus annus
> Trans pontum fugat et terris immittit apricis.
> —VERG., *Aen.* VI, 310.

> Nec tanta gelide Strymones fugiens minas
> Permutat hiemes ales et caelum secans
> Tepente Nilo pensat Arctoas nives
> Quot ille populos votis eduxit sonus.
> —SEN., *Oed.* 625.

Cf. Deseritur Strymon, tepido committere Nilo
Bistonias consuetus avis. —LUC. III, 200.

The migrants overtaken by a cold storm:

> Quales instanti nimborum frigore maestae
> Succedunt ramis haerentque pavore volucres.
> —VAL. FLACC. VI, 505.

October is the month for fowling:

> October pinguis dat tibi ruris aves.
> —*Anth. Lat.* 395, 38.

In winter there is no song:

Sed quantum, volucres cum bruma coercet,
Rura silent mediusque iacet sine murmure pontus,
Tanta quies. —LUC. I, 259.

The following passages, chosen from many, will show the tone of our own poets regarding the autumn flight of birds:

Brown meadows and russet hill are all alive with birds.
—BRYANT.

A gray bird rising forever more,
And drifting away toward the Mexican seas.—MILLER.

The birds have left the shivering pines
To flit among the trellised vines
Or fan the air with scented plumes
Amid the love-sick orange blooms.—HOLMES.

And when the lengthening nights have chilled the skies,
We fain would hear the song bird ere he flies.—HOLMES.

Like rainbow-feathered birds that bloom
A moment on some autumn bough
That with the spurn of their farewell
Sheds its last leaves.—LOWELL.

Cares the cuckoo for the wood
When the red leaves are down?—SILL.

Even the little field-fares in the corn no longer twitter.
—LONGFELLOW.

Southward the clamorous sea fowls wing their flight.
—LONGFELLOW.

Drove the loon and sea gull southward.—LONGFELLOW.

The robin and wren are flown
And from the shrubs the jay.—BRYANT.

I had a crimson robin
Who sang full many a day,
But when the woods were painted
He, too, did fly away.—EMILY DICKINSON.

Instead of lark or linnet
Shall whirl dead leaves and snow.—LOWELL.

And the swallow he swingeth no more aloft.—ALICE CARY.

Behold, the fleeting swallow
    Forsakes the frosty air.—TABB.
  (*October.*)

With mournful cries the wild geese fly,
Hurrying to the red-lipped South.—HIGGINSON.

A haze on the far horizon,
    The infinite, tender sky,
The ripe, rich tint of the cornfields,
    And the wild geese sailing high:
And all over upland and lowland
    The charm of the golden-rod,—
Some of us call it Autumn,
    And others call it God.—CARRUTH.

Overhead the wild geese fly,
Honking in the autumn sky.—CARMAN-HOVEY.

O'er us, the south land heading,
Screams the gray wild goose.—WHITTIER.

With mingled sound of horns and bells,
A far-heard clang, the wide geese fly,
Storm-sent, from Arctic moors and fells,
Like a great arrow through the skies,
Two dusky lines converged in one,
Chasing the southward-flying sun;
While the brave snow-bird and hardy jay
Call to them from the pines, as if to bid them stay.
—WHITTIER.

"I am ready to go," cried the querulous wren,
"From the wind-swept homes of these northern men."
—SIGOURNEY.

Then the glad birds, from their migration held
By his warm smile, pour'd forth their grateful strain.
"He gave us food, and with no stinted hand
Scatter'd the seeds that pleased our callow young,
And chained the howling blasts that ere the time
Were wont to drive us from our nests away.
For this we love him."—SIGOURNEY.

Then tribe after tribe, with its leader fair,
Swept off through the fathomless depths of air.
Who marked their course to the tropics bright?
Who nerved their wing for its weary flight?
Who guideth that caravan's trackless way
By the star at night and the cloud by day?
  (*Birds of Passage.*) —SIGOURNEY.

NOTE III.

THE HIBERNATING OF BIRDS.

"But what struck me most was, that from the time they began to congregate, forsaking the chimneys and houses, they roosted every night in the osier-beds of that river (the Thames). Now this resorting towards this element, at that season of the year, seems to give some countenance to the northern opinion (strange as it is) of their retiring under water. A Swedish naturalist is so much persuaded by that fact, that he talks, in his calendar of the Flora, as familiarly of swallows going under water in the beginning of September, as he would of his poultry going to roost a little before sunset."

"I am more and more induced to believe that many of the swallow kind do not depart from this island: but lay themselves up in holes and caverns; and do, insect-like and bat-like, come forth at mild times, and then retire again to their latebrae."

"Summer birds are, this cold and backward spring, unusually late. I have seen but one swallow yet. This conformity with the weather convinces me more and more that they sleep in winter."

These interesting passages from the classic '*Natural History of Selborne*' show that Gilbert White could never quite free himself from this bit of northern folk-lore. He pondered over it for forty years, but, as Prof. W. Warde Fowler has noted, here he had advanced but little beyond the point reached by Aristotle. Nuttal (op. cit., vol. I, p. 395, p. 400) gives two or three explanations for this widely spread belief in the hibernation of swallows.

"Accidental fits of torpidity, like those which occasionally and transiently take place with the humming bird, have undoubtedly happened to swallows, without proving anything against the general migrating instincts of the species, which as long back as the time of Anacreon has been generally observed."

"This predilection (by swallows) for the borders of lakes and ponds led some ancient writers to believe that swallows retired to the bottom of the water during the winter; and some fishermen on the coast of the Baltic pretended to have taken them up in their nets in large knots, clinging together by their bills and claws in a state of torpidity."

Coues, *Birds of the Colorado Valley,* pp. 378-390, contains a long discussion of the problem, with a bibliography of astounding size. Dr. Coues seems still to cherish an almost believing sympathy for the myth, because of the apparent validity of the testimony. But cf. Alexander Wilson, op. cit. s. v. BARN SWALLOW.

When we turn to the records of Greece and Rome, we find this belief in hibernation clearly attested. Aristotle (*H. A.* VIII, 16) mentions at least ten species as hibernating birds. Pliny (X, 24 [34], 41, 29) repeats the account of Aristotle. The list is surprisingly large, and seems to point to a confusion of hibernation and migration. The ancient poets, however, are more accurately in accord with the real facts which produced the error, when they assign hibernation (in the main) to the swallow only. (Cf. Lunt. *Blackbirds,* supra, Note I, Spring Migration.)

Pischinger (op. cit. Kap. IV, *Winterschlaf,* p. 48), is convinced that Hes.,*Op.* 568; Phil., *Frag.* 208, and Ar., *Av.* 108 ff. are best interpreted on the assumption that they reflect a belief in this phenomenon. It seems to me, however, that the more commonly attested observation of migration is quite adequate for the full understanding of the passages in question.

In the Latin poets we find at least two citations which clearly refer to this folk tradition:

> Vel qualis gelidis pluma labente pruinis
> Arboris immoritur trunco brumalis hirundo.
> —CLAUD., *In Eutrop.* I, 117.

> Conglaciantur aquae, scopulis se condit hirundo:
> Verberat egelidos garrula vere lacos.
> —*Anth. Lat.* 760, 101.

Two other passages also may possibly hint at this doctrine of hibernation:

> Tum blandi soles, *ignotaque prodit hirundo*
> Et luteum celsa sub trabe figit opus.
> —OV., *Fast.* I, 157.

> *Hibernos* peterent solito cum more *recessus*
> Atthides, in nidis una remansit avis.
> —MART. V, 67.

Gesner (op. cit., p. 529) turns the matter as an earnest for our own bodily resurrection.

"Iam visum est quod hirundines in plantis quibusdam concavis se abdiderunt; et hoc accidit in quadam silva superioris Germaniae, ubi incisa quercus putrida inventa est plena hirundinibus. Idem hoc Pompeius Columba, vir maximus rerum naturae rimator, in Germania se reperisse in concavo cuiusdam arboris in imo fluminis exortae. Comperi latere hieme hirundines in nido suo tamquam mortuas; proinde non puto avolare eas. Totam hiemem habent secum recentia ova, reviviscunt autem sub aestatem. Quare indico mirabile quoddam opus esse, ac imaginem resurrectionis nostrorum corporum."

Thomson vacillated between hibernation and migration:

> Clinging in clusters,
> Beneath the mouldering bark or where,
> Unpierced by frost, the cavern sweats,
> Or *rather* into warmer climes conveyed,
> With other kindred birds of season, there
> They twitter cheerful, till the vernal
> Months invite them back.—THOMSON.
> (*Seasons. Winter.*)

Naturally it is not a motive which easily lends itself to the demands even of nature poetry, and our own poets (so far as I have been able to find) have recorded it only a few times—although it may possibly lurk in these lines from Holmes and Freneau:

> And when and where the homeless swallows went
> To pass the winter of their discontent.—HOLMES.

> The birds are to their haunts withdrawn,
> The leaves are scattered through the plain.—FRENEAU.

The earliest certain reference is from Michael Forrest's *Travels through America,* published in 1793. He refers to both migration and hibernation:

> All the tuneful reluctant quit the grove,
> And each in search of winter-quarters rove;
> Quick to'rds the south to meet the genial ray,
> On hasty pinions, some do bend their way;
> Others, less knowing, or as fate design'd,
> In hollow trees, seek shelter from the wind;
> 'Till the genial ray, and the smiling spring,
> Dispel the gloom, and call them forth to sing.

The next two references are within the same decade:

> Yes, winter's power must shortly pass away,
> And all his dread appendages decay;
> For now a short-liv'd glow of vernal heat
> Invites the swallow from his close retreat.
> (*Winter,* 1800.) —SAMUEL LOW.

When bank-lodg'd swallows doze in demi-death.
(*Hamiltoniad, Canto III,*
Winter, 1804.) —JOHN WILLIAMS.

The next reference, in greater detail, is from the E. R. Campbell's poem on the *'Chimney-Swallows.'* (*Poets and Poetry of Vermont,* p. 34). Campbell, like Thomson, wavers between migration and hibernation:

Whence they come, or whither go,
Only swallows ever know;
Mortals only know they're here.
. . . .
Whether at the south they rove,
Sporting in the orange grove;
Whether housed in lakes, or fens,
Caverns low, or mountain dens,
Matters not.

The last indubitable reference is from Whittier's *Flowers in Winter,* where the poet records the magic powers of an ancient wizard:

A wizard of the Merrimack,—
So old ancestral legends say,—
Could call green leaf and blossom back
To frosted stem and spray.
The dry logs of the cottage wall,
Beneath his touch, put out their leaves;
The clay-bound swallow, at his call,
Played round the icy eaves.

This is, I believe, the last American allusion to this hoary bit of folklore and I think we may safely assume that it will never again find expression in verse.

NOTE IV.

RUSCINIA.

In an Old-English Glossary—published by Goetz in *Corpus Glossariorum Latinorum*, v — occur the words *acalantis, vel luscinia vel roscinia, nectegela,* which are assigned by Goetz to the eighth century. Their meaning is of course obvious. The form *ruscinia* as a parallel for *luscinia* appears also in a ninth century Ms. given by Diez, *Romanisches Wörterbuch*, s. v., citing Mone's *Anzeiger*, VII, 148. These are the Roman sources for the word *ruscinia*. In Latin, as is well known, the everyday name for the nightingale is *luscinia* or *lusciniola,* but in the Romance languages the corresponding names have regularly an initial *r-*, as in *rossignol, rossignuolo,* and others.

This paper is an attempt to interpret the glossema above, with its association of the *acalanthis, luscinia,* and *ruscinia,* and to present two or three possible theories for the shift from *l-* to *r-* in the two forms. It assumes that the initial *r-* in the Latin variants is the source of the *r-* in the later Romance forms. It attempts to treat the matter, in a broad way, with a glance at the natural history, the folk lore, and the poetic associations, which are inseparably connected with the problem. The subject is of no great importance, and is perhaps justified only in the light of the rather considerable occasional literature that has grown up about it.

The last discussion, so far as I know, is by Professor E. W. Fay, in *Modern Language Notes*, XVIII, 195. He also limits the problem to Latin times, and asserts the conviction that the explanations of the shift from *l-* to *r-* in the Romance languages, which attempt to trace the *r-* forms from *luscinia,* are beside the mark. He states the problem with the query "will not the variation of *l-* and *r-* in the Romance languages meet its most satisfactory, as well as its simplest, explanation by appealing to *ruscinia* as a popular etymology, in Low Latin times of *luscinia?*"

He then attempts to establish this popular etymology by supposing that the nightingale frequents the *ruscus* of ancient times, now known as *ruscus aculeatus* (thorn-bush or butcher's broom), which is, we may add, a low shrub found distributed over large areas in Southern Europe. Thus in popular parlance the true name *luscinia,* shifted to *ruscinia,* connoting the 'thorn-bush-singer,' because of this assumed direct association of the nightingale with the shrub *ruscus.*

---

[1]Reprinted from the Transactions of the American Philological Association, Vol. XXXVIII, 1908.

First, however, before discussing in detail Professor Fay's hypothesis, for the sake of completeness, an earlier theory should be examined in this connection. This was first suggested, I believe, by Grammont, in his monograph, *La Dissimilation consonantique*. It is based upon the theory that the *r-* in the derivatives of *hirundinella* may have changed the *l-* of *lusciniola* through the association of the two birds. While preferring this theory, Grammont apparently did not wholly give up the idea that the shift in question may be due to initial dissimilation in the original *lusciniolum* (*op. cit.* 118). Grammont seems to have been unacquainted with the glosses, for he ignores them and apparently assumes that the shift took place after Roman times. The most cogent points of contact cited by him are the myth of Philomela and Progne, the association of the two birds as harbingers of spring, and the association of the *rossignol de muraille* and the *hirondelle* in the country life of modern France.

His evidence for the shift, taken as a phenomenon of the later times, is inadequate and unconvincing. The average reader will agree with Gaston Paris, *Journal des Savants,* Février, 1898, where, in a review of Grammont's work, he refers to both hypotheses: "M. Grammont, tout en croyant que les formes romanes de *lusciniolum* qui remplacent l'r initiale par une l peuvent être dues à une dissimilation, préfère expliquer l'r par l'influence de *hirundinem.* Cette hypothèse me paraît peu vraisemblable; mais il faut réellement admettre que l'r de *rossignol* et de ses pareils n'est pas due à la dissimilation, puisqu'on rencontre en bas latin la forme *roscinia,* où la dissimilation ne saurait être en cause." The statement of the distinguished reviewer is seemingly conclusive for the dissimilation theory. In the earlier life of Roman times, however, the association of the two birds was so intimate and many-sided that the association theory must not be so hastily dismissed. The Romance forms for *hirundo — rondinella, rondola,* and others—may point to a common, perhaps dialectic, byform of *hirundinella* without the initial syllable. Similar cases of procope are easily found. Even in the realm of popular ornithological nomenclature an example is not wanting. Ernout, *Le Parler de Préneste d' après les Inscriptions,* 16, gives among others, *conea* as the Praenestine form for *ciconia,* 'stork.' His source, of course, is the well-known passage from Plautus, *Truc.* 688:

AST. Perii, 'rabonem.' quam esse dicam hanc beluam?
Quin tu arrabonem dicis? STR. 'A' facio lucri,
Ut Praenestinis 'conea' est ciconia.

If *ciconia* was shortened to *conea, hirundinella* shortened to *rundinella* is not surprising. Now, would (*hi*)*rundinella* react upon *lusciniola* and produce the result sought for? With no theory to prove, Otto Keller, *Thiere des classischen Alterthums,* 319, remarks, "Einer der eigenthümlichsten und bei andern Völkern nicht vorkommenden ist die enge Verwandschaft Philomelens mit der Schwalbe; sie beruht auf manchen Berührungspunkten, in welchen die beiden Vögel nach der Anschauung des Alterthums zusammentrafen."

Let us examine this in some detail. First there is the well-known myth of Philomela and Progne. In nearly all Greek writers Philomela is the swallow, and Progne the nightingale. In this connection we should note that they are *sisters,* the daughters of Pandion. In nearly all Roman writers these names are reversed, which, again, was a constant source of the confusion. In the sixth Eclogue of Virgil, Philomela seems best taken as the swallow, following the Greek tradition. Yet the ambiguity of the whole passage is such that Conington leaves it with the remark that it "certainly looks like a confusion of the habits of the nightingale and swallow." The same ambiguity appears in Hor. *Od.* iv, 12, and in a most remarkable way in Sen. *Her. Oet.* 200 ff. Much of this confusion in the Roman poets is due, doubtless, to the fact that the habits of the two birds and the dramatic incidents of the metamorphosis were never, in fact could not be, completely harmonized.

In the fourth Georgic Virgil clearly follows the Roman tradition and makes Philomela the nightingale. A later writer, however, speaks of Philomela as the swallow, "who, trustful bird that she is, hangs her nest in the homes of men." Virgil has the swallows in mind in the two graceful lines:

> Evandrum ex humili tecto lux suscitat alma
> Et matutini volucrum sub culmine cantus.—*Aen.* VIII, 455.

Both birds were thought of as harbingers of spring, like the robin and bluebird in our own Eastern States. For the nightingale in this regard, cf. Hom. *Od.* xix, 519; Arist. *Av.* 684; Sapph. fr. 39. Among the Romans the swallow, here, plays the chief rôle. Among many other passages the following are rather striking:

> Ver blandum viget arvis, et adest hospes hirundo.
> —Varro, *Sat. Inc.,* Baehrens, *P. L. M.* IV, 223.

> Te, dulcis amice, reviset,
> Cum Zephyris, si concedes, et hirundine prima.
> —Hor., *Epist.* I, 7, 12-13.

Fallimur, an veris praenuntia venit hirundo
Nec metuit, ne qua versa recurrat hiemps?
Saepe tamen, Progne, nimium properasse quereris,
Virque tuo Tireus frigore laetus erit.
—Ov., *Fast.* II, 853 ff.

The two birds seem to have been associated in the rites of Adonis, which were celebrated in the early springtime. Cf. Thompson, *Glossary of Greek Birds,* 13-14.

The element of sadness in the songs of the two birds was well-nigh universally recognized as a common trait throughout the poetry and lore of both Greeks and Romans. Among the latter this idea so outshadows all other attributes of the nightingale's song that *luscinia* itself seems best taken as **luges-cinia,* the 'grief-singer.'[1]

Pischinger, in his monograph, *Der Vogelgesang bei den griechischen Dichtern des klassischen Alterthums,* shows that this tone of sadness is, perhaps, the most common trait in the songs, not only of the nightingale and swallow, but also of the halcyon and swan. This attitude was based upon a conception of the song as an outpouring of grief, supposed to be felt by the unfortunate metamorphosed being, whose life had been merged in that of the bird in question. In this regard the Roman poets followed the Greek tradition almost *in toto.* For the nightingale's song from this point of view, cf. Cat. 65, 13; Verg. *Ecl.* 6, 78; *Geor.* iv, 511; Prop. iii, 11, 4; Ov. *Tr.* ii, 389; *Fast.* iv, 481; *Am.* ii, 6, 6; Mart. xiv, 75; *Cons. ad Liv.* 105; *Pervig. Ven.* 86. In several of these citations (and there are others) the nightingale is clearly portrayed, as we should expect, as singing by *night,* a fact which adds point to the remark of Keller (*op. cit.* 467): "Sprachwidrig ist die gewöhnliche, auch bei Weise, *Griechische Wörter im Latein. S.* 107, wieder vorgebrachte Etymologie von *lux* und *canere.*" This derivation, with its companion **luscicinia,* 'the twilight-singer,' strangely enough, continues to find defenders. Walde, *Lat. etymologisches Wörterbuch,* s. v., wavers between the two.

The more modern touch of joy in the song, as in the following passage, is relatively speaking very rare in the ancient poets:

Ceu patrio super alta grues Aquilone fugatae
cum videre Pharon, tunc aethera latius implent,
tunc *hilari* clangore sonant; iuvat orbe sereno
contempsisse nives et frigora solvere Nilo.
—Stat., *Theb.* XII, 515.

[1] Vid. s. v. Luscinia.

Evidently as a mourner, and a singer of sad funereal refrains, we find the *luscinia* portrayed in the wall-paintings of Roman grave monuments. The *hirundo* plays the same part; in fact, on Sophocles' tomb we are told that a swallow was represented. A Roman grave on the Via Latina has the two birds side by side, and an accompanying distich gives their names. This association of the two birds with the dead can rest only upon the ancient feeling that there was inherent sadness in their songs. This feeling, no doubt, also underlies several of the bird metamorphosis myths, for without this assumption they cannot be rationalized.

The describing epithets of the two birds are interchanged in such a way as to defy, at times, all rational individual identification. Both, for example, are lugubrious, both are garrulous, both in Greek are ξουθός in song and color.

In Moschus (if the text be sound) the two birds are associated in the same habitat, and to-day, according to Kaup's *Thierreich,* in both Greece and Italy the swallow (*hirundo urbica*) and the nightingale frequent in strikingly common proximity the same chosen localities.

And lastly, to add one more touch of contact, we are told by Artemidorus that in the dream lore of the Greeks the two birds have almost the same symbolism. Thus much for the lore. For several of the above and many other points of association, vid. Keller, op. cit. 315.

I can at this time point to only one close parallel in Latin for such a shift of the initial *l-* to *r-,* due to association. Porphyrio, on Hor. *Epist.* ii, 2, 209, seems to imply that the festival of Lemuria was called Remuria by the people, who associated the festival, with its appeasing of ghosts, *lemures,* with Remus and the walls where he met his death. Tradition, too, ascribed the origin of the festival to Romulus. Cf. Otto Keller, *Lateinische Volks-Etymologie,* 40.

This theory for the change, through association, is attractive, and to some it may appear adequate and convincing, yet is it cogent enough to have produced the change demanded? If we accept it, how shall we explain the presence of the bird *acalanthis* in the glosses and in a Servian note to be presented immediately?

This much, however, is certainly true, that if the origin of the form *ruscinia* can be established on some other theory which will more nearly meet all the phases of the problem, then the absolutely unique associations presented in support of Grammont's theory may well have been a very strong influence in sustaining the parallel forms in *r-*.

To return now to Professor Fay's suggested solution of the problem;

namely, that the form *ruscinia* is due to the direct association, in the folk-etymology, of the nightingale with the *ruscus*. In the *Cl. Rev.* XVIII, 307, he repeats this hypothesis and adds that "he will be grateful for any evidence to confirm or disprove the fact supposed; namely, that the butcher's broom (*ruscus aculeatus*) in Southern Italy is a favorite haunt of the nightingale."

This hypothesis is very plausible. It meets the philological situation admirably, and we must be grateful to Professor Fay for suggesting it. There is, however, one thing against it which will soon appear. Not trusting my own amateurish observations of the bird in question, which did not confirm the theory in hand, I asked my colleague, Professor Harold Heath, who was spending a year at Naples in the International Zoölogical Station of that city, to observe the nightingales, especially in relation to their supposed association with the *ruscus*.

I am deeply grateful to him for his report, which is further confirmed by the following note from Professor Umberto Pierantoni, a distinguished professor of zoölogy at the University of Naples.

"The nightingale," says Professor Pierantoni, "is very common in Italy. It is *not* found in the plant (*ruscus aculeatus*), but dwells among the high trees, frequenting especially the poplar tree. It lives also in the forests, near humid places, where it breeds in May, and sings preferably during the spring, in the evening and by night." Professor Pierantoni's observation seems conclusive as regards the problem before us, and at the same time adds new reality to part of Virgil's beautiful though touching scene in the fourth Georgic, where he portrays the nightingale in a poplar tree bemoaning the loss of her nestlings.

Considering all the evidence, the writer is inclined to believe that the following may well be the true solution of the difficulty. The name *ruscinia* was first applied by the people to a bird which really does frequent in great numbers the wide areas of *ruscus* so common everywhere in Italy. This bird was known also to the more learned, by the Greek name *acalanthis*. This bird was then associated in the folk-observation with the nightingale, and in time from this association and the popular confusion of the two birds, the name *ruscinia* was applied also to the nightingale. This theory explains the associations in the glossary: *acalanthis, vel luscinia vel ruscinia, nectigal*. Such confusions are commonplaces in ornithological nomenclatures. Our own mocking-bird furnishes many parallels. In many parts of this country the brown-thrush, likewise a great singer and mimic, is dubbed the French mocking-bird. In other parts the name "mocking-bird" is applied to two different species of wrens remarkable for the sweetness of their songs. In England the name "mock-nightingale" is frequently applied to the black-cap and to the sedge-warbler. The latter, in fact, furnishes almost a complete parallel to the case in hand. The bird is called the sedge-warbler from its habitat. So the ruscinia, by our theory. It is then named the mock-nightingale from the sweetness of its song. So the ruscinia may well, from its song, have been associated with the real nightingale (luscinia), resulting at last in a confusion of the former name with the original (luscinia) until the two existed side by side as names for the nightingale. If other parallels are needed, one may instance the cardinal grosbeck, which in the East is very commonly known as the Virginia nightingale, while in France the redstart is commonly called the *rossignol de muraille.*

The real identification of the acalanthis is, however, as yet uncertain. Thompson in his *Glossary of Greek Birds,* and Neri in his monograph *Gli animali nelle opere di Virgilio,* identify it with the goldfinch. This is not fully convincing, on grounds which I cannot discuss at this time. Warde Fowler, though in this regard not so well known in this country, is an ardent observer of the ways of birds. In one of the charming books, which have resulted from this delightful pastime, *A Year with the Birds,* 243, he makes a very strong case for identifying the acalanthis as one of the warblers. He notes in passing that at least one of the silvidae, the sedge-warbler, ofttimes carries its song far into the night.

Aristotle, *Hist. Anim.* ix, 17, speaks thus of the acalanthides: κακόβιοι καὶ κακόχροοι, φώνην μέντοι λιγυρὰν ἔχουσιν. These words might be applied equally as well to the nightingale. No bird of equal fame is perhaps less known from actual observation. It should be remembered also that the nightingale is not a thrush, but one of the silvidae, or warblers. Pliny, *N. H.* x, 205, has *acanthis in spinis vivit.* The acanthis is the same as the acalanthis. Another gloss from Goetz gives us this information, *acalanthis avis vepribus adsueta.* Both words, *spinis* and *vepribus,* are in harmony with and point to *ruscus. Ruscus* is glossed in Du Cange as μυρρινακάνθος, which again points to the bird acalanthis, just as *ruscus,* by the theory under discussion, points to the ruscinia.

Now if the luscinia and acalanthis were confused, we should expect to find traces of very high appreciation for the song of the latter bird. This is exactly what we do find. There were, as we have already noted, only four bird-singers of high esteem among the Greek and Roman poets. It was well-nigh impossible for others to break into this highly esteemed traditional group. We need not, therefore, be surprised that only two references to the acalanthis occur in the Roman poets. The lesser first:

Nyctilon ut cantu rudis exsuperaverit Alcon?
Astyle, credibile est, si vincat acanthida cornix,
Vocalem superet si dirus aedona bubo.—CAL. *Ecl.* 6, 5.

These associations, of course, are symbolical of the impossible. Here the songs of the acalanthis and the nightingale are obviously taken as types of the highest beauty in bird-song, in antithesis to the "raucous calls" of the cornix, and the "lugubrious plaints" of the owl. Erasmus classified the above as popular proverb. The association of the acalanthis and nightingale on the same side of the equation is instructive. The more so if we recall that here the acalanthis takes a place in the proverb usually held by another of the immortal four.

Tum tenuis dare rursus aquas, et pascere rursus
solis ad occasum, cum frigidus area vesper
temperat, et saltus reficit iam roscida luna,
Litoraque alcyonem resonant, acalanthida dumi.
—VERG., *Geor.* III, 338.

Here we have in Virgil a calm summer scene. Evening approaches. The background of bird-song is portrayed without its usual touch of sorrow, as, for example, in Hor. *Epod.* 2, 26, who in a somewhat similar situation uses *queruntur* of the birds as they sang. Cf. also Ov. *Her.* 15, 151. The association here of the acalanthis with the halcyon, again in company with one of the immortal four, indicates Virgil's high appreciation of the little singer. As Glover points out, it may well be a reminiscence in the master poet's mind of his boyhood days on the banks of the Mincio. There are only these two references in the Roman poets. But surely if two appreciative nature poets like Virgil and Calpurnius thought so highly of the acalanthis, there is nothing *a priori* improbable in a confusion of the birds and a blending of their names in the folk-mind and observation. Virgil says that the *dumi, i. e.* the thickets, resound. This word and its parallel *dumetum* are glossed by ἀκανθεών, which again points to the bird acalanthis. In this connection Warde Fowler, referring to Lenz, *Botanik der Griechen,* observes that the word ἄκανθις in Greek does not necessarily mean the thistle, but is applied to all kinds of thorny trees and shrubs, such as the *dumi* in which Virgil makes the voice of the bird resound.

I do not believe for a minute that Virgil confused the acalanthis and nightingale. He was far too good an observer for that. But later, as we should expect, if our hypothesis be correct, others *did* confuse the two birds. Observe now, in view of our discussion, what Servius says in a note on the acalanthis passage in hand: Acalanthis alii lusciniam esse volunt, alli . . . carduelim. This means, if it means anything at all, that in the time of Servius the confusion assumed as the source of *ruscinia*, and clearly implied in the glosses, was already in evidence. On this hypothesis alone can we explain the glosses and this Servian note, with their double association, of luscinia on one hand and acalanthis on the other. If this theory for the origin of *ruscinia* be accepted, its survival in the *r*- forms of the Romance languages seems to present no serious difficulty.

BIBLIOGRAPHY OF THE PRINCIPAL LITERATURE CONSULTED.

Allen, Katherine: Treatment of Nature in the Poetry of the Roman Republic.
Madison, 1899.

American Poets: Vid. Preface.

Baehrens, A.: Fragmenta Poetarum Romanorum.
Leipzig, 1886.

Baehrens, A.: Poetae Latini Minores.
Leipzig, 1879.

Baethgen, E.: De Vi ac Significatione Galli in religionibus et artibus Graecorum et Romanorum.
Göttingen, 1887.

Buchholz: Ueber die homerische Naturanschauung.
Erfurt, Prog., 1870.

Buecheler, F.: Carmina Epigraphica.
Leipzig, 1897.

Burroughs, John: Birds and Poets.
Boston, 1899.

Burroughs, John: Songs of Nature.
New York, 1906.

Burroughs, John: Wake-robin.
Boston, 1886.

Browne, T.: Vulgar Errors. Ed. by Wilkin.
London, 1888.

Check List of North American Birds. Ed. by A. O. U.
New York, 1895.

Cheney, S. P.: Wood Notes Wild.
Boston, 1892.

Columbian Muse, The: A Selection of American Poetry.
New York, 1794.

Coues, Elliott: Birds of the Colorado Valley.
Washington, 1878.

Coues, Elliott: Check List of North American Birds.
Boston, 1882.

Coues, Elliott: Key to North American Birds.
New York, 1872.

Duyckinck, E. A. and G. L.: Cyclopedia of American Literature.
New York, 1855.

Elliot, D. G.: Wild Fowl of North America.
New York, 1898.

Fairclough, H. R.: The Attitude of the Greek Tragedians toward Nature.
Toronto, 1897.

Fowler, W. W.: Summer Studies of Birds and Books.
London, 1895.

Fowler, W. W.: A Year with the Birds.
London, 1902.

Fowler, W. W.: Tales of the Birds.
London, 1903.

Fowler, W. W.: More Tales of the Birds.
London, 1902.

Gesner, Konrad: Historiae Animalium L. IIII, qui est de Avium Natura.
Tiguri, 1587.

Gemoss, W.: Die Realien bei Horaz.
Berlin, 1892.

Glazer, E.: P. Vergilius Maro als Naturdichter und Theist.
Gütersloh, 1880.

Glover, T. R.: Studies in Virgil.
London, 1904.

Griswold, R. W.: The Poets and Poetry of America.
Philadelphia, 1842.

Hartung, J. E.: The Birds of Shakespeare.
London, 1871.

Hammerschmidt, K.: Die Ornithologie des Aristotles.
Speier, Prog. 1897.

Häcker, V.: Der Gesang der Vögel.
Jena, 1900.

Hehn, V.: Kulturpflanzen und Hausthiere, etc.
Berlin, 1902.

Holbrook, R. T.: Dante and the Animal Kingdom.
New York, 1902.

Holland, R.: Heroenvögel in der griechischen Mythologie.
Leipzig, Prog. 1895.

Hopf, L.: Thierorakel und Orakelthiere in alter und neuer Zeit.
Stuttgart, 1888.

Hudson, W. H.: British Birds.
London, 1895.

Kayler, B. von: Jagd und Jagdrecht in Rom.
Göttingen, 1894.

Keller, O.: Thiere des classischen Alterthums.
Innsbruck, 1892.

Kettell, Samuel: Specimens of American Poetry.
Boston, 1829.
Knappitsch, A.: De L. Caeli Firmiani Lactanti 'Ave Phoenice.'
Graz, Prog. 1896.
Knowlton, F. H.: Birds of the World.
New York, 1909.
Kuhns, L. O.: The Treatment of Nature in Dante's 'Divina Commedia.'
London, 1897.
Lebeda, Th.: De Animalibus et Herbis ad Cenas Romanorum praecipue adhibitis.
Braunau, Prog. 1891.
Lang, A.: Myth, Ritual and Religion.
London, 1899.
Le Breton, A.: De Animalibus apud Vergilium.
Paris, 1895.
Longolius: Dialogus de Avibus.
Coloniae, 1544.
Lorrenz, B.: Die Taube im Alterthume.
Wurzen, 1886.
Mackie, A.: Nature Knowledge in Modern Poetry.
London, 1906.
Marx, A.: Griechische Märchen von dankbaren Thieren.
Stuttgart, 1889.
Miller, M.: Das Jagwesen der alten Griechen und Römern.
Munich, 1883.
Morris, F. O.: A History of British Birds.
London, 1857.
Neri, F.: Gli animali nelle opere di Virgilio.
Pisa, 1896.
Newton, A.: A Dictionary of Birds.
London, 1896.
Nuttal, T.: Ornithology of North America.
Boston, 1897.
Pascal, C.: Sul Carme 'De Ave Phoenice' attribuito a Lattanzio.
Naples, 1904.
Pischinger, A.: Der Vogelgesang bei den griechischen Dichtern des klassischen Alterthums.
Eichstatt, 1901.
Pischinger, A.: Der Vogelzug bei den griechischen Dichtern des klassischen Alterthums.
Eichstatt, 1904.
Poetae Latini: Vid. Preface.

Ribbeck, O.: Comicorum Rom. Fragmenta.
Leipzig, 1883.

Ribbeck, O.: Tragicorum Rom. Fragmenta.
Leipzig, 1891.

Riese, A.: Anthologia Latina.
Leipzig, 1894.

Schmid, G.: De Luscinia.
St. Petersburg, Prog. 1904.

Schmid, G.: De Aquila.
St. Petersburg, 1898.

Seager, H. W.: Natural History in Shakespeare's Time.
London, 1896.

Shairp: Poetic Interpretation of Nature.
Boston, 1889.

Siecke, E.: De Niso et Scylla in aves mutatis.
Berlin, 1884.

Sladen, D.: Younger American Poets.
London, 1891.

Stedman, E. C.: An American Anthology.
Boston, 1906.

Stedman, E. C., and Hutchinson, E. M.: Library of American Literature.
New York, 1888.

Thompson, D. W.: A Glossary of Greek Birds.
Oxford, 1895.

Thompson, D. W.: Bird and Beast in Ancient Symbolism.
Edinburgh, 1895.

Thoreau, H. D.: Notes on New England Birds. Ed. by F. H. Allen.
Boston, 1910.

The Time of the Singing of Birds.
London (Henry Frowde), 1910.

Trumbull, G.: Names and Portraits of Birds.
New York, 1888.

Wackernagel, W.: Voces variae Animalium.
Basel, 1869.

Wegelin, O.: Early American Poetry. A Bibliography.
New York, 1903.

Wheelock, I. G.: Birds of California.
Chicago, 1904.

White, Gilbert: Natural History of Selborne.
New York, 1895.

Winteler, J.: Naturlaute und Sprache. Ausführungen zu W. Wackernagels 'Voces variae Animalum.'
Aarau, 1892.

INDEX OF CITATIONS FROM ROMAN AUTHORS